Wild Life

Memories of wildfowling and fishing around the Blackwater Estuary

Jack Hoy

ISBN 978-1-78792-045-3

Book design, layout and production management by Into Print
www.intoprint.net
+44 (0)1604 832140

Dedication

I would like to dedicate this book to my family, friends and acquaintances who instilled in me the love of wildfowling and an appreciation for the wildlife and landscapes of this jewel of an island. It is often said that those who have the least, give the most.

They speak to the watchman. Drawing by **Fid Harnack.**

Mid-Winter's Night

In one Essex creek when
the wind's in the East and the
honk of wild geese can be
heard.
    The salt air freezes.

Two gunners go out on the
rising tide and lie prone in
their flat-bottomed punts :
    With their paddes and sticks
they work down the creek in
the lee of the saltings.
Past the withies.

Presently; they come to open
water and the sea is choppy.

The rising moon guides them.
    By listening the fowl are
heard feeding.

At last they see them under the
tail of a sandbank and some
in a deep gulley. The punts
move warily nearer.

A watching goose spreads
an alarm and a cloud of
fowl jump at close quarters
    Two guns are heard and they
pick up three geese and float
around with the tide to, search.

Three more birds are found
and the two punts decide to
return. They speak to the
watchman.
    As they land on the shingle
hard,
ice crackles under their boots
and cordials are taken. Four
hours have passed.

The gunners are satisfied and
with six plump birds slung from
their belts they go to their
warm vessel.
A hatch is closed.

Norman O. Searle

4

Contents

Foreword

IT IS A privilege to write a Foreword for Jack's book although I do have a confession to make: prior to reading the text, I had no inkling as to what wildfowling involved. Even worse: to my mind wildfowling conjured up images of the senseless slaughter of innocent birds and wildfowl on a colossal scale with no apparent motive. *Wild Life* has corrected this rather distorted view of wildfowling of mine, and I have gained a new-found respect for this most ancient of pursuits. Wildfowling is, I have since learned through my research, almost as ancient as fishing and has been undertaken since time out of mind. Our ancestors from way back fished and pursued the art of wildfowling as a means of survival and providing food for the family and community; without it, they would simply have starved. This noble sport has been followed through the centuries and generations of wildfowlers have learned the techniques from their fathers and passed it on to their sons and daughters. In my previous (pre-book) incarnation, I would never have thought of using words such as "art" and "noble" to describe wildfowling. Jack's book has changed that perception.

During the many email exchanges between Jack and myself, he often referred to his raw text as his "ramblings"; well, the only ramblings I came across in the book were those he undertook across the marshes as he pursued his quarry. I found his words poetic, at times deeply moving, and his powers of description are to be admired. There is one particular passage that always tightens my throat and moistens my eyes, where Jack describes the disappearance of a particular tree from the familiar landscape of his youth. To avoid any spoiler alerts, I will let you find the particular passage and draw your own conclusions as to why it affects my emotions so strongly. Jack certainly tells a good story, and in his tales of wildfowling with family and friends you can almost sense being alongside them all on the salt marshes, in among the creeks, or out on a wind and wave-tossed trawler on a stormy day in the River Blackwater.

Jack's love of nature and his strong views on conservation shine strongly through this book. He has a deep respect for the natural landscape and is passionate about keeping it wild and free. His frustrations with Government organisations and quangos that seek to regulate a sport that has been freely pursued without interference and needless bureaucracy over many years is transparent; his views are undoubtedly shared by many whose love for wildfowling, and the environment in which it is followed, is paramount. Even club rules can sometimes obfuscate the purity and purpose of wildfowling, leading to resentment and disbelief. All of these obstacles are eventually overcome and the deep love for the life of the wildfowler eases the frustrations and angst suffered in these stressful times.

The book also covers Jack's experiences with fishing and trawling both in the Blackwater and further out to sea. The stories that unfold during these joyous times on the seas are both enlightening and humorous. So many of the characters that have graced this glorious island must have had, or still have, saltwater running through their veins. We take so much for granted in our lives, but we should always remember the hard lives and sacrifices made by our fishermen in providing fish for our suppers. *Wild Life* shines a light on, and amplifies, this aspect of island life and demonstrates the wonderful times that could be experienced by boys and girls growing up in the mid-20th century. This was a character-defining pursuit, and it was greedily lapped up by Jack in his youth.

One of the biggest themes in the book, and the one that comes across so clearly, is the sense of comradeship among the characters of this story. Family and friends were, and are, a hugely important part of the rich fabric of Jack's wildfowling and fishing life. The sense of adventure and fun is there for all to see but it is the binding friendships that glue the community together. Jack's close family – his father, grandfather, uncle and cousins – all played a major role in fostering the deep love of wildfowling that Jack retains to this day. *Wild Life* covers just two decades of his time pursuing this ancient sport. There is a fund of other tales he could tell but for now we must content ourselves with the rich pickings to be found in this treasure trove of memories. I think this book is a triumph and an important piece of social history. It will appeal to all those who love wildfowling, fishing and the magnificent landscape of our most treasured island.

Trevor Hearn
June 2024

1: Early Memories

My earliest memory of Feldy, Sampsons Fleet, Copthall, Newhall and the surrounding fresh and saltwater marshes and farmland goes back to 1953-4 when I was eight or nine. I started beating on the farmowner's shoot with my father, Jack, and his brother, Din (Nathan), who did the gamekeeping and vermin control on the two farms of Copthall and Newhall. Also in the beating line was another brother of my father, Syd, who had just retired from the Royal Air Force after serving 25 years, together with my grandfather, Alan, and my cousin, John, who was six months younger than me. They were beautiful, incredible, nostalgic days. As a nine-year-old I shared all this with my father, his brothers and my grandfather and I also forged a friendship with my cousin up until his tragic death in 2004, and with another boy which would last a lifetime. I got to know the wonderful freshwater marshes and fields intimately as I walked them in the beating line, driving pheasants and coveys of wild English and red-legged partridges towards the line of guns that were awaiting them in the low ways that were once a saltwater creek. There, the tide used to ebb and flow for three or four hundred years until the Dutch drainage engineers enclosed the saltings behind an earth bank and formed an area that, in my view, was richer in nature and wildlife than when it had been tidal. It was all rough and uneven, interwoven with the low ways that were once the creeks that drained the saltings once brimming with salt water. There were anthills by the thousand and rabbit earths on the higher, drier ground amongst the acres of thistles. Hares and leverets leapt from their forms as they were disturbed while walking through an open area, or through long, coarse grass that was too unpalatable for the sheep and rabbits to graze. Wily marsh pheasants would prefer to run than fly. They would break cover and reveal themselves, only for a tenacious dog to scent its line and force the bird into the air to escape. The hunter became frustrated in its effort to chase the prey without success, as the triumphant bird made its escape, only to land a hundred or so yards away and continue once again on foot.

All the time, as you walked over the marsh, with every step forward there was an expectation that a bird or animal would flush from its hiding place: always rabbits every few yards, and grey and red-legged partridges in coveys would burst up in front of you, calling in alarm as they skimmed over the marsh. Short-eared owls, barn owls, tawny owls and little owls all prospered. Hen harriers were never very common, turning up during the winter to hunt the sea walls and marshes, but never a marsh harrier or buzzard; these turned up years later. There must have been an abundance of small rodents. When it was particularly freezing cold for weeks, bitterns used to find some form of sustenance in the borrow dykes just inside the seawall, and snipe (always snipe) would flush from all over the wet marsh singly or in whisps.

Jack Hoy as a lad about to embark on his wildfowling career.

As the winter progressed, after a few days of rain, the old, low creeks held water. Some you couldn't cross with wellies while others, with just a few inches of water, lined the bottom; these were a haven for waders of all species, probing the soft earth and grass. Snipe particularly loved these places along with, surprisingly, woodcock especially at dusk. Curlew, redshanks, green sandpipers (not so common then), and lapwings by the thousand haunted the marsh. On the bigger fleets which held water all year round, teal would spend the day there sleeping, resting, and feeding on the club rush seeds dropping into the water. At dusk dozens, sometimes hundreds, would fly around the marsh in tight bunches, only to drop suddenly out of the sky into a fleet to feed. Mallard, too, would circle around quite high for several minutes before making sure it was safe committing to a dark fleet. Wigeon also loved the sweet grass that floated on the freshly flooded marsh, their presence given away by the white and brilliant green droppings that they left behind.

On the abundant thistle heads, flocks of goldfinches would feed, together with red linnets, chaffinches, skylarks, meadow pipits, yellow hammers and corn buntings. A host of seed-eating small birds would fly from one source of food to another, their undulating flight giving some clue as to their identity. Amazingly, even with all the anthill mounds and nests, I can never remember seeing a green woodpecker. Also, blackbirds were always common both in the summer and winter. Din always referred to them as "marsh blackbirds", as if they were different genetically; who knows, perhaps he was right? Likely as not, they were the same species that we get on our garden bird tables summer and winter. But there was a large migratory influx of blackbirds that came with the redwings, fieldfares and others that fed on the berries adorning hedges and bushes surrounding the small arable fields during the winter months.

The arable fields were mostly sown with spring wheat or barley and the harvest always seemed to be much later. Some crops were still standing, or at least not finished being cut, until well into October. If the crop was flattened by rain and wind, it was not long before the local population of ducks, particularly mallard, just couldn't resist the easy pickings of a field of laid barley. They seemed to like one field in particular and they would fly from Old Hall mainly. If they weren't disturbed, dozens and dozens would drop onto the barley crop or stubble to gorge themselves and not all of them made it back to Old Hall to digest the easy pickings; nothing tastes better than a stubble-fed mallard. Canada or greylag geese, which today would share the crop with the ducks, were unheard of, and we only read about the pursuit of them in stories from the regular weekly contributors from a borrowed *Shooting Times*.

Sunday mornings were devoted to ferreting the huge rabbit population that did untold damage to the crops around the field margins. Some of the warrens on the marsh were huge. The task of netting each hole would be virtually impossible and these were hardly ever worked. Earths which were smaller, with ten or a dozen holes, were the ones we favoured; the chances of losing a valuable animal was much less likely. Digging and finding one in the maze of tunnels in heavy Essex marsh clay was hard work and locating the ferret on a rabbit in a smaller earth was so much easier. The electronic locating collar and finder wasn't invented then. We would divide up into teams: me, my cousin, and a mate would go and work one lot of earths while my dad, Din and my grandfather would work another. On several occasions the other brother, Syd, would bring a mate, and they would go and work another set.

The one thing that was at the back of the adults' minds was the fact that three wives and mothers were busy slaving away in the kitchen to prepare the Sunday dinner to be served at precisely 1.30pm, so at midday you thought twice before putting ferrets into holes and being late. It nearly always happened. One of the teams would get laid up and a lot of sweating, swearing and digging resulted; sometimes, an animal was lost and left to its own devices and hopefully caught a couple of days later, or even the next weekend. You dare not be late for dinner. The rabbits were paunched and legged, threaded onto the thin metal burrow probing rods, which we termed "spears". We counted nets, made sure all the ferrets were accounted for, cleaned the mud and clay off spades, and carried all the gear back to my uncle's Morris 10 car parked somewhere as close by as possible. The adults were in the car with the boxes of ferrets; all of us boys, dogs, bags, and the rabbits were bundled into a trailer hitched to the rear bumper of the Morris. The rear door was closed, and a net thrown over the trailer, just to, hopefully, hide us from some eagle-eyed policeman. The trailer was what Din used to take a fattened pig to Colchester market to sell, so the sides were quite high which would hopefully hide us from prying eyes. The trailer was also used to transport the dogs and us boys every other Saturday when we went beating for the shoot at Great and Little Wigborough.

On shoot days, which were always every two weeks on a Saturday, the guns and beaters would arrive at 8:30am, either at Copthall or Newhall Farms. The farmer at the time, whose face I can't remember at all, was a Mr. Burrell. Shortly afterwards, the farm was sold to Mr. Sammy Sampson, and he became the new owner and joined the shoot. Mr. Victor Gray owned and farmed the neighbouring Newhall Farm. The guns would all go to the farmhouse to plan the drives for the day and have tea or coffee; the beaters used a barn with straw bales for seats. The bales, I remember, were always held together with wire instead of baler twine, the type of bales that were produced by a threshing tackle and baler that had been contracted out. I remember Mr. Frost from Barrow Hill, who used to work for Mr. Jones (a contractor from Rowhedge), going from farm to farm threshing and bagging the wheat and barley.

The beaters all used to turn up by whatever form of transport they had. If they lived locally near the farms, they used to walk or have a bike, but there were only two or three locals. The rest came from Mersea or, like my uncle Sydney and his mate, from Rowhedge. Sid used to drive an Austin Devon or Somerset A40, an insipid green colour, and, sitting on the back seat in all of his splendour, an Irish red setter. He thought the world of that dog. On shoot days my father would be up early preparing sandwiches and hot flasks for the both of us and also cooking a fried breakfast. We would set off on our bikes to pedal the two miles to his brother Din's bungalow in Rosebank Road, with the dog trotting beside my dad's bike. We would arrive at 8.00am then hitch up the trailer. Three or four of us lads, with at least four dogs, would pile into it and make ourselves as comfortable as possible, sitting on empty corn sacks with big dogs lolling all over the occupants. The trailer, I remember, had very hard suspension (if any) and it was a rough ride to Wigborough. The Morris 10 passengers consisted of my grandfather, Alan Hoy, in the passenger seat, and my father Jack was in the back with Tiddler Mole, an old shooting and gardening mate of Din who, obviously, was driving the car. When the Morris 10 arrived at Copthall, we were set free from the trailer with our canine companions. We put our lunch high up on hooks in a building so the dogs and, probably, rats couldn't get to it. The beaters' place that we used for our midday break was a small red brick building that was part of the farm, and which is still there today. It had a small fireplace and, if the weather was particularly cold, a fire was lit. Logs were in another shed and we banked up the little fire so it would be still alight when we got back to the farm at lunch time. Standing on the floor would always be a crate of 12 bottles of brown and light ale for us to drink; the beer, I remember, was brewed by Cook's from Halstead or Truman & Daniell's at West Bergholt.

The first drive at Copthall was from the farm buildings heading down towards the seawall where the walk is today. The beaters would spread out in a line from the farm to the seawall towards Abbots Hall farm boundary. The guns would go down the farm lane to the lower brick barn, then head towards the marsh and line out from the old counter wall to the working seawall near Copthall Creek, where the bird hide is today. There were no radios or mobile phones then so you had to give the guns time to get into position, then we would all move forward as one in a straight line pushing any game ahead of you. The beaters would reach the edge of the marsh and turn in a sweeping left-hand movement. The beater on the left would have to wait and mark time, but the beater on the right flank, usually on top of the seawall, would practically have to run to keep up with his colleagues as they swept to the left. Then when all were in line and straight again, you would move forward as one. Coveys of partridges were pushed forward in front of the beaters, and you knew that they were hopefully in between the beaters and guns. Slowly, the beaters moved forward trying not to rush the quarry somewhere on the rough terrain, but these birds are full of self-preservation, and they knew there was danger ahead. A covey would lift and, instead of flying forward, they would turn either left on right or fly straight back over the beaters. There was a lot of arm waving and shouting but it was of no use, they knew exactly what they were doing. Some did fly forward and over the waiting guns; some paid the price, but the vast majority got away unscathed to live another day.

There were usually eight guns in the team stretched out across the marsh 40 yards apart, reaching across to the seawall, and all usually standing low in an old dried-up creek to try and be out of sight as much as possible. Most of them were quite young as I remember, but the shoot captain was a retired army officer, Major General (Squirrel) Lewis. He couldn't hit a barn even if he stood inside, but he was an absolute gentleman: extremely friendly and courteous and, of course, it seemed as if every bird on the farms flew towards and over him. There would be a groan from the beaters. "Look at that lot heading for the general", and, as usual, not a feather floated to the ground. But one day he left us all open mouthed in astonishment as a covey flew over him and he managed to shoot a right and left – that is, one with the first cartridge and another with the second.

Everybody congratulated him on his marksmanship, but it didn't last. After the drive was finished the dogs would work behind the line of guns retrieving and picking up any birds that were not picked up by hand. The group of beaters and dogs were then picked up by a tractor and trailer at Copthall Marsh, and then transported back up the lane to the farm, then along Copthall Lane to Newhall Farm and down the farm lane and track to Sampson's and Feldy marshes. We would line out across the marsh from the old counter wall to Sampson's sluice and seawall, then drive and beat back the marsh to the waiting guns.

We had walked and beat another smaller piece of Copthall Marsh back to the boundary ditch and sheep fence separating Copthall from Newhall. There the guns again would line out and wait for us to push whatever came forward towards them. Ground game were never shot as it was too dangerous for fear of a person or a valuable dog being hit by ricocheting pellets, but foxes were an exception, though only if it was safe to shoot. My dear uncle Din used to carry a gun in the line of beaters; if any birds broke back, he would have a shot at them to add to the bag. All of his shooting life he would have used a 12 bore with hammers either side of the breech to detonate the cartridge. He was a brilliant shot – nothing would he miss. As he walked along with the beaters, the hammers of the gun would be pulled back ready to fire but the barrels were in an open position, so it was relatively safe so as to not discharge a cartridge accidentally. As soon as a chance arose, he would close the barrels to the breech and fire at the departing bird. His brother Syd sold him a K.D. Radcliffe 12 bore hammerless shotgun. All you have to do with a hammerless shotgun is to slide the safety catch forward and it is ready to fire. It is situated on top of the gun just in front of your thumb; very quick and very safe. Usually with a S/S hammerless shotgun, when you push the top lever across to open the barrels, it automatically pushes the safety catch back to a safe position. Din would be in his usual place in the line of beaters with his newfangled gun, barrels open but loaded. However, he had forgotten the safety catch was pushed back to safe when he had opened the gun. A dog would flush a pheasant or partridge and Din would snap shut the gun, throw the gun into his shoulder to shoot at the fast-departing bird, and everyone would be watching to see the bird crumple at the sound of his shot. Sadly, of course, the gun was on safe and however hard he pulled on the trigger it wouldn't fire. "What the hell are you doing boy?", his father would shout at him. "This bloody gun, the safety keeps going back so I can't fire the bloody thing", came the reply. Everyone was in fits as poor old Din sucked on his pipe, his face red with frustration, but it wasn't the last time. It happened quite regularly. In the end he gave up and let someone else be walking gun.

After three or four drives we would all go back to Copthall, pair and brace up the bag, and have "dinner": sandwiches, a flask of tea or coffee, and, of course, the crate of beer. Some used to take a bottle home with them instead of drinking it there. They were duly reminded: "Don't forget to bring the empty back when you come next time", as there was a thruppence deposit on the bottle. One or two of the old boys who used to come beating bought a doorstep of bread and a block of cheese, and sometimes a raw onion, instead of sandwiches. They were produced from out of a coat pocket wrapped in a piece of white linen cloth, and out of another pocket an apple, which all would be cut up with his pocketknife, after wiping the blade clean on his trousers! For a drink, a "Corona" bottle full of cold tea was produced! When the team of guns were shooting at Newhall Farm, the Grove woodland right next to the farm were the first drives of the day. The guns would stand on the fields on what we used to call "the east end" and form a "U" shape. The beaters would enter the Grove at Copthall Lane and push through the woodland, hopefully flushing out any pheasants or partridges (usually red-legged or, perhaps, French which used the woods more than their English cousins; the latter preferred the open fields and marshes). Woodcock was also particularly common after the October and November full moon cycle. When that drive was finished the team of guns walked and did the same operation at the north end of the grove. Any pheasants that were present moved ahead of the beaters, so the last fifty yards was driven very slowly, just to trickle and flush them out. The undergrowth was incredibly thick, with nettles and brambles blocking your pathway and hiding every pheasant, woodcock or partridge. Dogs were the only way to flush these tight sitting birds and it was a very keen springer or cocker spaniel that would face such painful tight cover. Labradors just looked at you with disdain and thought, "you must be joking mate, I'm not going in there to be torn to shreds", so, inevitably, many birds were missed and stayed exactly where they were concealed. They then flew out low behind you as you passed by, away from danger.

Afterwards the team of guns would all head off down the farm track towards the marsh, and line out from the old counter wall and behind the raised track that heads towards the sluice that drains under the seawall into Sampson's saltwater creek. The beaters would line out from the Grove across the fields of stubble or plough to the deep ditch that divides New Pots Farm from Newhall. This ditch collects all of the rainfall that falls on the land up as far as St. Stephen's Church in School Lane in Great Wigborough, channelling into the ditch to the left of Copthall Lane through the Grove, and down between New Pots and Newhall. In times of heavy and persistent rain it was a torrent, but it reduced in force as it entered the old, wide creek of Sampson's with the ground level dropping from shrinkage as it had dried out over millennia. The water slowed down, filling the

Beaters at Copthall 1967 – (L to R) John ("Hoss") Hoy, Doug Sawkins, Jack Hoy senior, Steve Green, Barry Swiggs, Billy Jowers and Syd Hoy.

Dogs: Bess, Bruce, Judy & Judy.

old creek from side to side with acres of shallow water. The sluice pipe passing through the seawall was of a very small diameter and it would take weeks for the water to drain away down the muddy saltings creek into the Ray Channel.

Din would give a shout and we would all move forward as one. Boys were never allowed to be together and there was always an adult in between to keep an eye on us, or to reprimand us (as Din would say: "to stop us buggering about"); but we still did bugger about. Everyone had a beating stick that was used for hitting branches and hedges in the hope of moving any pheasant or game bird hiding there. As you walked across the heavy clay fields, the earth and mud would build up on your wellies and increase the weight threefold, so you were constantly scraping off the clinging clay to lighten the load from your feet. The clay was also perfect for making "ammo": clay balls were formed with your hands about the size of a baseball and then pushed onto the end of your beating stick and about 6 inches up the shaft. Then it was the same action as casting a fly or baited hook with a fishing rod. You would choose an unsuspecting target and lob the ball of clay over the supervising adult next to you on your left or right to one of the lads you shared the trailer ride with. It took a few attempts to get any kind of accuracy and after a while you were deadly; but all of the time you had one eye on Din. When he wasn't looking, a rain of mud mortar balls would descend on one chosen target, then one of the older beaters would inform you that had been spotted by Din, so you would carry on behaving yourself for a while. However, Din had you sussed when the next mortar was lobbed and there would be a screaming bellow from the left or right flank where he was walking. "John, (his son – the architect of mayhem and mischievousness), will you and the rest of you bloody boys stop buggering about, and keep in a straight line".

16

I always remember my other cousin, David ("Labber") Green when he used to come in the beating line. He was of a slight, nervous disposition and so unsuspecting David was picked on as a victim and target. As we slowly moved across the field, when Din wasn't looking or had gone the other side of a hedge that put him out of sight, it was then that David got the full treatment. We would fashion three or four mud balls, put them gently into our coat pockets, and, at a given signal, all three of us would lob them at David as fast as you could get them onto the end of your stick. The first salvo would land all around him and he would look up to see what was going on, only to see another salvo raining down on him. David would be ducking and diving, trying not to be hit, but he took it all in good heart and it wasn't long before he was doing the same. All the time, we were waiting for Din to "whisper" at the top of his voice and give us another severe telling off for "buggering about".

We would continue the drive. The guns we could see in the far distance down by Sampson's Creek were lined out waiting. We would beat and drive a piece of marsh to the left of Feldy track that was called "The Pig's Ear", although I never found out why. Din would send me to to the far-left boundary bordering Andrew Davidson's marsh and farm. I remember walking past some trees which must have been elm trees that subsequently died of Dutch elm disease, the roots being exposed by rabbits, sheep and the digging and rooting of free-range pigs that were on the marsh. I would reach the ditch or brook taking the rainwater to Sampson's sluice and cross over onto what is called Ray Hill marsh, driving whatever was in front of me to the waiting guns. I can remember the fleet and brook very well; it was not a deep ditch like it is now, but a wide depression that resembled the creek when it was tidal hundreds of years before. As you got within 300 yards of the seawall, it widened out quite considerably. The old saltings edges were still so visible that you had to step, or jump, down into what was the creek bottom, but hundreds of years of wind, rain and grazing animals had eroded the cant away to a lesser degree. I would carry on walking towards the seawall. My fellow beaters would be on my right-hand side pushing forward what was in front of them. A covey would lift and fly towards and over the guns, and a staccato of shots would sound as the fast-flying birds passed over the waiting guns.

The seawall in front of me was now only a hundred yards away. I stepped out of the old dried-up creek and walked up the anomaly of a relatively steep incline which gives the name of the marsh: Ray Hill. I could never imagine this high area of land ever being covered by any high tide, and when the whole area was saltmarsh, it would been an island, as a spring tide surrounded it in its entirety. I got to the top of Ray Hill. I could see over the low seawall, as it was then: the saltings and Sampson's Creek, Ray Creek, and the saltings of Ray Island to the south, all came into view. Over on Mersea Island I could pick out the landmark elm trees that were then so common; they towered above everything else. One huge tree was close to my grandfather's garden gate at the top of Firs Chase. It was half in the road and half on the footpath, and you virtually had to squeeze through the gap between the fence and tree as you passed by it. Another stood close by in Din's smallholding, where he and my aunt worked long hours growing flowers for the seeds under a contract for Suttons, the celebrated seed firm. Din and my aunt also fattened a pig or two for the Colchester market, and sold fruit, vegetables and eggs to the local shops and neighbours, in what is now Blackwater Drive. The tree in the smallholding was massive: it was probably the tallest on the island, it towered above everything. It was a real eye-catcher. The others that I could see were the swaying, elegant poplars that stood in the garden of the Passadora's family house close by, which was called "The Firs".

As my gaze looked east along the top spine of the Island, I could see another landmark which I used to pass regularly on my bike: with its red brick structure and, in those days, tiled roof, the water tower in Upland Road dominated the skyline. I carried on walking, crossing over the dry borrow dyke and up the steep incline onto the top of the seawall, then turned to my right with all of my fellow beaters who were stretched out across Feldy Marsh, heading for the line of guns in front of them. I continued along the top of the seawall with Sampson's saltings and creek to my left. I could hear the occasional report as someone took a shot, but my attention was distracted by the hull of a barge lying in line with, and under the shelter of, the seawall at the head of the creek. She was virtually intact; her mast and rigging were missing, as were the covers that sheltered the hold, so she was open to the elements and the crashing waves and spray that, at high tide, hit her broadside in a south-easterly gale. On the wide transom, her name was carved: "UNITY" and "IPSWICH". Apparently, she was given to William Wyatt as part payment for a debt. Then she was laid to rest a couple or three years after the Second World War; probably a plank on her once-proud hull was smashed in to let the tide flow and ebb through her, so she would never float again. Her remains are still visible in the soft mud: if you look on Google Earth, you can see her outline and shape just below the surface of the green waters.

The wide, coastal, muddy creek, so typical of Essex, ran away from me to my left. On the south side of the creek was just a relatively narrow stretch of saltings, and the sluice that drained the surface water from the land that had collected in the low-lying fleet and borrow dykes. On the north side was a large triangular section amounting to several acres. Quite close to the cant edge were the remains of a low seawall that extended away from me for a hundred and fifty yards, and then just disappeared down to the level of the saltings. These continued away from me towards the Ray Channel, and abruptly stopped where it had been breached. Now a creek came through, and on the other side of this deep, 20 yard-wide, muddy gutter, the saltings appeared again, running in line and bordering the Ray Channel, then heading north towards the shingle factory at Johnny Millgate's at the head of Ray Creek. This, as well, was an old seawall. When was this structure built? How long did it last? When was the storm and huge tide that topped and breached it, and the unrelenting North Sea took back? On the inside of this old wall, a borrow dyke was dug, and the spoil was then formed on top of the saltings to enclose that area in order to keep out the sea. When it breached, why didn't they repair the breach instead of building another seawall, going across at an angle to where it is at this present day?

The saltings that are formed either side of Sampson's Creek are particularly rich in coastal vegetation. The muddy, small creeks are full of samphire and, on the salting top, purslane and sea asters grow in profusion. When these plants drop their seeds, teal in particular gorge themselves on the tiny seeds floating in the creeks at high tide. Where the wind and tide collect and leave them, the teal will find them. Curlew, oystercatchers, redshank, greenshank, dunlin, godwits, knots, shelduck: as soon as the mud is uncovered, each and every one is using their specialised bill to find their favourite form of sustenance, either on the surface, or hidden under the soft ooze, pushing their bills right up to their eyes as they search. Green plovers would spend the day roosting on a firmer area of mud before they were washed off their last legs by a flooding tide, only to fly up in the sky for hundreds of feet, then glide and parachute down on broad, feathered wings to stand on a nearby field with their golden and grey cousins.

I heard Din's whistle and call for the line of beaters to stop. Syd was going back one hundred yards with his red setter to look and search for a stricken cock pheasant that had been hit and had flown back over the beaters, landing on the marsh by a large area of tall grass and thistles. He

Syd Hoy at Rowhedge in the 1950s with his spaniel and Irish red setter.

19

took the elegant-moving dog downwind of the thick cover and cast it off with a "hi loss" command to hunt and use its incredible scenting ability. To see a setter moving, questing and hunting is an amazing sight; they seem to glide and float over the ground as they turn this way and that, following a tiny whiff of scent as it floats towards its nose. After a few minutes, the questing dog suddenly turned into the wind, and stopped dead in its tracks. It was pointing to a thick clump of grass. It lifted one front leg, held its tail horizontally, the long red ribbons of his coat swaying as it caught the breeze, and froze to the spot. Nothing moved: only its incredible, scent-sensing nose. Syd was about forty yards away. He moved closer, within five yards, and the setter hadn't moved an inch. As Syd got closer, the dog took a step nearer to the thick area of reedy grass, his front leg lifted once again in the classic pointer/setter pose. Syd gave it the command to fetch. It dived into the thick cover, then, after a second or two, it lifted its magnificent head and, within his jaws, held the cock pheasant. Syd called the dog to him and took the bird. He smoothed down a few ruffled feathers, then placed the bird in his game bag, the long tail feathers protruding from out of the top of it. Then, praising and making a fuss of his charge, he made his way back to the line of beaters.

I stopped short of the gun that I was heading for; he was positioned around a bend in the seawall. If any bird had gone his way, he probably wouldn't have been able to shoot because I would have been in his line of fire. I stopped on the top of the seawall. I was right in the middle of Sampson's Creek, had it been tidal. I noted the soft, shiny mud to my left. I then turned to my right, and looked up the length of Sampson's Fleet, heading inland. The first thing that really struck me was how much lower it was compared to the creek that was tidal. Had the land inside shrunk as it had dried out, or had the mud built up in the creek when the seawall was built, damming the flow of water which was keeping the creek free of mud as the ebb tide rushed out into the Ray Channel? The difference between the two levels was incredible. I walked down the inside of the seawall and stopped to where I thought the mud was level with the top of my head. The bottom of Sampson's Fleet inland, I guessed, was at least 10 feet lower. I can't imagine it had shrunk that much; I can only guess that, when it was tidal, Sampson's Creek was a very substantial waterway, keeping it clear of silting mud like it is now.

The beaters were now close to the guns. Din blew his whistle, and the drive was over. The dogs worked behind the guns, hunting for any birds that weren't picked, but were eventually retrieved. Guns and beaters got onto the tractors and trailers, which were driven by either Gordon Purtell or Bernard Radcliffe, both of whom worked at New Hall for Mr. Gray, before being taken back to

Copthall. The bag of birds was laid out on the lawn, counted and recorded. The guns were given a couple of brace of birds each, and anything that was left over, the adult beaters had.

Back then, in the 1950s, the pace on the land was very much slower. I can remember some of the farms on the Island still used horsepower to plough and cultivate the land, but most of the farms had a tractor or two of relatively low power. Consequently, those with horses had a smaller plough and implement, and it took longer to turn in and cultivate the land, but it gave all of the wildlife using the farmland time to adapt to the changes. Most wheat and barley stubbles were left all through the winter months; partridges, pheasants and a host of smaller seed-eating birds would be sustained throughout. Root crops were also grown. Sugar beet, turnips and mangolds would be fed to sheep to eat and graze, and kale for cattle. All of these crops were full of weeds that seeded, and which gave food and cover to a host of birds and animals.

At the end of the day, the General summoned Din to him, and between them they would work out how much the wages of the day came to. One pound for an adult, and 5 shillings (25p) for us boys. We were over the moon. Everybody bade their farewells, saying, "See you in a fortnight's time". The passengers got into the Morris, both us and the tired, soaking wet, steaming dogs, clambering into the trailer for the bumpy ride back to Mersea, and then the two-mile bike ride back home.

2: First Flight

ALL, OR MOST of, the rainfall that fell onto the surrounding marshes and fields eventually found its way into the wide, low way of Sampson's Fleet. In times of persistent heavy rain, the area was totally flooded, but in normal conditions the fleets and low ways would hold just inches of water, and these were a haven for mallard and particularly teal. Mallard would feed on the drowned worms and seeds, but also on acorns that had floated down from the Grove at New Hall, the oak trees overhanging the fast-flowing ditch dropping them into the water as it made its way eventually to the Ray Channel. Club rush seeds were what the teal loved; it grew in abundance on the fleet edges and, at flight time, in the area around Sampson's, and particularly Ray Marsh, the large, twisting fleets were a magnet for these lovely small ducks. Ray Marsh always held water, even through the summer months. I can never remember it being dry. Mallard nested close by, their offspring only having to walk a few steps before they were in the relative safety of a reedy piece of water to hide. Redshank nested in the tussocks of reedy grass, and lapwings nested in profusion everywhere; as you walked close by a brooding female, the guarding male bird would dive bomb you if he thought you were a danger to his mate and their nest.

At about this time, Alan Gray, who farmed Bocking Hall at East Mersea, used to graze his sheep at Ray Hill marsh. Every year a Welsh shepherd used to come to Bocking Hall for a few weeks to attend to Mr. Gray's flock. As a boy I went to Bocking Hall quite frequently, as my mum used to work at the farm, riddling and bagging potatoes. She also worked in the fields, picking potatoes and peas; lots of women would be out in the fields working, bent double all day picking these crops. It must have been back-breaking work. At school holiday time several children were helping their parents in the fields to earn some extra cash to pay for Christmas presents, or just to earn some money for the everyday expenses. I used to bike to the farm and help the shepherd attend the hundreds of sheep owned by Mr. Gray; it was probably during the Easter and summer holidays that I used to go with him in Mr. Gray's Land Rover and drive to wherever the sheep were. Every day we would drive over to Ray Hill marsh and attend to the flock. As a result of the undulating marsh, the sheep would somehow get onto their backs in a hollow and lie there upside down, unable to get back onto their feet. We would split up and search all of the marsh looking for these animals; if you came across one, you would grab a couple of handfuls of woolly fleece and turn them back over the right way up. You would have to hold them for several minutes before the feeling and use of their limbs were back to normal. Some unfortunates were not quite so lucky and not found until it was too late: the sad carcass having been discovered eaten by foxes, crows, magpies, and both black-backed and herring gulls.

I was in my element walking through this incredible environment, never knowing what was going to surprise you at every step as you searched for an unfortunate animal. The shepherd used to bring his sheepdog down from Wales with him; I remember the dog was very tall and long in the leg with the usual black and white coat and very friendly. I also thought at the time that the shepherd never gave him much affection, unlike our dogs at home which were doted on and always made a fuss of. I always made a fuss of the collie whenever we were together, and when we walked the marsh, he used to come with me instead of the owner. He was also a good hunting dog, chasing rabbits into their burrows, and hunting the fleets for moorhens. All dogs love to hunt moorhens; they must give off a strong scent that is irresistible to canines. On one occasion the shepherd's dog was hunting the reeds when this brown bird flushed and flew ahead low in front of him, about the size of a moorhen, legs dangling from its body. It only flew a few yards and landed back into the fleet. The dog carried on hunting when suddenly the bird lifted out of the reeds again, but this time it kept flying and flopped into another fleet hundreds of yards away. When I told the shepherd about the bird I had seen, he said it was probably a water rail. Several years later, I was shooting on a reedy fleet waiting for a duck at evening flight. The light was fading fast, and it was nearly time to pack up and go home. Suddenly, and without any warning, there was a blood-curdling scream, as if someone was being attacked, or a pig objecting to being manhandled. It made the hairs on the back of my neck stand on end, so frightening was the noise. A few seconds later, a teal flew past. It fell on the other side of the fleet in some tall reeds; I sent Otto, my labrador, over the wide water-filled fleet to retrieve it. He had marked the little duck's fall, so he had a good idea of where to search. The reeds were dense and tall; it never fails to amaze me how these wonderful dogs find these birds in the jungle of reed stems and darkness but, as he was searching, he flushed a water rail. A few seconds later, I could hear heavy breathing and snuffling through his nose, a good sign that he had the bird in his mouth as he swam back to me. I have seen many water rails over the years as my dogs flush them. They are a very secretive bird. I have heard a rail scream only once after that; the noise is as if out of a horror film. Totally unnerving. I spoke to Dave ("Doodle") Whiting later that evening, describing this scary scream. He said it was probably a water rail.

I met up with the shepherd at the far end of Ray Hill marsh, and we walked back to the Land Rover together and back to Bocking Hall. I was never to see him again until our paths crossed more than 50 years later. I had to go to Bocking Hall to repair a plumbing problem for Mr.Gray (he was living in the house at the time), so I was having a chat about the farm and other things, when the back door opened and in walked the shepherd who I hadn't seen since I was about 11 or 12 years old. I recognised him instantly; he looked exactly the same as when I last saw him, and when Mr. Gray introduced me to him, he also remembered me as a young boy. He had come down from Wales for the day, and I had just come to the farm for an hour. Fate, perhaps? I sometimes wonder!

Din had access to both farms as a result of his duties: gamekeeping together with vermin, continuous predator and winter rabbit control. He took full advantage of shooting duck on the stubbles, the flooded marshes, and the fleets. My grandfather lived on the other side of his garden fence, and it was quite a regular trip when the pair of them and, very often, Tiddler took the Morris over to Feldy where they would each select a favourite fleet or flooded stubble field to await flight time. This was around the time of World War Two when before, during and after, cartridges were in short supply and relatively expensive, so the shooting was very selective in terms of what species you were after. Teal were only shot to add to the bag if the mallard didn't turn up; back then mallard were very common. It was a bit of a sin to waste a cartridge on something as small as a teal, however sporting and good eating they are. These men were pot hunters: they had families, grateful neighbours, and customers that relied without question on the sustainable and bountiful harvest that was provided. It was not only by my relatives, but several expert local people who specialised in supplying natural food for the table, be it ducks, geese, game, and, of course, the humble rabbit.

I can remember my very first flight on one of the flooded areas of water that was once a large saltwater creek. It branched off from Sampson's Creek from when it was once tidal, then headed southwest towards Copthall lower barn. It then turned again to the south and headed towards Little Ditch and Salcott Channel. If it ever joined up with the wide creeks, I would never know, but we left our bikes that night on the end of a counter wall which, at some point, was constructed across the creek to stop the tide coming in, at the place where Copthall Creek comes up to the seawall today. Back down the old creek towards

Newhall and Sampson's freshwater fleet and saltwater creek, another counter wall was constructed which is still the farm track used to this day. It stopped the tide in Sampson's Creek from the east, and one of the first areas of saltings enclosed are the two fields to the left of the track, adjacent to the lower barn at Copthall. It must have been in the Christmas school holidays in 1954 or 1955 when me and Dad went over to Copthall. We passed the lower barn, went another three hundred yards, and lay our bikes down in the coarse grass at the end of the counter wall where the low-lying land, which flooded every winter, stretched away to our left: two hundred yards long, twenty-five yards wide and ankle deep. It was absolutely perfect for dabbling ducks. Dad stayed up the end nearest the counter wall while I walked a hundred yards further along.

I was using a s/s 28g hammer gun that Mum and Dad had just bought for me for Christmas. It had been in Vin Thorpe's bike shop window for sale; I think at the time it cost £10 which, back then, was more than a week's wages. Vin always had guns for sale, just propped up in the corner of the shop window, along with the new and second-hand bikes. All the lads who were interested in shooting were always looking in Vin's window to see what was for sale and what he had acquired recently.

I splashed along the shallow waters edge towards where I was going to await flight. I found a suitable spot and knelt down, concealing myself in some tall grass and reeds. I opened the breech of my new gun and looked down the pitted barrels to make sure it was clear of debris. I put my fingers into my coat pocket, took out two gorgeous, shiny orange, Eley Grand Prix no.5 cartridges, and slipped them into the chambers of the gun. I waited. I would take a cartridge out of my pocket and feel the smoothness of the varnished paper case. I read all of the black lettering and the words "Eley Kynoch" imprinted in the brass end and notice the different colour of the copper percussion cap that awaited the firing pin to dent it, as the dainty hammer fell on it. I would gaze along the browned barrels, feeling the smooth cold metal in my hands. I put the gun into my shoulder and would aim at something in my imagination. I looked to my right, and I could just see Dad's (beret[1]) hatted head and wisps of blue smoke as he exhaled on his "rolly" (roll-up cigarette) of St. Julien's tobacco. I looked forward and, in front of me, a bird was swimming on the water on the other side of the flood. It was by now getting quite dark, so much so that the bird looked completely black. Is it a moorhen? I wasn't sure. Then, when I looked again, there was two more. I cocked the little gun, aimed, and fired. One of the

---

1   Nearly all of the older generation wore a beret when shooting: was it something they were demobbed from the forces with? They also wore a gabardine raincoat with a wide belt, called a "mac" (macintosh).

birds stayed on the water. I ran out and picked it up: a drake teal. I came back to my hide and knelt down again, removing the fired cartridge from the chamber; the pungent smoke drifted up to my nose from the open gun. I inhaled the intoxicating fumes, just as I had done so in the past after my father had taken a shot. I put the spent open cartridge to my nose and just breathed in that wonderful aroma. Even to this day, if I am standing behind someone at a clay pigeon shoot and a cartridge is fired and ejected, and which I catch, I still have to put the fired cartridge to my nose and take a deep breath.

I reached into my pocket again and placed another cartridge into the gun. I picked up the teal and stroked the feathers of the little duck back into place and laid it gently on the grass. When I came back to reality, on the water were 5 or 6 ducks swimming about. I picked one and fired. The rest jumped off the water and flew past me to my left; I fired at them again and, amazingly, one fell from the bunch. I was ecstatic. I didn't know which one to go for first, so I ran across the water and picked the first one, then searched to my left to where the other one should have been; nothing lay there. I was starting to panic, it was getting darker by the second, and I had no torch and no dog. My eyes and head were spinning as I looked this way and that, and then I heard a familiar voice behind me. "Is this what you are looking for?" Dad had it in his hand. I had miss-marked it in my inexperience and walked over it by 10 yards. We both walked back to our bikes as I recounted about them landing on the water without me hearing, or even seeing, them. My first three ducks. How much pleasure and enjoyment those little birds have given me over the years. I still get just as much of a thrill now as I watch them flying at breakneck speed across the wild, open estuaries and saltings, turning as one in a tight ball as they race off to a chosen destination. We found the bikes in the darkness and pedalled the 7 miles to home. I couldn't get home quick enough to tell my mum.

Using the little 28g gun, I would accompany my dad over the summer months pigeon shooting on two or three farms in the evenings and at weekends somewhere on Mersea. We would always end up under a favourite sitty tree[2], get into the ditch below, make a bit of a hide to cover us, and then get under it and wait until an unsuspecting bird would land on its favourite branch. I would quietly cock the little gun, find a hole in the canopy, and poke the muzzle through. I lined up the target and squeezed the trigger; they didn't hear the bang. They would roll forward from their perch and dive head-first to the ground. I would hand Dad the gun, nip out through the hide, and look for my prize lying somewhere beneath the tree. I would then squeeze back in and take my place sitting

---

2   A "sitty" tree is one with bare branches or a branch devoid of leaves where pigeons would sit or roost.

in the ditch and wait. I can remember one day, a couple of years before I had the 28 bore, sitting under our favourite tree waiting for a pigeon. Dad's 12 bore was leaning against a branch, loaded. We had been sitting in the ditch for quite a while when suddenly a "dow"[3] landed on the top of the oak. I looked across the ditch to my father; he was fast asleep. He had probably started on an early shift that morning, so I didn't wake him but reached across the ditch to the 12g. I quietly cocked one of the hammers, lined up the pigeon, and fired. The pigeon released its grip from the branch and fell tumbling to the ground. The bang very quickly woke up my father who didn't know where he was for a second or two. I was 7 or 8 years old. That was my first pigeon. I can still remember seeing my father's startled face as he was so rudely awakened. As I recall his expression, his wide eyes and slightly open mouth, I have often thought and recalled that summer day as I got older, and later heard the subsequent stories of his time during World War Two, with the frightening and horrific episodes of war. Was he being jolted out of an exhausted and battle-weary, overpowering sleep somewhere in North Africa or Sicily where his war abruptly ended? Or was he, frighteningly, back in France with the BEF as Wehrmacht, Luftwaffe bombs, bullets, shells, and mortars rained down on him as he took the same useless cover lying behind a spindly bush or tree, and a similar looking ditch as he lay in fear for his life? Indiscriminate mayhem broke all around him, trying to claim the young lives of him, his mates, and comrades in battle. All of this was so fresh in his mind as it was only 10 or so years before!

Dad used to get me to take shots at flying pigeons. I would walk on one side of a hedge, and he would be the other; he would be five yards further in front than me. Consequently, the bird would come out my side offering me the chance to shoot as it flew across or straight away from me. It also taught you to shoot quickly and snap shoot at your target, knowing the little gun had a smaller pattern of shot and range to be effective. But it was effective; it was a brilliant little gun. It used to bring down a pigeon in a puff of grey feathers as they tried to evade me. Also, if we were going to wait somewhere for evening flight for a duck, we would go an hour or so earlier, and flight "dows", as my dad called them, at a little spinney on our way. If it was windy from the west, we would position ourselves on the eastern side of the wood, as they flew low across the fields towards us to try and bed down and roost for the night in the sheltering trees behind us. We would sit together in the ditch, me usually on his left as it is easier for anybody right-handed to swing a shotgun from right to left. I would always shoot first, letting them come as close as possible, and not moving an eyelid so

---

3   A dow is a local name for a pigeon.

as not to alarm or make them turn out of range. Dad would say, "NOW!". I would pick a bird on my side if there was more than two; he would shoot at the twisting turning leftovers, alarmed by the report made by my gun. He used a rusty s/s underlever hammer gun 12g, years before the top rib had lifted from off the barrels. Fred Hayward, a brilliant local engineer, had braised it back on; it looked like scrambled egg all the way from the chamber to the foresight. The gun was only blackpowder proofed, I'm sure, but things like that didn't seem to matter back then. Some of the other pieces that were used locally were death traps, but no one had a hand blown off as far as I can recall. Dad used to fire Eley maximum! no.5 through it; he was a brilliant shot, but when he did miss, I used to give him loads of ribbing.

We would continue on our way, not leaving it too late to await flight, to quite a wide piece of fresh water that, once again, was the extreme end of a former tidal creek. Most of the fleet, or at least the best bit, was owned by the neighbouring farm. It was never artificially fed with grain: the depth was a constant ten inches in the middle, shallowing off on either side. It was a haven for mainly teal, but mallard also used to feed on the natural seeds and from the club rush that grew around its edges. It was on that area of water on Mersea that I learnt to shoot ducks at flight time; and in the failing light, where your hearing and vision pick up on a small duck, they give you not a second of thinking time as they fly past you. If you can see it or them in the darkness, it is in range; the gun is mounted in an instant, and as soon as the stock hits the shoulder the trigger is pulled. More often than not, there would be a satisfying splash as the little duck hits the water. Dad was always on the alert for mallard, and if he heard or saw some flying about or heading towards us, he would give me a whistle or a quiet call to attract my attention so as not to shoot at teal but wait to see if the mallard were going to come to us. What a prize a mallard is in the bag! They are a beautiful bird, either duck or drake, and such fine eating.

The bag was never large. If we got six between us, which was very rare, it was a good flight, but the knowledge I gained from my father was to put me in good stead about the ways of wildfowl, birds, nature and the countryside. I still have the little 28 bore which I haven't used once since 1959. The massive oak tree that, for years, we used to sit under, which attracted so many pigeons, finally died, and is no longer standing on the corner of the boundary hedge. It sadly disappeared from the landscape in about 2001, the same year as my dad. I bet if you root and scratch about in the shallow bottom of the ditch you will still find the non-ferrous remains of the 12-16 and little 28g cartridges.

It must have been in the early season of the following year when my dad borrowed, and later bought an s/s 12 bore hammer gun (which I refurbished and rebrowned in memory of his 100th birthday in 2014) from Bill Rudge. Bill was Dad's driver, Dad being the conductor of the bus company that they both worked for operating from the depot at West Mersea. He thought the 28g was not man enough to knock down a duck at any sort of range, so the 12 was the gun for me. A trip over to Feldy was planned. Mallard were using their favourite stubble field, Sampson's Fleet had a few inches of water from side to side, and teal were using the fleets. Over on Ray Hill marsh the fleets were being fed with grain to encourage more ducks; every species of the duck tribe is incredibly greedy when it comes to the easy pickings of liberal helpings of either wheat or barley. The shooting on Ray Hill was rented by Mr. Wass. He owned a bike shop in Short Wyre Street in Colchester, and on that particular evening Mr. Wass and other people were also shooting. I can't remember too much of the evening, but I can remember two or three people standing on the other side of Sampson's Fleet with white flags, so when teal or mallard tried to drop into the fleet, the flags were waved to frighten them off, and for us not to have a chance of a shot. It worked; all I can remember is trying to wield the heavy 12g trying to get a bead onto fast moving birds in the failing light. Din, Hoss (my cousin) and my grandad, and perhaps Tiddler, flighted the large favourite stubble field. Dad was near Sampson's with me; he had shot a mallard earlier. Din and the others had a couple of mallard but Mr. Wass and his guests was having several shots over on Ray Hill marsh.

Ray Hill was the best of all the fresh marshes, stretching from Salcott to the Peldon Rose pub. It was very low lying, and the fleets were quite wide and relatively deep as they meandered, twisted and turned, making the water area quite extensive on relatively few acres. It was a haven. Even today, after days of heavy rain when the land drains can't cope, on what is now a flat field, the old twisting fleets flood and reappear just as I remember them. I have often wondered over the years how much of a problem Din was to Mr. Wass for him to organise people to scare birds so Din couldn't shoot them legally on his side of the fleet. Or perhaps Mr. Wass was a problem for Din!

3: "Never fear, we have just passed Boadicea."

MY FIRST EVER outing on the saltings was with the 28 bore on the 1st of September 1955. Din drove the Morris over to Copthall and I walked with my father, Din, Hoss and Tiddler to the salting of Abbots Hall. It was, of course, pitch black as I followed along; after half an hour or so Dad stopped, and the other three carried on. Dad showed me a path which went out onto the marsh. I hadn't gone but a few yards when I stepped into a tiny water-filled creek that had been covered by tailings of corn which had been discarded onto the marsh. It was black and stinking, and putrid water splashed up the front of my trousers, coat, and gun. I reeked as I carried on out onto the saltings. In one hundred yards or so I found a small creek to my left and settled in to wait for whatever. Shots kept going off in the darkness. Occasionally I could hear wingbeats passing over-head but I never saw a thing; one double shot went off quite close to me, making me jump, but I never did see who it was.

As it got slowly lighter, I could see a little further as birds started to move and flight. A curlew passed to my right; I shot at it but missed. All the time, there was shooting and guns going off all around me. I couldn't see what everybody was shooting at. As it got still lighter, I could make out the shapes of people hiding in the marsh where I had shot at the curlew. Suddenly a person came into view; I must have shot right over his head! I could see a lot clearer now as the dawn broke; the shooting was more frequent as ducks and waders were a clearer target. Teams of mallard passed over sky high, and bunches of teal, all miles out of range, were shot at as they flew over someone, but not all of the ducks were out of range; occasionally there would be a bird shot and someone would scurry across the marsh to claim their prize. I could see the wide channel of Salcott

Creek in front of me now; it was lined with smacks, skiffs, and all manner of different craft at anchor.

As the early morning progressed, and as it got lighter, the birds ceased flighting. In front, and to the left and right appearing out of the marsh, people started to climb out of their muddy hiding places, and walk off the marsh back to their punt, dinghy, skiff or smack for home and breakfast. I was amazed just how many gunners there were. At my naïve young age, I thought the only people who had guns and went shooting were the members of my family and friends. I looked down Salcott Creek and heading east was a flotilla of craft. I looked behind me and I could see Dad on the seawall; Din, Tiddler and Hoss were walking back along the bottom of the seawall towards my father, so I got my gear together and joined them. I still reeked from the putrid, black liquid that I had stepped into earlier. As I walked up to them, the greeting I got as I showed them the stinking creek was, "Bloody hell, boy. What is that smell?" Din, I remember, had shot a mallard but that's all that was shot in our little group.

We went back to Abbots Hall again for the evening flight. I found a better creek in the daylight and settled in to watch and wait. It was bright and sunny with a gentle warm September breeze coming from the southwest. I looked behind me and, in the distance, I could see my father still puffing away on his rolly, keeping the mozzies at bay. Din and Hoss were further to the west on the other side of the barge quay, on the saltings in front of Abbots Hall flight pond. Tiddler didn't come, so my grandfather took his place in the Morris 10. Gunners kept arriving and walked to their chosen favourite spot and creek; not so many boats were at anchor in the channel that evening. I could also see gunners on the other side of Salcott Creek, on the south side from Quince's Corner heading towards Pennyhole to the east. Beyond the seawall to the south, between me and Tollesbury, was the incredibly wonderful duck marsh of Old Hall, and it was from there that I could hear a lot of shooting; all of these wonderful places were still new and a mystery to me, but I would get to know them with intimate fondness as I discovered them all in the following years. Then I looked high up in the sky. I could see the reason for all the shooting: mallard – teams and teams of mallard – flighting to the fed-flight ponds. The shooting seemed to be continuous as party after party, and bunch after bunch, of mallard, teal, pochard and tufted ducks streamed over my head. What an incredible sight it was; a two-way traffic as the birds that had been shot at were heading back to Abberton reservoir, and then those, together with more birds, were coming back later to try their luck, once again, for their evening meal. I was enthralled.

The daylight was now fading, and the whistling wings of the flighting birds was the only indication as they flew high overhead in the darkness. Not all flew over out of sight and range; as it got darker, a lot more flew lower, and so the fowlers in the marsh would get their chance as the birds flew out of a dark sky into the light for a split second. The bigger the duck is, the longer you can see it in the gloom, so for a better chance with anything smaller, like a teal, you have to be very quick off the mark for success. However, their presence is given away before you sometimes see them. Mallard are nearly always talking and calling to each other as they move about in the darkness. Wigeon are very vocal, whistling and growling as they flight. Teal are usually quiet in flight; they tend to call more when they fly around the saltings and creeks as they look for somewhere to feed. Noisy, fast wingbeats are usually what the fowler hears first;

John ("Hoss") Hoy.

they can pre-warn you two or three seconds before they pass by, or over, you. The more there are in the bunch, the more noise they make; and not just in the dark, but also in broad daylight, as they catch you unawares daydreaming, and bring you fully back to your senses as a rush of pinions passes by, or over, you. Your head and eyes are on a swivel as you try to locate it, or them, before they pass by out of range and unshot.

The local gunners that were sharing the saltings with me were now popping away with more regularity as it got darker; I still really couldn't see what they were shooting at. I could hear wingbeats that seemed quite low over me, and perhaps catch a glimpse of something moving swiftly overhead, but I never had a shot. I found the path and walked back to the seawall where I met up with my dad and the rest of my relations. I asked how they had all got on: Din had a pair of mallard, my grandad had a teal, my dad had bagged nothing, and Hoss also had nothing, although he had had four shots at some teal.

At the beginning of the summer school holidays in 1958, I got a job with Alfie Pavey as a milk-boy; we used to start at six am, meeting at Alf's bungalow and dairy in Suffolk Avenue. While Alf loaded the van, Derek or Graham

32

Waring (two of the other boys) would load the trade bike and deliver milk at Empress Avenue, and through to Prince Albert Road. Terry Mole and I would deliver to his customers in Suffolk Avenue; by the time we had done that, Alf had driven the Standard Vanguard to load up at the bottom of Suffolk Avenue, by East Road, to pick up crates of milk that had been delivered at some unearthly hour earlier in the morning. The road was so bad, the delivery lorry couldn't get to Alf's dairy; it's unbelievable how bad some of the roads were on the Island then. Suffolk Avenue was like a ploughed field; huge ruts from top to bottom. How the Standard made it up to Alf's bungalow is a miracle. All of us boys were ordered to jump off by Alf and push to give the Standard a helping hand when it was wet, slippery and muddy.

My wages for the week were 15 shillings (75p); of this, I saved as much as I could. I wanted a bigger shotgun. It took me 18 months to scrimp and save £20.00 towards my future purchase; every week, I would scour through the pages of items for sale in the Essex County Standard which was pushed through the letterbox every Friday. Then, one day, there it was: an advertisement, with a telephone number, selling a 16 bore s/s hammerless shotgun for £25:00 ono in Colchester. Dad rang up from the Mersea bus depot the next day to ask when it would be convenient to view the gun. The following week was arranged. Dad was at work and, as I couldn't wait, my sister met me after school some-where in Colchester. We caught a Corporation bus to Boadicea Way off Layer Road; we had no idea where the road was, so we asked the conductor to let us know where to get off. I can remember it now: when we were a hundred yards from our destination, the bell rang for the bus to stop and the bus conductor sang out, "Never fear, we have just passed Boadicea". We found the address in Montgomery Avenue and knocked on the door. When the front door opened, a man dressed in an army uniform stood there, and looked at us as if to say, "What do you kids want?" We explained that my father had rang a few days before but couldn't make it, so we had come instead to look at the gun that was advertised for sale. He invited us in, disappeared for a few moments, and then handed this beautiful German gun for me to look at. It was a thing of beauty; I had never seen any other gun like it in my short, shooting life. Instead of the whole gun being a rusty brown colour, and with hammers sticking up like all of the others I had handled, on this model the barrels were blued, and the action was polished steel with the usual, quite heavy, engraving of Germanic guns. The stock was a dark, well-figured piece of walnut, with a cheek piece which is commonplace on German guns. The trigger guard was of horn or bone and the oval at the end of the pistol grip was also of the same material. Behind the action fences, projecting out either side of the blued top lever, were two cocking-indicators. I pushed the top lever across to open the gun and peered down each barrel: not a pit or mark. Engraved on the rib was the maker's name: Sempert & Krieghoff, Suhl. Nevertheless, there was one fault that my inexperienced eye didn't see: a crack in the hand of the stock.

I just had to have that gun. I couldn't let go of it, I wanted to take it home right there and then. Reluctantly, I handed it back to the owner. He put it back into a brown canvas gun slipcover, something else I had never seen before. He asked me, "What do you think?". I spluttered out, "I love it; will you take £21.00 for it?". "No, sorry", he replied, "I want £25.00". I was gutted; all I had was the £20.00, hoping I would be able to borrow a quid from Dad to seal the deal. We left. I got home and told my parents about the wonderful gun, and how I didn't have enough money to pay for it. Unbeknown to me at the time, Dad rang up the owner again and offered him £23.10 shillings, and he accepted. I got home from school a few days later, and when I walked through the back door there, on the kitchen table, was the brown canvas gun slip, a cleaning rod, a blue-coloured box of Eley 16g cartridges, and, laying on the gun slip, the gorgeous 16. I was overjoyed.

It was incredible; what a difference that gun made to the number of pigeons, game, ducks, and rabbits that went into my game bag. I now had a gun that would equal any game- designed 12 bore, and I shot well with it. I had so much faith in it, that it was a rare occurrence if I missed. As soon as I was home from school, I would be on my bike with a pocket full of cartridges, the 16 in its slip, heading for one of the farms and walking around the fields, adding something to my family's larder. What a joy it was, walking and exploring fields and hedges, coming across rough corners of cover that would hide a rabbit or a pheasant. It also taught you how to be canny and observant; not just a gun's range in front of you, but sometimes hundreds of yards away. It might be a pair of ducks dropping into a ditch or pond somewhere, or pigeons feeding on a stubble, then working out what was the best way to get them into range for a shot. Whenever you went through a gap or gateway into another field, you would creep forward and peep left and right down the side of the hedge to see if a covey of partridges or a pheasant was feeding on the field, then show yourself slowly so as not to frighten them into flying away. A covey of partridges will sometimes sit tight and let you get into range for a shot, but a pheasant will usually run straight into a hedge or cover to hide; mark the spot where it went into the hedge. If you have a dog, hold him back until you get to your mark, then cast him off on the hot, fresh scent; almost every time, the bird comes out on the other side of the hedge and flies away unharmed. If it flies forward from you, try to watch it and see where it goes; you might, if you're lucky, get another chance. Always be ready for another bird; if it was a cock, he might have his harem of hens with him.

If Dad wasn't working on a Saturday afternoon, we would go on our bikes, together with the dog, to one of the farms and shoot together, with Dad usually on one side of a hedge and ditch, me on the other, and the dog hunting in between us. It was a well-trained animal that stayed close and wouldn't run ahead on the hot scent of a pheasant; sometimes it would flush the bird out of range at the far end of the hedge when it was forced to break cover. As I was young and fit, I would run trying to keep up with the dog as it hunted the ditch and hedge, and hopefully get a shot when a bird or two broke cover at the far end. Poor old Dad, with his shot-up leg, hobbled and limped as fast he could on the other side of the hedge to catch up and get into range.

About that time, Dad had, for several years before and after, kept a few pheasants. They were mostly dark melanistic and kept in an enclosure with his hens and chickens in the garden; he would collect the eggs and then would place them under broody hens. He also used a paraffin-heated incubator in his shed to hatch them, rearing them until the birds were old enough to be released into favourable areas on the farms where we shot. He must have released hundreds onto the Island over the years. Foxes were quite uncommon then on the Island, and it was a very rare occasion if you saw one. I was 12 before I saw my first, so you could release young pheasants without too much worry of a fox attack. Ted Woolf, an oysterman who lived in Victory Road, had a collection of pinioned wildfowl, mainly Brent geese and several ducks that he kept for many years. They were kept on an area of grass beside his bungalow enclosed behind a four feet-high wire netting fence; they weren't attacked or killed by foxes at all for all the years that he had them, right up until the mid-sixties. After that, he lost them all to repeated fox attacks. Din also lost birds from his flock of laying hens, and Bert ("Cooty") Hoy started to lose hens from his large, free-range flock in Cross Lane in daylight raids. From about that time, they were more commonly seen. The rabbit population had been hard hit by myxomatosis, but they were still very abundant on the farms on the Island, except at Barrow Hill Farm where I never, ever saw one. I am sure it wasn't the lack of rabbits that caused the attacks; the island's population of foxes was getting more common and urban. The surplus of eggs produced by my father's pheasants would go to Din to be hatched under his broody hens and bantams, then released over at Feldy and the Grove at Newhall, along with the other pheasants brought in from Colonel Round's estate at Birch. Din would obtain as many melanistic dark pheasants from Birch as he could in order to place them on the farms at Wigborough where he could have a visual check as to which were his birds when they were seen and observed or were flushed over the guns and made their way into the bag.

As boys, we were always down on Wyatt's hard talking to the fishermen and oystermen, and the older gunners, about wildfowling and duck shooting when they came ashore from working or after a morning's flight. I seem to remember that they hardly ever shot a duck; in the bottom of the punt or dingy would be the muddy corpse of a King Solomon or two, or a handful of tukes and oxbirds[4]. You would ask if they had seen many ducks: they would reply, "Ain't clapped oiys onner duck for weeks, bor". There was one chap who lived locally; he was always out in his punt both early morning and nights within the creeks and marshes. Ernie Hart was his name, and as young lads we were well impressed with him as a tough wildfowler. In actual fact, he wasn't that much older than us; he was probably in his late twenties when we were just finishing school, but he was a very good wildfowler and shot. He used to bring home loads of ducks, but incredibly, for all the hours he spent sitting in a punt, or a muddy freezing cold creek, the bag for his best-ever season was 99 birds. The years he got that number of birds were 1958, 1959 and 1960, when the Izillmere and the Zuyder Zee were being drained on the Dutch coast; it displaced thousands of ducks, mainly teal, wigeon, and waders which flocked to the estuaries of Essex, Suffolk and Kent.

With the money I earned while working for Alf Pavey, I bought my first pair of long boots which were three-quarter length Hood bullseye. My new waders were used when I would cycle to Jack Marriage's farm at Barrow Hill and hide my bike behind a concrete block building standing in Jack's field at the bottom of Barrow Hill. In actual fact, the building belonged to a Major D'Manby who lived at Barrow Hill House before the Frost family lived there; he also owned the saltings and some of the fields in which Jack used to grow crops. The saltings were free for anybody to shoot, and everyone who had a gun did so if they fancied it. I would walk to my favourite spot out on the saltings, my new waders allowing me to cross and stand in muddy, water-filled creeks, keeping me dry while awaiting flight. My favourite ducks used the marsh just as they do today; teal would flight and zip around at flight-time, as I would pop away at the sporting little birds. Shooting ducks from a muddy creek where your feet are firmly fixed in the ooze is totally and utterly different to shooting on an inland piece of water where you have natural cover or can soon find some to make a hide. There is no comparison, and to be able to position your feet pointing the correct way to, hopefully, make a successful conclusion, you have to think that out before you plant yourself in deep sticky mud, using the wind (if any) and the failing light to be facing the right way to stand any chance of success. On the marsh right up near the seawall was a small freshwater pond; well, it used to be before the North Sea topped

---

4   These are local names for birds; they are curlew (King Solomon), redshank (tuke) and dunlin (oxbird) respectively.

and breached the seawall in 1928. My father could remember horses grazing on Barrow Hill fresh marsh before that fateful night. The grandfather of Colin, Alan and Tim Cook owned it at the time; he sold up shortly after that. Teal would come to that tiny pond, and some found their way into my game bag. The little pond is still there, unlike the dead, small oak tree that was near it and is now gone.

I remember Jack Marriage senior asking me one day to have a go at the pigeons that were attacking his field of young peas. I settled into a ditch to take cover, and several flew off as I walked down the headland to my hiding place; it was under a big elm tree and, as I waited quietly and patiently, I noticed a small brown bird above me the on the tree trunk. I watched it for ages as it searched the nooks and cracks in the bark: the only treecreeper I have ever seen on Mersea. I can't remember now how many pigeons were in the bag that day; not many, but I am sure I kept the field clear.

At the far eastern end, the old, breached seawall heads towards the large tidal channel that separates and divides Mersea Island from the mainland; it is called the Mersea Channel which runs up to the Strood causeway. Over the far side is a large area of saltings; the creek is wide and deep with soft mud. I was flighting one evening at the far-end of Barrow Hill, when I noticed a regular flight of mallard passing over Bonner's saltings heading north-west inland towards Abberton reservoir. They were probably feeding on a stubble field somewhere that way, and by the direction they were coming from off Mersea, they were leaving Reeves Hall marsh and fleets. I went back the next night with my gun and sat on the end of the old broken wall and waited; again, sure enough, as the sun set, the mallard appeared right on cue, heading on the same line. The flight didn't last long; probably five or ten minutes from what I could see in the failing daylight, but there must've been upwards of fifty ducks passing over the same spot. If only. The creek is wide and deep, the mud soft and clinging, and the tide rushes back really fast. I sat there on the seawall and debated in my mind the pros and cons of crossing over. I must say, it worried me; the thought of getting stuck in the middle, and the tide flooding back and surging in and around my legs, and then over my head, made me shudder. I made the decision that I was going to try the next night. The tide empties from the creek two hours before low water, so in effect it should be two hours before I see any water coming back on the flood.

The following night, I rode my bike right across the headlands and fields to the seawall, walked out to the end of the old broken wall, and sat there waiting for the sun to set. I watched the last of the ebb tide disappear out to sea, then, to cross the wide deep 150-yard channel to the other side, I slipped down the cant onto the mud and strode off into the unknown towards the bottom of the creek.

The first twenty yards were soft, then suddenly, to my surprise, I was walking on hard stony ground under four inches of mud; it went right across up to the other side of the channel! Where the last twenty yards was nearly up to your knees, that made you gasp as you pulled each foot up out of the clinging ooze, and plough forward. Back then, I weighed virtually nothing, so could skip across soft mud like a tuke. I made the other side quite easily. l made my way into a creek that emptied into the channel then got onto the saltmarsh top.

I got my breath back, then made my way further into the saltings, crossing smaller creeks to look for somewhere suitable to hide. I chose a creek that was narrow and about 4 feet deep with a neap tide shelf that I could kneel on as I faced to the east, hopefully under the mallard if they came. I kept staring towards Reeves Hall hoping to spot them as soon as I could; then suddenly a pair went past me on my right-hand side, out of range. What shall I do, move or stay? I stayed. I kept looking in front; another four were coming straight for me. I buried my face into the vegetation that hung over into the small creek; I kept perfectly still, just the top of my head was showing above the saltings. My eyes were looking through the vegetation as the birds came swiftly to me. I checked that the safety catch was pushed forward again for the umpteenth time. NOW! I straightened up to take the shot, but then realised that I had got up too soon; the ducks were still a long way out, and when they saw me, they all flared and fell back. I fired a desperate shot, but they all flew away unharmed. Another six birds flew past, wide to my left, and another pair to my right, just out of range. Bloody hell! Then a pair were going to pass me again to my left; they were a few yards apart, but the nearer one was in range. I swung the 16g through it and fired; it collapsed at the shot. I was just about to shoot at the other when I noticed that the mallard I had just shot at had recovered and was levelling out to carry on flying away. Once again, I swung the 16 and fired. It didn't hear the bang; it folded up and went into the marsh.

I marked the spot and sprinted to the fall; there it was, a drake mallard in all its splendour, laying there without a speck of mud on it. I picked it up and smoothed down the feathers of its handsome plumage as I went back to my creek. I laid the fabulous bird on the saltings in front of me; I couldn't take my eyes off it, it was pristine. I knelt down once again and waited for more. It was by now getting quite dark; I said to myself that I would give it another five minutes. I kept thinking and worrying about the tide coming back and stopping me crossing the Creek; if I couldn't cross it would be a very long walk back to my bike. I heard wings and the reedy-sounding quack of a drake mallard right over my head. I saw them in the dark sky as they flew over me twenty yards up; again, I swung the 16 as they swiftly passed over me. I fired. The duck folded and hit the saltings behind me with a resounding thud; I ran to the fall, and again, another drake mallard. l was elated: two big, fat mallard. Brilliant!

Suddenly, it came to me: the tide! I put the ducks in my bag and hurriedly retraced my steps back to the edge of the saltings to the main channel. I peered into the gloom to the channel bottom. I needn't have worried; the tide hadn't moved. I retraced my footsteps in the soft mud and crossed back to Barrow Hill and to my bike at the bottom of the seawall. When I got home and told my dad about the flight, he suggested that I should go back again the next night before the tide stopped me from getting over. I could see it in his face that he also wanted to come and flight them, but with his disability he knew it was impossible to walk through the soft, clinging ooze. We worked out the tides; it was possible that I could beat two sets before it was too deep to cross. I went back three nights on the trot. I shot four more mallard and had a couple of good chances of a right and left but missed; it would be another two more seasons before I achieved that. On the last night, I didn't even see a bird.

4: Shooting with Friends

ALL MY LIFE as a wildfowler or puntgunner, when the weather turns in the fowler's favour either in a full-blown gale, or below-zero, freezing temperatures, when I see hundreds and sometimes thousands of birds that offer up the slimmest of chances of, maybe, just a tiny percentage of their number being put in the bag, either with a shoulder gun or in the gunning punt, the urge to get at or under them is so incredibly overwhelming and challenging. However, with the risks sometimes involved, it makes me break out in a cold sweat as I recount the episode in my thoughts, sitting safe and sound in my armchair. Yet I know I am not alone in this tunnel vision obsession to observe and pursue those wonderful web-footed birds; I know a handful of like-minded fowlers who are just as keen, so hopefully, if my body holds up to the rigours, they need to keep a wary watchful eye for just a few more seasons.

As kids, we were never really worried about soft mud and getting stuck in the clinging, black ooze. As youngsters, at the weekends, evenings, and during the hot summers and school holidays, groups of us who lived by the Fox pub and in Dawes Lane would meet up, get on our bikes, and head off to swim in the saltings and creeks, usually at Barrow Hill and the "Bomb Hole", a breach in the old seawall near the Strood roadway coming onto Mersea. When I was about eight or nine, and even older, with a long run up you could jump over the Bomb Hole from one side to the other; it was probably only 7 or 8 feet wide but very deep, the flooding tide poured through it as it was squeezed. We would jump and dive into the filling creek and let the fast current wash us through the gap, at some speed, into the saltings behind to play in the hot muddy creeks, covering each other in black muddy goo as we threw handfuls at each other. As the flooding tide filled the saltings, we would chase each other, catch someone, and throw them into a watery creek; then, when it ebbed, the water inside the old wall was trapped. It was then that it really poured back through the breach with a torrent. We would get in the water fifty yards away and let the fast-ebbing salty water wash us through the narrow gap at high velocity, down the creek to the Strood causeway, then climb back out onto the saltings, run back, jump in, and repeat the exercise time and time again. The "Bomb Hole", as countless tides have ebbed and flowed through, is now 60 feet wide, or more. So really, we were quite used to our saltmarsh environment from a young age, swimming and playing in the summer, and using it for shooting during the winter. It wasn't alien to us at all, but it was treated with the utmost respect as it could bite back!

I used to look at the injury and deep scar on the back of my father's left thigh, and never really thought too much about it. As a small child, I can remember putting my fingers right into the deep wound; it must have been 2 inches deep and 9 inches long. I was fascinated. He wore an iron on his leg with a spring arrangement that was attached to a small steel ring on his shoe at the toe. At the bottom of the leg iron was a 3-inch metal pin that was pushed into a hole on the heel of his shoe. What caused the injury was probably a British shell; he was ordered back behind his battle lines to an ammunition dump, driving a lorry or a Bren gun carrier with a sergeant and a major to pick up more shells and ammunition for the big guns and troops at the front. It was the first assault on Sicily with the 8th Army; they drove into the ammo dump and were loading up the vehicle when the dump received a direct hit from a German shell. The whole lot exploded, killing both the sergeant and the major. Dad was knocked unconscious by the explosion and blast; when he came to, he tried to move but his injuries prevented him from doing so. He lay between both of his dead comrades, waiting to be found and treated temporarily. He was taken to the military hospital in Alexandria, Egypt and operated on. A piece of shrapnel as big as a match box from his thigh was removed; it had severed all of the ligaments and tendons in his thigh muscle which operates the foot. As a result, he was unable to lift his foot up from his ankle joint, and if he didn't wear the leg iron, his foot would drop. The spring arrangement fixed to the toe of his shoe kept his foot up; if he wore wellies and was walking in deep clinging mud or a muddy field whilst beating, he couldn't lift his foot to keep the wellie from slipping off. Din would know about his brother's handicap and, if the fields were particularly clinging, Dad would walk a grassy flank or track; but that was the only thing I can remember that his injury prevented him doing, apart from the fact he now couldn't walk in soft mud to go wildfowling.

On the school bus coming back to Mersea every afternoon, I made friends with a boy who lived at Haycocks Farm: his name was Stephen Rodwell. I used to go to Haycocks after school and at weekends and help him exercise his pony as well as riding it. I used to enjoy it, but he was also interested in going out with his father's 12 bore. Also, being situated next to Maydays Farm, we had permission to shoot on that farm as well which gave us access to the small spinney (Maygrove) that Dad and I used to flight the pigeons on the outside in the ditch. Johnny Jowers ("J.J." – a future Colchester mayor in 2023) lived a couple of hundred yards away from Haycocks, and his uncle Alan farmed the neighbouring Bower Hall. John would borrow his 12 bore, then the three of us would meet up at evenings, weekends and school holidays to shoot on the three farms. Alan also owned a large area of saltings and occasionally we would go there. I think J.J. bought my dad's hammer gun if my memory is correct; he paid £1.50 for it. I think he was robbed! My friendship with Stephen was short-lived; he was sent to a private boarding school when he was about 14, and I haven't seen him since. The pony (Paddy) was still at the farm, and I used to ride and exercise him until he went also.

One of the beaters who also came from Mersea was Pat Clark. He was in his mid-twenties back then and he was also a keen shooter and wildfowler. He drove a 1940-50s red and white Chevrolet, a left-hand drive. On some mornings and evenings, I used to see it from my school bus, parked on the old barge quay at the Strood. I asked him one day when we were beating together why was it parked there, and he told me he used to go wildfowling out on Bonners' saltings. I then asked him if I could go with him at some point if he wouldn't mind, and he agreed. He was going to go the very next morning on a Sunday, if I wanted to come, and he would pick me up at 6am from my house next to the Fox pub. There was no milk round on a Sunday, so I could go. I was up early the next morning and stood in the front room looking out of the window, waiting for Pat. Headlights shone through the window as a car came towards the house, and the big Chevy pulled up. Pat opened the boot lid and I put my gun and bag in the cavernous area before climbing in and sitting where the driver normally sits, and away we went down to the Strood to the Barge Quay where Pat usually parked. It was still very dark as we walked and stumbled along the top of the seawall towards our turn off which was 400 yards further on near the houseboat belonging to Ernie Richardson. We followed the defined trodden path out onto the marsh. We used Ernie's low, single-board bridges to cross muddy creeks and continued for 10 minutes, then Pat said, "I am going to turn off here". His path went left, so I continued further out and found a creek to comfortably kneel and hide myself in. The sky was getting lighter all the time as the dawn broke. The sky overhead was cloudy, but far to the east over the North Sea the sun was still hidden by the curvature of the earth, and there was an incredible coloured light; the sky was clearing out of cloud on the far horizon, the sun's rays were reflecting back to Earth from the clouds, and in this clear area of sky was an indescribable palette of colour: red, green, orange and yellow. It was breathtaking.

I looked behind me to see if I could see Pat. I couldn't; he was well hidden. Then suddenly, the world woke up, or, as it seemed, gulls organised themselves into groups and started to flight. Curlews bubbled and called out on the muddy foreshore, then headed onto the fields to probe and feed. Flocks of dunlin moved ahead of a young flooding tide, criss- crossing the saltings in front and behind me as they dashed off to feed along the water's edge. I was yet to see a duck; every redshank was scrutinised in case it suddenly metamorphosed into a teal as I instinctively lowered myself into the creek and thumbed the safety catch. Hundreds of lapwings were flying over me towards the fields and marshes while over on Mersea, flocks of waders were flying over the island making a beeline for the huge open mudflats of the Blackwater estuary to the south. The sun was still to make an appearance but the sky to the east where it was due to rise was turning a brilliant reddy-orange colour. There was a chilly breeze blowing on my back and neck; I turned up my coat collar and fastened the top button under my chin, thrusting my hands deep in my warm trouser pockets and waited. There weren't many in the bunch of teal that were well wide of me to my left, but from the direction that they were heading, I imagined they must be going towards Pat. They carried on at breakneck speed. Suddenly, they were all flying vertically as I watched them; one second, they were skimming the marsh and the next, they were 30 yards up at the top of their descent. One of the little ducks fell out of the bunch, the very quick double report of Pat's gun coming to me a second or two later. His two shots woke up and moved everything near him; there were all different species of coastal birds on the move now, mostly waders and gulls. Four shelducks passed behind me and flew to the big channel on the Mersea side and some wigeon were far-off to the east, by the point of Bonners. I watched as Pat searched for his teal, taking several minutes before I saw him bend down and reach over to pick the duck up, then disappear back into the marsh once again.

All of a sudden, the sun broke over the far horizon. I looked at my watch for the time: 7:46am. I knew Pat wanted to be away early this morning, at least by 9am, so I kept an eye on the spot where he was hidden. When I saw him make a move, I would also go. Flocks of woodpigeons started to flight towards the west, coming from the direction of Alresford; over they came, flight after flight and bunch after bunch, numbering in their hundreds as they flew high over me. I looked to see if I could see Pat; he was now out of his creek and putting the strap of his bag over his head onto his shoulder, and then walking about the marsh on his knees, cleaning and wiping the mud from his boots on the lush saltmarsh vegetation. I thought to myself at the time that it was a good idea, so I did the same, and continue to do so to this day. I started to walk back to Pat, my gun in the crook of my left arm Davy Crockett- fashion, still loaded and my thumb ready on the safety catch in case a duck jumped out of the saltings near me. Suddenly, there was a rush of wings as about twenty teal passed over me from behind, quite low. I pushed off the catch, threw the gun into my shoulder, and fired one hurried shot. I didn't even have time to pick a bird; in my panic, I shot at the thickest section as they were getting further away from me every second. Then one very unlucky bird peeled away from the bunch as the rest of them flew vertically at the report. The single teal kept flying low over the marsh. I didn't take my eyes off it. It reached the seawall where we would walk back to Pat's car; on the corner of the seawall is a concrete World War Two pillbox. When I last saw the teal, it was near the pillbox, so a good mark. I met up with Pat; he, too, saw the stricken bird come down. It took us quite a while to walk off the marsh back to the seawall by the houseboat, and then another few more minutes to the pillbox. We both searched in the long, rough grass for the little duck. I knew Pat didn't want to be late, so I felt obliged to forget about it. I saw the entrance to the pillbox and crawled inside and there, hiding in a dark corner, was my unfortunate teal. Pat dropped me off at home. I thanked him very much for taking me out and he said, "Do you want to come again sometime?". "Yes, please, I would love to!" I exclaimed. I gave him a wave, the Chevy's powerful engine growling as he accelerated the big car up the road. My father was in the garden, feeding his chickens and pheasants, when I recalled the events of the morning to him. "Well done", he said.

The owner of the houseboat that we passed on the way to the marshes, Ernie "Marshie" Richardson, was a character in himself. A paraffin oil lamp gave a dull light through the rag of a curtain hanging over the window of his tiny abode, tied up to four posts on the high-water mark, right under the seawall fifty yards further on. Ernie used to net the creeks and catch flounders, dabs, eels, and mullet. As the tide emptied from the saltings, he would go to his net and recover what he had caught. He would rake the foreshore for cockles, and where a creek had bladderwrack seaweed at its entrance into the marsh, he would lift the seaweed and gather winkles and boil them in a large cast iron saucepan over a paraffin oil stove. Then, as the Peldon Rose pub opened at lunchtime, and at night, he would load up his trade bike with strings of fish hanging from the handlebars, and jars of cockles and winkles in a wooden box on the front of his bike. He would sell or barter them, either to Mrs Pullen, the landlady, for beer and cooked food money, or to the local clientele that used the pub. He always wore a pair of Hood Bullseye thigh boots both in the summer and winter and he always sat on his favourite stool at the bar. He was educated and well-spoken, and before his life of voluntary solitude, it was said he was an accountant. When the pub closed for the night, if he was lucky, one of the regular customers returning home to Mersea would give him a lift and stop by the entrance through the hedge to the track that went down to the seawall, and thence to his houseboat. He would leave his bike at the pub and pick it up the next day.

Sometimes he would catch a bus back to the Rose; all the local bus crew knew him. The driver would slow right down without stopping; Ernie would grab hold of the upright pole on the open platform at the back and swing himself onto the platform and stay there. Then, when the bus got to the pub a few hundred yards further on, it would slow down again without stopping. Ernie would lean back to counteract his forward momentum and step off the platform onto the road, giving a friendly wave to the crew as he walked into the pub. He never paid! However, disaster struck several years later when he had an accident with an oil lamp or burner; somehow, it got knocked over and his boat and home went up in flames and was destroyed. Ernie's hands were quite badly burned trying to put out the flames; after that, he lived in a caravan standing in one of the meadows belonging to the pub. I can remember when I used to go with my dad for a pint or two in the Rose a few years later; you would push open the low front door of the pub and walk through a dark corridor where the unmistakable aroma of beer and ale would hit your senses as you entered. The smell of stale cigarette smoke would permeate from the two or three bars: typical of any pub back then. There was also an unmistakable smell of rubber! When we turned left into the public bar, there would be Marshie, standing with his back to a huge open log fire, his thigh boots slowly cooking from the fierce heat. He was a very nice man. The

The burnt out remains of "Marshie" Richardson's houseboat.

burnt-out remains of his boat are still there.

Pat hadn't been beating over on Feldy for a few weeks, so it was quite a while before I saw him again. He asked me if I wanted another fowling trip. It was in the new year of 1961. I had just left school that Christmas, 1960 and was about to start my working career as a plumber for a building company in Colchester, so it must have been in early January that I accompanied Pat once again out onto Bonners' marsh. I jumped at the opportunity when he asked me, so it was arranged that he would pick me up at the same time as the last outing on the

45

following Sunday morning. All that week leading up to Sunday, the airstream came from the east-northeast. It was a freezing, bitterly cold period and snow showers blew across the country. At night the sky cleared out, the wind dropped, and the mercury plummeted. On Saturday evening, I got my gear together for my trip in the morning. Mum kept saying to me as we huddled around the open coal fire together watching TV, "You don't want to go out there in the morning, do you boy?" How many times she said that I can't remember. Dad kept looking at the TV with a straight face. "You had better make a hot flask to take with you", she said. "Yes, mum, good idea", I replied. I went up to my bedroom about 10pm, put a hot water bottle under the bed covers, and then set the alarm 15 minutes earlier than usual. I walked over to one of my bedroom windows which was north facing and peered out. I went to wipe the condensation from off the glass to see better, but I couldn't as it was frozen. I ran my fingernails down the pane of glass and scratched four lines in the ice. It was snowing quiet heavily as I closed the curtains. I opened the wardrobe doors and got out dad's bus company great coat and laid that over the eiderdown quilt just for a bit more lagging. I got undressed but left on my vest, shirt and socks, then pulled my pyjamas over the lot. I put my trousers, jumpers and the rest of my gear for the following day beside me under the bed covers. I lay on my back motionless, sandwiched between the icy cold freezing linen sheets, clutching the rubber hot water bottle to my stomach, and shivered.

The alarm clock rattled out dead on time at 5:15am. I put the rest of my warm clothes on by the light streaming through the west window from the streetlight on the other side of the road. I peered out through the window; everywhere was covered with snow four inches deep.

As I came out of my bedroom, mum came out of hers. "I'll make that flask for you", she said. "Mum, there's no need, I'll do it", I replied. "No, I insist" she said and hurried down the stairs in front of me. She soon had the Primus paraffin burner going and put a saucepan of milk to heat while I had a cup of tea and cereal as she made my flask. After breakfast, I checked all of my gear again, put the flask of coffee in my bag, and waited for Pat. Mum went back to bed, telling me, "Be careful, and don't fall in and get wet". I stood once again looking through the window of the dark room towards the direction Pat should arrive, with just the streetlight dimly lighting up the front room and onto the decorations and reflective baubles adorning the Christmas tree. The clock on the mantelpiece over the now dead and black fire chimed: 6 o'clock. The headlights of Pat's car were not yet in sight. "Ah, here he is", I thought to myself. However, the vehicle didn't slow; it was Mr. Field, the milkman, heading to East Mersea after picking up his crates from Muggy Mason's dairy near Digbys. I looked at the clock again

46

as the chimes rang out: 6:15am. "Come on Pat, where the hell are you?" At 6:20am two headlights suddenly came into view; the big Chevrolet pulled over and stopped. Pat got out and apologised for being late; the car's battery had not been able to cope with the freezing temperatures, but luckily Pat had a charged spare battery in his dad's garage and, using jump leads, the car fired into life.

We got to our usual parking place at the barge quay, but Pat reversed in and pointed the engine and radiator away from the freezing wind, then lifted up the bonnet and laid an old blanket covering both engine and radiator to insulate it. The sky overhead was clear of clouds, the stars shone in the heavens, and the freezing northeast breeze hit the exposed parts of my uncovered body as I got out of the warm car. My ears hurt as the cold air hit them, and my face felt like it was going to crack. We loaded ourselves up with guns and bags, and then headed into the wind along the seawall once again. We came to Mushies houseboat; surely that bloke was not in there? But there was the dull light behind the curtain. Hells bells! The saltings were covered in snow as we turned to head out onto the marsh; you could still make out the depression of the path as we walked. The bright starlight sky illuminated the way ahead of us as it reflected off the snow. Pat came to where his path turned off to the left which would take him to a big creek that came into the saltings. He had it in his mind that, as the tide rose, birds would be pushed from off the muddy, cold foreshore and find some shelter in the saltings. He was in no rush to leave today, so the only thing that would force us off was the tide; it was due about midday, and it was forecast to be quite big.

I carried on further out. I no longer had Pat's footsteps to follow as I made my way; the path was easy to see as it was brilliant white, but the creeks either side were black in contrast where last night's tide had melted the snow. I passed by where I sat last time and kept going. I was now quite warm from the exercise of the long walk. A black creek cut across the path in front of me, not very wide, but quite deep. I crossed it thinking that I had to be the other side of that when the tide comes back, or wet feet would result. Just to my right-hand side was where I had shot the six mallard the season before. I carried on a bit further and had to cross another creek, but now they were getting shallower which made it awkward to hide oneself properly. It was still quite dark, so I had that to hide me for a while. I found a creek with a shelf to kneel on and made myself at home, loading up the 16g. It was now just light enough to see if anything came in range for a shot. Redshanks would startle you as they passed close by, screaming abuse at you for being in their space and making your thumb instinctively push the safety catch forward. I noticed that the once-clear sky and stars had gone; now it was dark again. The dawn had been put on hold. I looked towards the northeast where, before, I could just make out the land and trees over at Brightlingsea and Alresford. Now they had disappeared, and a few minutes later I knew the reason why: SNOW. It was a complete white- out in blizzard conditions. I knelt there in the relatively sheltering creek, with my neck pulled down into my shoulders. I pulled my woolly hat down tighter over my head, covering my ears. I turned my polo necked jumper up over my nose, wriggled my gloved hands into narrow pockets, and peered out from under my eyebrows, for the little shelter they provided from what was being thrown at me.

The blizzard didn't last long, probably twenty minutes, if that, but it was still overcast and dark. I could now see the Pyefleet Channel much more clearly, the water matching the sky in colour and appearance; they both appeared as one. It looked cold and foreboding. As the blizzard and squalls were passing through, I could hear the reports of Pat's gun in the far distance. He was much less than a mile from me, but his shots were being attenuated and dulled by the snow and atmospheric conditions. He was also, of course, downwind of me. He sounded as if he was quite busy, and the ducks were doing what he thought they would do. There were a lot of wigeon on the move, flying from further down the Pyefleet, and from the Colne and Geedons. They were heading inland towards Abberton reservoir, but far out in the middle of the channel, hundreds of yards away, and some were very high in passing over me.

I could still hear Pat's gun krumping away every now and then, but I had nothing in range of me at all. It was still bitterly cold. I kept sipping at mum's hot flask, then lighting up another cigarette which I had rolled while waiting for Pat in the dark front room. I flailed and flacked my arms back and forward around my shoulders to get the circulation back, sucking and putting my numb trigger finger into my mouth to warm it up, then spitting out the flavour of mud, blood and salt.

I don't know where it came from but suddenly a duck was passing across my front. Luckily, I had just finished drinking, smoking and flacking, so I was holding the gun ready once again for a shot. It was fast; I swung through it and fired. It closed its wings and immediately fell out of the sky in a graceful arc. When I got to where it had gone into the marsh, it had dropped into a wide, flat, muddy creek. It left a depression in the icy mud from where it first hit, then bounced six feet and slid along over the slippery goo for another ten feet. Only the steep edge of the creek stopped it going any further, and it was plastered in mud. I picked it up by the tip of a wing feather; in its last movements it had flapped its outstretched wings and had covered itself. I held it up at arm's length away from me as I walked back to my creek, trying to identify what species it was. I cleaned the unfortunate bird as best as I could by wiping it on the vegetation and in the snow, but even when it was relatively clean, I still didn't know what it was. Its legs and feet were back towards the rear end; it had a short squat body, and its colour was a uniform brown. I thought it might have been a pochard or a tufted duck. It was too big for a goldeneye, but it did have one identifying feature; over the top of its beak, and up its forehead, the feathers were white.

I lay the duck in front of me on the marsh, occasionally looking at it, racking my wildfowling grey matter in order to try to identify it. I then took stock of what was happening around me; I could see over the wide creek to the Mersea shore that the tide was two-thirds up the previously muddy, but now white, foreshore. It was lifting and floating the ice and snow which had settled on the mud, all the way down the Pyefleet and Mersea Channel. It looked cold and uninviting as it scrunched along the channel. A pair of teal took my hat off as I watched the ice; I didn't get a shot at them. Then another pair on the same line. One dropped at the first shot, but I missed with the second. Just as I got back to my creek another tight little bunch passed me wide. I thought they were worth a shot, so I fired; the tighter choked the left barrel and two fell out. I found one quite quickly, but it took me ages to find the other. As I was searching, another pair took me by surprise, and I missed them clean with both barrels. I looked over the wide creek to the Mersea shore again; the water was up to the cant edge and starting to enter into the saltings. It was time to make a move. I walked back to the creeks that I had crossed earlier, and to my amazement they had water in them; not enough to come over the tops of my thigh boots, but if I had left it another 30 minutes it would have been wet, cold feet.

I started to walk back along the path towards Pat. I could still see my footprints, although it had snowed since. It was now about 11am and the high tide was due about 12:30pm. I could now see Pat; once again he was scouring the marsh, looking for a bird that was lost under the deep snow and thick vegetation. He held his arms out, gesturing to me as to where the bloody hell could it be. As I got to his path turn off, I waited for him. Eventually, he turned up after finding the duck and we walked off the marsh, negotiating Ernie's slippery bridges that were just under the water. We arrived at the seawall by the houseboat, and then walked back to the car. We washed our boots and birds in the tide, now close to the car. Pat lifted the bonnet and removed the insulating blanket as I looked back up the Mersea channel; it was a sea of ice from one side of the wide channel to the other. I climbed in the car, out of the freezing wind. The Chevy's engine roared into life, then on the way home Pat recounted his hits and misses. In his bag were ten ducks: two mallard, seven teal, and one wigeon. I showed him the strange duck that I had shot, and he couldn't identify it either. Pat dropped me off outside my house. I thanked him once again for taking me out. "We will have to do it again some time" he said, but sadly we never did. I think he got married!

Dad was at work doing a Sunday shift on the buses, so I couldn't ask him to identify the strange duck. I found my 'British Bird Book' and searched the pages on wildfowl. There it was: a female scaup. The next time I was to see a scaup was in 2015; it was on the Pyefleet, about 300 yards away from where I shot the first one I had seen. Martin Cock had got a group of three in his spotting scope. When Dad came home from work, he looked at the duck and shook his head. "It looks like one of those dunbirds[5] to me", he said.

---

5   "Dunbird" is a local name for a pochard duck.

5: Three Men in a Boat

MY FRIENDSHIP WAS forming with my cousin and one of the other occupants of the trailer: Barry ("Swiggy") Swiggs. All three of us were mad keen on shooting; me and Hoss were lucky by the fact we came from a shooting family, but Swiggy was an only child living with his mum and grandmother, so the only shooting he had done was with an airgun of a mate that lived near him in the same road. We had all left school by now, so we were earning a weekly wage. I was working as a plumber in Colchester, Hoss was working for a local builder as a carpenter, and Swiggy was working for William Wyatt, the boatbuilder, at Mersea. Swiggy had bought a 10ft flat-bottomed dinghy from Wyatts, and this little boat was our vehicle to another world in which we would explore all the saltings and creeks, taking turns rowing as we didn't have an outboard engine or could afford to buy one.

Another boy who lived in Upland Road, Trevor ("Basky") Hart, was also starting to shoot about the same time, and going out with his older brother Terry, borrowing punts from mates and using them. However, the owners were also very keen and active, so they weren't always available. Trevor built his own 18ft. typical Blackwater punt based on William Wyatt's design (but decked in), a design that was so common at Mersea at the time. He built it in his mum and dad's front garden over the summer months, ready for the start of the wildfowling season. I would stop as I passed by on my bike, talk, and help him do some two-handed jobs.

Barry Swiggs ("Swiggy").

On the right-hand side of Wyatt's hard and slipway, the mud and foreshore were where most of the gunning punts were anchored, so it was named, and still is called, "punt bay"; at its peak there were probably a dozen or more there, and they were all regularly used. The craft weren't gunning punts in the strictest sense that they were used for puntgunning but were used to transport a fowler to his chosen location somewhere in Salcott Channel, Ray Channel, and the Tollesbury channels, together with the islands. The area was very extensive, so it was quite rare that you bumped into someone else; the more often you went, you got to know the favourite places of the older generation of fowlers, so did your best to keep out of their way.

The punts were designed with practically a flat bottom but not quite; they had a slight curve built into them of 1 3/4 inches fore and aft, and across mid-ships of about 1 inch or less. The shape of the bottom is quite critical; if the curve fore and aft is too much, they look like a banana. They also row like a pig, not keeping a straight line, and the water slaps on the bottom just aft of the stem making them noisy when rowing. When at anchor in a breeze, they yaw about not wanting to head the wind. Hideous things! They were quite high, the side boards being about 10 to 12 inches, then decked in fore and aft; the cockpit where the gunner sat and rowed was just big enough to seat two people and perhaps a dog. They were very seaworthy and could withstand a very rough sea. Also, with the shape of the bottom, they would push over mud with ease. On several occasions when coming back down Salcott Creek after a morning or evening flight, if it was an easterly wind blowing on your back as you rowed for home, we would push the punt over the mud from Salcott into Little Ditch ("Doitch") for a shorter and more sheltered passage; not just in a punt but also Swiggy's flatty. In the flatty, when we had the wind behind us, all three of us would stand up and hold open our coats so they acted like a sail. The person in the stern would have an oar in the scull hole, steering the wave- skimming dinghy for home. Brilliant!

I remember one Sunday afternoon in the mid-winter season of 1961-2; we borrowed Rod ("Steeljoints") Hayward's punt to try our luck at evening flight on the saltings at the top end of Tollesbury Channel. We left punt bay just after high water at about 1 o'clock. It was a drizzling wet atmosphere with a southwesterly breeze as we started on our three-mile journey. Rowing down the Thornfleet on the now ebb tide, all three of us were in the punt: me and Hoss were rowing and Swiggy sat on the foredeck with his feet in the cockpit behind Hoss. As we crossed the mouth of Salcott Channel to round Old Hall point, we started to ship a few lippers as the wind was increasing and roughing up the water. We eventually rounded the point and had water over the floorboards slopping about from side to side, wetting the hem of our coats, and trickling into the tops of

Peter Dawson's salvaged punt.

our thigh boots. We turned the punt into a saltings creek, unloaded all the gear, and pulled her up onto the top of the marsh. We tipped her up on her side and emptied her out. We got back in and away we went again. The wind was now gusting, and the punt's stem was heading into the strong ebbing tide and waves which were rolling down the foredeck and into the punt, and once again over the top of the floorboards. We got another 200 yards and had to do the same again, but we were pigheadedly determined that, as we had got this far, we could reach even further to get to flight. Hoss moved to the stern oar, Swiggy on the bow oar, while I got down on my knees in the stern so the wind wouldn't impede our slow progress as much. Thankfully, the tide was now dropping down the mud; we were rowing in 2 feet of rough water, not going too far offshore in case the punt capsized and tipped us into deeper water. I kept bailing and sponging out as quickly as it rolled in; we made slow but steady progress along the dirty north-channel shore, taking a little shelter from Flaxy on our starboard south side.

The two rowers were now pretty tired, especially Hoss who had been rowing from the Mersea hard non-stop. We were still about 200 yards from where we wanted to be, so the punt was turned inshore, and we pushed it up the mud into a small creek where we anchored it. We walked along the seaward side of the seawall towards Joice's Head further to the west, then spread out along the saltings to await flightime. The sky was now very dark, and low threatening black

53

clouds rolled down the Blackwater. Six wigeon passed over me high; I fired two shots, and one of the ducks fell from the bunch and set its wings into a glide over onto Old Hall marsh. I marked its course, the wind taking the duck 200 yards or more away from me as I watched. I topped the seawall and strode off to find it; I was lucky in the fact that it lay on its back, belly up, so I could see its white plumage contrasted against the dark marsh grass. A hen wigeon. I got back to my muddy creek just as a regular flight of wigeon were leaving the exposed, wind-blown, muddy shore of the Blackwater and passing over us to try and find some shelter in the Old Hall marshes, but well out of gunshot range. One little lot, I remember, (and I have never seen or witnessed it ever again), were actually disappearing and flying through the clouds as the atmosphere was so dense and low.

It was now raining very hard, and the wind was screaming. I gathered up my gun and game bag, then took some shelter in the lee of the seawall. I looked further along and noticed my other two mates were doing the same. The ducks that flew that evening, as they headed the wind, were incredibly low and hardly moving, or so it seemed. None of us touched a feather; I think we were more worried about our trip home than shooting ducks. We met up and decided that it was time to go. We topped the seawall, and the wind and horizontal rain hit us, soaking through our inadequate clothing in seconds. We found the punt and pushed it down the mud into a very rough sea. We clambered aboard. After rowing for a few minutes, the waves came straight in and filled the punt immediately. As we were in shallow water, we could stand and bail her out; we jumped in again, only to go a few more yards when it filled up once more. We emptied her again and decided the only thing we could do was push it along out of the water over the muddy foreshore ooze. It was still blowing incredibly hard, and the rain made the visibility disappear as we headed east, pushing the punt towards the point of Old Hall. It seemed as if we would never get there, but eventually we came to the muddy point and spit, which we rounded to find some shelter from the wind. We looked across Salcott Channel, the normal route that we should have been taking as we headed for home, but as far as we could see in the darkness, huge waves and breakers were rolling before the wind. Our punt wouldn't stand a chance heading into seas as rough as that. We bailed out the rainwater and took a long look at the direction in which we would be heading: straight downwind with the wind and waves on our stern.

The rain was still torrential; it blocked out all visibility, even of a light or a landmark. We were relying on luck and our knowledge of the area and instinct as to where the wind was going to take us. We jumped in the punt again and cast off towards an unknown shore where, hopefully, we would make landfall quickly. Me and Hoss were on the oars, Barry once again on the foredeck, just to keep the stern a little higher out of the water in order to try and prevent any breaking waves from rolling inboard. We rowed for all we were worth, just to try and keep straight, and in pace with the big waves that were trying to swamp the little boat. I can't now remember how long it took us to make landfall, but what I can remember is how scared and frightened we were, as we rowed for our lives in total darkness over a chaotic, rough sea. The punt yawed and wallowed as the wind drove us before it. Occasionally, an oar would catch a crab as it missed the water in a deep trough, losing some momentum for a second. After what seemed a lifetime, suddenly the waves were different; they were higher and more pointed. They broke over the stern deck, the oar blades touched the seabed, and we had made it ashore somewhere. We jumped out and pushed the punt as quickly as we could out of the water before it filled up again, standing on a dark muddy shore and looking all around us, still trying to see a light that would give some indication of our position. We had to guess where we were; with the gale from the southwest, it was more than likely we had landed somewhere on Cobmarsh Island, east towards the Monkey House, (the island was 30% bigger then). Again, we pushed the punt uphill to where we thought the edge of the saltings should be. We never saw the saltings as we came over the top; all we saw were the few streetlights dotted along the coast road. The relief was indescribable.

We started to push the punt down the steep foreshore mud. The punt wanted to go, so we jumped on board with me and Hoss kneeling on the side decking, and with a firm grip on the cockpit coaming. Barry threw himself on the long fore-deck on his knees, holding on as best he could as the punt went like a three-man bobsleigh, careering down the rain-soaked slippery mud. As it drew nearer the creek edge, it suddenly turned 90 degrees sideways and hit the water, the angular bottom and side chine stopping her dead in its tracks. Me and Hoss managed to hang on to the punt's cockpit washboards and stay onboard, but poor Swiggy was literally catapulted and flung from the deck, landing in the cold water on his back. He disappeared for a second, resurfaced, then floundered about trying to get to his feet. He stood there with his arms outstretched, spitting and sputtering, and looking even more like a drowned rat than we were. Hoss and I just couldn't help it; looking at him standing there dripping, then staggering, blaspheming, and searching about looking for his woolly hat in the black water, we just couldn't help but laugh. In the end, we were all killing ourselves, more in relief and joy than the misfortunes of Swiggy. After Barry had emptied his boots and wrung out his socks, we clambered aboard and rowed down the sheltered creek of Buzz'n (Besom) and to the hard. We pushed her once again up the mud and anchored her in punt bay. As we walked up the hard to our bikes, a person stood there in the dark. "Is that you, Barry?" a female voice inquired. His mum had been worried about him and had come to find him. "Do you know what time it is, boy? Where have you been? Me and your grandmother have been worried sick!"

I put my soaking wet bag with the bedraggled wigeon inside and the gun slip over my head onto my shoulder, then jumped onto my bike. Hoss turned off at the top of Firs Chase into Rosebank Road. I made for home in the still-pouring rain and with the strong wind behind me. Going past the police station, a voice shouted out, "Oi you, where are your lights?". I shouted back, "I know, but I am soaking wet and want to get home!" and carried on. When I did get home, I stripped off all my wet clothes in the garden shed and left them hanging over my bike. I hung up the wigeon, then took my gun indoors. I dried and cleaned it, then found some dry clothes and joined my mum and dad in the front room. They were watching television. Dad looked up. "You're a bit late. How did you get on? Did you get wet?" he asked.

I went to work the next day; it took me about three days to get over the fact that I was still alive and hadn't drowned. Eerie! We never had a chance to go back and retrace our footprints of our escape, and truthfully to this very day, I still don't know our exact route home over Cobmarsh Island. We would bring it up in conversation over the years; we would just look at one another, grimace, and shrug our shoulders.

My mum was always dusting the soot and smuts made by the coal-fired kitchen cooking range from off the various surfaces and, in particular, the mantlepiece. At some point in the afternoon, a new fire was laid and lit. The ashpan was pulled out a couple of inches to get some air into the newly lit fire, but, unintentionally, while she was dusting, a damp and swollen paper-cased cartridge was knocked over. It rolled, fell from the mantlepiece, and went straight into the ash pan, then under the fire grate. A while later, we were all sitting around the table having a teatime meal, my sister and I with our backs to the fire about four feet away, and mum and dad sitting at either end. Suddenly, without any warning, there was a terrific bang which made us jump out of our skin and the room was then showered with hot ash, soot and cinders; we all ducked and dived, trying to take cover. What the ....?

6: All at Sea

AT ABOUT THE same time, when we were 15 or 16, we decided that we wanted a boat with an engine to take us to our various fowling locations. Three people in a punt in a rough sea, as we had found out, wasn't ideal. Ben Clarke had a boatyard at the bottom of The Lane by the Scout's hut, and there we found a 14-foot clinker-built one and, what Ben referred to as, a western jolly boat! Also, sitting on beds, a small petrol engine. After not finding anything else, we eventually made up our minds and would approach Ben to ask how much he wanted.

We rode our bikes down the Lane from Hoss's home to the boatyard and searched him out; he was working. "Hello boys, how can I help you?" he enquired. "We are wondering how much you want for the boat," we replied. He had obviously seen us looking at it previously so straight away he said, "Forty pounds." We looked at each other, a bit taken aback and shocked at the price. "Oh, all right," we said. We jumped on our bikes and rode back to Hoss's and talked about it.

On a piece of land next to my grandad, which was owned by Din, there were a couple of unused chicken sheds standing there slowly going to disrepair. Din was thinking about selling the land as a building plot, so he wanted to get the land clear before making up his mind. Hoss decided he wanted one of the sheds to use as a workshop, so we took them both apart and made one good one out of the two. We then cleared an area in the garden behind Din's garage and erected the shed; it was quite large, probably 20 feet by 12 feet, and in this building, we spent hours and hours talking, working, and planning about boats, trawling and shooting. This shed was our HQ for the next thirty-odd years, particularly on a wet weekend when nothing can be achieved; we would idle away the hours waiting, standing in the doorway or gazing out of the window, bored to tears waiting for the rain to cease. In the evenings and at weekends, we would rendezvous at the "boatshed", as it became to be known.

We decided to buy the Ding which was her name-sign written on the transom. She was in quite good condition overall, but lightly built with thin planks and timbers; her petrol engine was a twin-cylinder, horizontally opposed "Norman" with a three-quarter inch gunmetal shaft running aft to a gear lever that operated a variable pitch propeller. We made the deal with Ben, and he towed her to the bottom of The Lane, leaving her anchored on the mud by the Dabchicks Sailing Club. We then moved her to the other side of the causeway in front of Alf Parish's shop, Fleetview Stores, on an area of clean sandy foreshore out of the mud, so we could work on her and give her a paint job. The Norman engine was air cooled so we could run it without the worry of overheating while she was not in water, but from the beginning it was always a problem. It always started quite easily; it would run for a few minutes on the two cylinders then, after a while just on one. We tried everything to get it to run as it should; all of our expert mates scratched their heads, but all failed. We launched her and took her for her maiden voyage, making sure the flatty was tied to the stern. The engine, as usual, ran perfectly for a few minutes, then one cylinder cut out, so she putt-putted along on the one as we motored up the Strood Channel. We tried everything to get her to fire on both cylinders, but with no luck. Hoss was on his knees beside the engine, puffing away on a dog-end dangling from his bottom lip, fiddling with the carburettor. Then Swiggy moved and sat on the gunwale near him watching. I left the tiller, so she was steering herself, and sat on the gunwale beside Swiggy. Suddenly, the engine picked up and started to run on both cylinders as smooth as you like! "What did you do, Drib?" we enquired, as we all looked at each other in amazement. The Ding surged through the tide; I went back to the tiller while the other two moved to level her up on an even keel. She ran beautifully for a few more minutes, then the one cylinder cut out, and once more she putt-puttered on the other one. Hoss moved to the port side followed by Swiggy; I stood on the port side of the tiller, then suddenly she fired up on two cylinders and she ran perfectly once more. Once again, we moved to put her level and once again she ran on the one cylinder. We could never get her to run properly, so whenever we used her, she had a permanent list to port! We never trusted Ding, so in the short time that we had her, we were looking for another boat.

Around this time Mr. Gray from Bocking Hall was keen to have a couple of driven shoot days on the Island. He was a member of a shoot near Thetford, and Dad would accompany him on several occasions. Alan Gray would get together his team of guns, mostly farmers and friends on the island, while Dad would organise the beaters. Guns and beaters would all meet up at Bocking Hall and set off for the first drive of the day, beaters in a tractor and trailer taken to the first drive, and the guns in three or four Landrovers. The first drive in the morning started at Mr Herbert Cock's farm in High Street North. The beaters would line

Beaters 1968-9. L to R: John Green, Pinky Hewes, Bob Sharp, Basky Hart, Hoss Hoy, David Conway, Graham Woods, Simon Cutts (kneeling), Graham McKillop, Russell Peck.

out by Firs Chase caravan site and walk across the fields where Woodfield Drive and Whittaker Way are now located, then walk across the fields and marshes to the waiting guns positioned from the Glebe playing field near Wellhouse Farm, and down towards the Strood. The second drive was from Jack Marriage's farm at Barrow Hill from the seawall down by the Strood, then across Alan Jowers' fields at Bower Hall. A few beaters would walk and drive birds from Wellhouse Farm, belonging to Lord Alexander and Dennis Sorrels at Weather Cock Farm in Dawes Lane, towards Bower Hall; the waiting guns would line out and stand behind Haycock's Farm and down to and behind Maydays Farm. The third drive was from Maydays Lane across the fields belonging to Alan Gray at Bocking Hall; the guns would be positioned on the boundary hedge of Weir Farm and Reeves Hall.

It was a shame that the owners of Reeves Hall didn't want to participate in the day. Then it was back to Bocking Hall for "dinner". The first drive after dinner was from the boundary hedge of Fen Farm, opposite the Dog and Pheasant pub, and then heading west over the land of Keith Cooper at East Hall, and Mr Sanafer or Ingram at Rewsalls Farm, the guns waiting in Rewsalls Lane from the little group of scots pines, down to the youth camp at Kiddiesland. The guns would then drive to and stand at Waldegraves Farm lane, the owner being Mr Jack Lord. The final drive was from Rewsalls Lane, across Waldegraves to Cross Lane, then back to Bocking Hall to count and record the bag and finish the day. It was incredible, the number of wild-reared birds that had been flushed and went forward over the line of guns, mostly grey and French partridges, but also lots of pheasants. Of course, most of the people shooting that day had hardly ever picked up a shotgun, so only the few better shots connected with the fast-moving birds. I particularly remember the drives over Rewsalls, Waldegraves and Cross Lane. It was a constant stream of wild game birds flying high and fast.

Living next to the Fox public house, I was very near Waldegraves Farm. I was frequently down Cross Lane walking the dogs, or with my gun or air rifle shooting on the fields behind my house and in the woods down by the old decoy. Next to a caravan near the seawall, I noticed a boat that hadn't been in the water for a long time. I went straight home and biked down to Hoss's and told him what I had discovered. Straight away we were on our way, went to find Swiggy, and headed for Waldegraves caravan site. She was a small ship's lifeboat, approximately 16 feet long, beamy, and traditionally double ended. The stern post had a stern tube fitted but originally, if she was ever used as a lifeboat, she would have been rowed and sailed if needed. I went down to Waldegraves regularly after I initially found her to find the owner, but it seemed like weeks before he eventually turned up. I knocked on the caravan door; it opened, and this pleasant cockney man smiled at me as I stood there. "Yus mate, what can I do for you?" he said. "I wonder if your boat is for sale?" I enquired. "Could be", he said in a broad east London accent, "tell you what, I'll fink abaart it this week; if you come back next weekend, I'll let you know, awlright?". On the following Saturday afternoon, the three of us were back to meet the owner. "Well, I've fought abaart it and I want to sell it. How much do you fink it's werff?", he asked. "Would you take take a fiver for it?", I said. "Yeah, that sounds fair enuuff", he replied. "Tell you what, if you give me annuvner quid, you can have the engine as well". We couldn't believe our ears; we had done the deal of the century. Six pounds for the boat and the engine! We paid him the cash and told him we would pick it up one evening during the week. We couldn't get the boat off of that site quick enough before he changed his mind or somebody else had made him a better offer. Hoss went to see Sam Webb to borrow a tractor and trailer. All three of us were officially too young to drive, so my dad, who had a driving licence but hadn't driven anything since he was blown up, was seconded to drive the grey fergie tractor and trailer.

I can't remember now who gave us a hand to manhandle and lift the boat up onto the high trailer, (I think it could have been Dougie Sawkins), but we did, together with the engine. We bought her down to Hoss's and put her on a narrow piece of land that belonged to Din in between the council houses in Firs Chase, with Louis ("Pinky") Hewes living on one side and Jim Gladwell the other. The engine was a 1930s Ford 10 sidevalve car engine and

All hands on deck: getting Boat seaworthy for fishing.

car gearbox. We discarded it immediately and put it in the boat shed along with all the other boating equipment, gear and junk that we had found and acquired, thinking that it might be handy one day! We started work on her straight away. She still had all the storage lockers fitted in her, which we removed. The two large hooks in the bow and stern which were used to hang her from her parent ship's davits, were still intact. We cut these out. She was in very good condition with oak planking, timbers and frames. One of the planks on the curve of the chine was split, so Pinky senior, living a few yards away and working at Wyatts as a shipwright, gave us loads of helpful, free advice. The split plank was cut out and a new one fitted. Where one or two timbers were broken, we steamed American elm, and bent and riveted new ones in place, fitted new gunwales and capping, followed by strong bow and stern knees to strengthen and tighten her up. With all of the woodwork and repairs done, we burned off all of the old paintwork and coated the woodwork with a metallic primer, undercoat and a gloss finish. While we were in the process of refurbishing her, we looked for an engine and gearbox, shaft and propeller.

All of this costs money of which all three of us had very little, so we made the decision *Ding* had to go. She was put up for sale. I can't remember how much we sold her for but Ian ("Pimp") Proctor, who worked with Hoss as a carpenter apprentice for the same firm, was probably persuaded, with the threat of a dead leg, that she would be perfect for him, so he kindly bought her. Mick Lungley was a marine engineer who had a barn-cum-workshop in Kingsland Road, and also worked for Clarke & Carter, the boat builders and shipwrights at Mersea. He had a marine engine for sale; it was a factory conversion of a petrol sidevalve sea water-cooled Austin 8 or 10 called a "Thetis", and a direct-driven marine gearbox. We went and found Mick at his "office" in The Victory pub; he was sitting on his usual stool by the bar with a pint of Double Diamond in reach and filling up the bowl of his pipe with a black shag tobacco. He was in deep conversation with Lennox Leavett who at the time also worked at Clarke & Carter. Lennox had his usual cigar projecting from the corner of his mouth as he drawled away in his deep Essex Tollesbury accent. Lennox piped up as we walked into the pub, "It's those three bloody poachers who keep shooting our ducks". We laughed at Lennox, bantering with him and saying, "The only reason you have got so many ducks is that there isn't a Tollesbury wildfowler who can hit one; and the only duck that makes it into an oven in Tollesbury is a tame domestic one hanging in the butcher's shop". He spluttered and sucked on his cigar as we took the mickey. Lennox's father was the legendary Will ("Tukie" or "Chippie") Leavett who was James Wentworth-Day's puntsman, made famous at the time by their exploits in Day's wildfowling books and the sporting press. I did meet James Wentworth- Day one evening in 1969, I think, as he was drinking and reminiscing with his old Mersea and wildfowling mates in the Soc and Sail, another well-known Mersea drinking establishment.

We then spoke to Mick about the engine. We made arrangements with him, and a couple of days later met him at his workshop and viewed the engine. He started her up easily, but he only ran it for a few seconds as it was sea water cooled, but it sounded fine, so we made the deal and paid Mick forty pounds. Mick also had propellers, prop shafts and stern tube fittings, which I am sure we acquired from him. We were to make good friends with Mick over the forthcoming years together with his

The *Boat* nearing completion in the "Boatyard".

62

mate, Ashley Upsher. Mick tragically took his own life, worried about his tax affairs with an HM Inland Revenue investigation pending! We fitted engine beds in our new acquisition and manhandled the "Thetis" over the gunwale and dropped it onto the new beds, then lined it all up with the shaft and propeller which we had machined by Albert and Jim Clarke. Pinky advised us as we proceeded.

Outside Fleetview Stores 1967. L to R: Barry Keene, David Mills, Hoss Hoy, Barry Swiggs, David Garrard.

After several enjoyable weeks and loads of laughs being with my young mates, we had her ready for sea. Mick borrowed a boat trailer and tractor from Clarke & Carter, and she was towed to the hard and launched. We started the Thetis, made sure she was pumping water through to cool, and away we went with the flatty in tow. She went like a dream; the engine didn't miss a beat as we flew up the channel to the Strood and back to the Mersea hard. We waited for the tide so we could float her onto a sandy piece of shore and left her near the high-water mark in front of Fleetview Stores to take up, but she was as tight as a drum and hardly leaked a drop. All the time that we had the *Ding*, we were looking for a clear place to put in a mooring. Initially we found a place on the right-hand edge in the Gut on Ray point, but it was close to another boat's mooring, and we got a bit of grief from a local owner. Thinking back, we had room to move it further away from him. We were still very young and didn't want to upset anybody, so we dug two clogs deep into the mud on the middle ooze on the opposite side of the Gut. Then we joined the two clogs together with some heavy chain and a strong swivel, connected the rising scope to the swivel, and tied the *Boat* to it. She came addry for two hours either side of low water but, fortunately, the prevailing wind coming from the southwest usually kept her close to the low water mark. Swiggy's flatty was anchored in punt bay, so it was only a short scull to the *Boat* where she was permanently secured. The mooring is still there today.

We used her a lot all that summer. We discovered that the Thetis wasn't very economical to run; there was always a can of petrol on board to top up the main tank which we used to leave with all the other cans owned by the fishermen and oystermen to get filled at Albert Clarke's petrol pumps in his front garden next to Fleetview Stores. Albert or Mrs Clarke spent several laborious minutes every day providing a wonderful service; I think, at the time, the pumps were hand operated. There were always several boys down on the "front", messing about in dinghies and boats, fishing for flounders and eels, and netting the creeks and channels for mullett, trying to spear them with a homemade harpoon as the gorgeous silver fish fed on the weed that would accumulate on the bottom of a neglected boat. I remember a few years later at morning flight in early October, I was in a salting creek near to the edge of a wide channel and I could hear mullet, sucking, feeding and grazing right at the water's edge close to the salting. I slowly walked out towards the channel and cautiously looked right and left along the shallow waters edge: mullet. Lots of them were feeding in just a few inches of water close to the marsh. I moved back out of sight, then crept forward on my hands and knees. As I neared the edge, I lay down and peeped over the edge of the salts so as not to alert them into swimming away. Several smaller mullet were grazing just in front of me, but just a few yards to my left was a huge fish. I shuffled back out of sight and crept forward again to where the mullet was; it's head and body were just under the water, no more than two or three inches covering it, and only 8 feet away, I aimed straight for its head and fired; a plume of water and mud showered me, but when I looked for my fish, there was nothing there. Just that shallow depth of water was enough to stop my charge of shot, and the fish swam away unharmed. I looked along the tideline and could see the telltale ripples and swirling water of some more fish feeding. I did the same approach and waited for another big fish. This time I waited until its head was out of the water and fired; it rolled over stone dead. I weighed it when I got home; it topped my mum's kitchen scales at just over 10 pounds.

A lot of the lads would spend time with the full-time fishermen, helping them bring their catch up the causeway to the top of the hard and going with them, spending weekends and all-night trawling for soles and roker, or drift-netting for herring. Several boys went straight into fishing as soon as they left school, some well before their official leaving date. Just like the wildfowlers, these full-time hard fishermen were our heroes, our gods. We wanted to be just the same as them and listening to their stories and of big catches of fish, we were enthralled.

The Blackwater estuary was a haven for fish and oysters. The boats then were relatively small fishing smacks, converted from sail to power. Just like the tractors that worked the land, they were of low horsepower so were limited as to where they could fish and to what size of trawl they could pull, plus they had to get it aboard at the end of a tow. If it had been productive and the net was heavy, it was hard work to manually haul a trawl up onto a smack; not all boats had winches. The nets and trawl or drift nets were hauled by hand or with blocks and tackle to make it easier.

The seabed of the Thames estuary and the Blackwater was particularly littered with debris. During the second World War, vessels that had struck a mine were blown to smithereens and had sunk, enemy aircraft had been shot down, and allied aircraft, in trying to limp back home after being shot up somewhere over Europe, crashed into the sea. Thousands of nets caught fasts. "Fasts" were anything that were too heavy to get onboard: ship's anchors, large pieces of aeroplanes (or even whole planes), posts jutting out of the seabed, prehistoric tree stumps, large rocks deposited by the ice age, mines, and bombs that had been ditched to lighten the load, not just of an enemy aeroplane, but also of a stricken British one trying to make a safe landing back to its airfield. Smaller pieces that had either been caught in a trawl or oyster dredge were dumped or brought ashore out of harm's way. The big pieces that couldn't be lifted remained where they were, and to the unwary, they always posed a potential risk of losing fishing gear. All of these obstacles would snag and hold a boat and trawlnet fast, some impossible to retrieve and pull off. In the worst case, the valuable net became wrapped around the wreck, never to get it back. The regular full-time fishermen knew where most of these "fasts" were and had them marked on a chart or stored in their memory, so as they approached a wreck or hazard, they knew by looking at stationary landmarks on shore that it was wise to haul the gear well before, or give it a wide berth as they proceeded. There was no GPS back then.

There were several "weekenders," mates that fished and trawled the river, and we wanted to do the same. We found a second-hand 12-foot beam trawl that was for sale; the trawl head "Ds" were joined by a wooden beam and was very light but too long, so we acquired a galvanised scaffolding pole and cut it down to 10 feet. Roger Butcher welded it to the metal "D" heads and made the skids six inches wider where they run along on the seabed. The net was hardly used, but we had to get it altered and reduced to fit the now 10-foot beam. Old Shaver Mills did the work on the net to make it fit. We took the net back to Hoss's, made up a ground chain, fitted a 6-foot-long chain and rope bridles from the heads to the trawl wings, then tied and fitted it to the beam and heads. Then we carried it on our bikes down to the hard, laid it across the flatty, and sculled it out to the *Boat*. It was laid on the port side, one "D" hanging over the gunwale in the stern and the other laying on the floorboards, forward towards the bow. The net lay folded behind the beam, neatly out of the way when not being used. A 70-foot cod-end rope and buoy also lay behind the beam on the net.

We just had to try the trawl. We met down on the Hard and sculled out to the *Boat*, started the Thetis, and motored out down Thorn Fleet on a dropping tide. It was a warm summer evening; as we motored out through the quarters on a flat calm sea, we took a short cut over the Nass spit and headed up-river towards Tollesbury pier. We slowed down about a mile or so west of the Nass beacon and turned the boat in a wide circle to port. Hoss threw over the cod-end buoy and line, then we slowly paid out the trawl over the side of the boat. With Swiggy on one end of the beam and Hoss on the other, they carefully dropped the beam over the rail into the water, held on to the trawl warp and slowly paid it out after taking a turn around a cleat to control the speed as it disappeared beneath the water. Then, when it was clear of the stern and propeller, I headed east with the ebb tide to the Nass beacon where we were going to haul.

Hoss let more warp out, and when it looked about the right angle, he made it fast to the cleat, slowed the engine down to a tickover, and went slowly with the ebbing tide to the beacon. We kept holding the warp to try and feel if the gear was on the seabed; at times the stern would drop deeper in the water as what we thought was the ground chain digging into some soft mud, stopping the boat briefly, then pulling it out and continuing on its way. As we got near to the end of our tow, we decided to haul to see what we had caught. We hauled on the single rope attached the trawl's bridle, the boat still moving forward in gear, and with the tide, we didn't anticipate that it would be so hard to pull the net to the boat. In the end we took it out of gear and pulled the boat back to the net. The warp shortened and eventually the beam came to the surface but to our horror and amazement it was upside down; we had dragged it for a mile or more along the seabed with the steel scaffolding pole bouncing along upside down. Somehow, we then had to turn it over the right way up. We managed and got it safely aboard; we pulled the net over the rail, peering through the meshes to see if we had got anything. We didn't even open the cod end; it was empty.

We steamed back to the mooring in a quiet mood as we pondered what had gone wrong. We tied her up, sculled ashore, then biked up to the Victory pub to have a pint to drown our sorrows. A few of our mates came in; they had seen us behind the Nass. We relayed the story of our maiden trawl and much mickeytaking and laughter at our expense was the order of the evening. Roger Butcher came in with Eccles Mussett; they had also seen us in the river sieving water and Roger asked us how we had got on. We told him of our mishap with the trawl and how hard it was to pull in and haul. "Have you got a block on the bridle?", he asked us. "No, we haven't", we replied. "How thick is the warp, can you grip it easily?", he enquired. "Well, it's that thick", as we stuck up a little finger. "Is that all?", he said, "you need it thicker than that", as he stuck up one of his fat fingers, "you want it that thick, and you definitely need a block on the bridle". He proceeded to draw a diagram in a notebook that he always had in the top pocket of his overalls.

We had a coil of thicker rope in the boatshed, and, in an aluminium fish box, we had lots of bits and pieces that we had come across and collected. We found a couple of single wooden blocks that would let our new thicker warp pass through, and a big cleat that we screwed and fixed to the stern thwart, so that we could tie one end of the warp too. Then a fairlead screwed to the gunwale either side of the rudder to pass the warp through to the block on the trawl bridle, then back to the boat through the other fairlead, and then forward to the Samson post in the bow to which the boat is tied and moored. Over the next couple of evenings, as soon as I had got home from work, I bolted down my dinner and then biked down to Hoss's. Straight away, the three of us were sculling out to the boat with tools and gear and did what Roger had recommended. We shackled the block on to the bridle, bolted and screwed the cleat to the thwart, and screwed the fairleads onto the gunwales to guide the new thicker warp. We didn't cut the warp; we left it long to trim and cut as required when the trawl was being used.

The next weekend we were back out in the river to try out the alterations we had made. The tide was once again ebbing as we shot the net and beam over the gunwale into the muddy water up towards Tollesbury pier. I headed for the Nass beacon again. The trawl was up on the water's surface the right way up, and level. Hoss slowly paid out the warp once more and straight away he noticed how much easier and lighter the warp was to handle and pay out as the trawl came into contact with the seabed. With the block on the trawl bridle acting as a reduction gear, it was now 2 to 1 thus halving the energy required to haul it back to the boat. After about an hour, we decided to haul; even with the 2 to 1 reduction it was still hard and tiring pulling on the thicker rope, so the engine was knocked out of gear and the boat was pulled back to the trawl. We were still moving forward with the ebbing tide.

The beam came to the surface and this time was the right way up. Hoss took a couple of turns of the warp around the Samson post, I put her in gear, opened up the throttle, and gave the net a tow at fast speed to wash anything down into the cod end. Then, by lifting the warp out of the stern fairlead, slowing down the engine and turning to port, the warp being tied to the forward post would quickly turn the boat, so the beam and net lay alongside ready to haul. The net was streaming away from the boat with the tide so as not to foul the rudders and propellers. We lifted the beam aboard, then the net; we opened the cod end into a fish box, and we were amazed at what we had caught: a few soles, starfish, crabs, limpets, dead shellfish, and some big native oysters. Excellent!

We were chuffed to bits at our success. When the tides were right, we were out in our little boat trawling the river at every opportunity; we couldn't get enough of it, so great was the fun. With all the practise we were having, we had the shooting and hauling of the gear down to fine art, and we did catch fish, mainly soles, dabs, plaice, bass and skate, with even a surplus to give away to family and friends and some to sell.

Some of the boys of around our age, either younger or a bit older, had bought thirty-foot-plus double-ended lifeboats on the whole and had converted them, mainly for trawling. Boys who teamed up, just like the three of us, were out occasionally trying their luck, so there was always the spice of competition amongst us. I am trying to think of a few names as I write this: Peter and Jim Clark in the Sea *Drift*, David and Stephen Conway in the *Storm Drift*, Eccles Musset and Roger Butcher in the *Noname*, Tony Smith and Ray Hempstead in the *Silkie*, Mick Lungley and Ashley Upsher in the *What's its name* (if you believe), Bob Open in the *Anne*, Graham Knott in the *Inchworm*, David and Peter Dawson in a boat of which I cannot remember the name, and Graham ("Hank") Woods in the *Woodpecker*. I am sure there were more, but the names are now forgotten. Also,

Woodpecker, Red Admiral & JBJ at anchor in the River Blackwater.

there were one or two from Tollesbury: Simon ("Crosby") Frost, Mac, Webby and Southerly Frost, who was always single-handed in his beautiful, elegant smack. Additionally, there was Tom Pouldon and his wife, Sue, and about three or four crew from Heybridge Basin that would anchor at Mersea, meet their Island mates in The Victory for a few raucous beers, and then sleep onboard overnight, ready for an early start out trawling the next day on Tom's big boat, *The Locker*.

As the confidence of the seaworthiness of our small craft grew, and with the reliability of the Thetis, we trawled the river and estuary further afield. There was always a professional or part-timer working the estuary somewhere every day, either over on the south shore at Bradwell, at the back of the Nass, on the Mersea shore fishing the sandy seabed by the Molliette wreck or towards the bench head and Colne bar, and Priory spit, and also over on the Main and Dengie flats. We made a mental note of where these boats were working, so where they went, we went; and so, it paid off. However, quite often we would forget how small she was; on a windless, calm day we would go that extra mile or so only for the wind to freshen and the sea to pick up rough from some direction out of the west. Then it was a scramble to haul the gear and get it into the boat before we were swamped, as we lay side on to the wind and with the waves pulling the net over the rail. As soon as the cod end hit the floorboards, the codend rope and buoy made fast, the little craft was stemming the waves and wind, heading for home and shelter. The deck-crew sorted out the catch on the floorboards as we steamed for our home creek, as quickly as the waves and weather would allow us.

When the sea was rough, and when we hauled and pulled on the trawl warp, the boat was virtually stationary in the waves, so consequently big waves rolled in over the stern and would cause us much consternation as they tried to fill our little boat. It took several frantic minutes on the hand pump to lighten the unstable load before the next green lipper hit us and came onboard. One day, we were trawling the back of the Nass on a floodtide, shooting the gear by the beacon and heading west upriver. We had been towing for half an hour or so when we noticed we had stopped moving forward; we were fast. We tried opening up the throttle on the engine flat out to try and move but she wouldn't budge. We decided to try and get the trawl beam aboard, so we heaved on the warp and got the trawl close to the boat underneath her; but however hard we pulled on the rope, we couldn't lift it off the seabed. We tied the warp to the centre thwart amidships but as the rising tide was trying to lift the boat, she was slowly sinking and listing further to port with very little freeboard as the net held her firm. We released the weight on the rope and the boat quickly righted itself. Then we transferred the warp over the stem and put it through the bow fairlead, making it fast to the mooring-cleat in the bow. As the tide kept rising, the bow was sinking deeper and the stern was lifting out of the water, but we were still stuck fast. We also pulled hard on the cod end rope, then tied and made that fast to a cleat. Everything was bar tight as the rising tide tried to lift us. Then Hoss said that we were moving; we looked at the shore and we could see that we were indeed moving, albeit slowly.

We started the engine; we decided that, as we couldn't lift onboard what we had caught, we would try to take the trawl and net above the low water mark and leave it there and come back at low water when it was addry so we could retrieve it. Slowly, very slowly, we made for the north shore into shallower water where we knew it would come addry at low tide. As the water shallowed, the net hanging under the boat would hit the seabed and stop us moving until the tide lifted everything again. We kept looking along the shore trying to guess where the low water edge was; the tide had about another hour or so to run so we estimated that we were now above the low water mark. We slackened off the ropes and let the trawl go down onto the seabed and hold us in position. As it was still quite early, we decided that we would wait for the tide to ebb, so we wouldn't have to leave the trawl overnight to retrieve the next day. Eventually, the tide turned, dropped, and ebbed away; as it got shallower, we were able to get the trawl bridle block onboard, then we could just lift the cod end up to the surface of the water. We peered through the murky water and then it was revealed what we had caught: LIMPETS! A ton of bloody limpets. Quickly, before we went aground, we untied the cod end and dropped it back in the water. We grabbed handfuls of net and slowly worked and shook the limpets out through the open cod end back onto the seabed. Then we put the trawl warp back onto the stern cleat, paid out the warp so we could take the boat back out into deeper water, then took a turn around the cleat, and gave the engine full throttle. Slowly the open trawl came with us as we dragged it into deeper water. We towed it for five minutes to wash it through, hauled and shook out the remaining shells, and got it back onboard. After that, we went home, knackered.

The ground chain on the trawl was literally a ⅜-inch steel chain that would fish too hard on the seabed. We noticed we would trawl up a lot of dead shells; these would lie in the belly of the net wearing it out as we proceeded forward. So, the net came ashore back to Hoss's, and we set to and made a new ground rope after seeking advice from the boys that knew our local trawlermen. They were always helpful with their advice as what to do and where to go; it was never a case of, "Go and find out for yourself the hard way". If we ripped a net, someone would come aboard and, in a flash of a swishing netting needle, it would be repaired. All my life, I have always held these tough men of the fishing community in the highest regard. They deserve every penny they earn, the ultimate hunter.

Another day, we were out towing the trawl at our favourite place at the back of the Nass. We were still using the heavy chain ground rope, for want of a better description. Knowing now how much dead shell and rubbish the trawl picked up, we would only tow for a half-hour. We hauled; the beam was in the boat, and me and Hoss were dragging the heavy net up and over the rail and shaking the contents down into the codend. Swiggy was kneeling on the floorboards, putting soles into a fish box that me and Hoss were pulling through the trawl meshes and throwing to Swiggy. Hoss untied the cod end rope, and the contents of the net covered the floorboards all around Swiggy who was on his knees sorting out the catch amongst the dead oystershells, crabs, jellyfish, seaweed and other debris. Suddenly, he recoiled back, pulling his hands quickly out of the pile as he stared at this large, gaping-wide mouth, which seemingly went for him. "What the **** was that?", he exclaimed as he gingerly probed back into the pile of rubbish with his fingertips. Me and Hoss were in fits at Swiggy's antics as he slowly uncovered this alien; when it came to light, what we had caught was a turbot, an absolute splendid fish of about 10 pounds weight. We stayed behind the Nass for the rest of the day, catching mainly soles and roker, one of our best days. We asked Dick Haward to sell some of our catch, including the turbot. The turbot was sold, and it fetched £10; our weekly wages between all three of us hardly amounted to £10. What a result!

We now had the gear to make up a new ground rope. We laid out the beam and trawl on the grass at Hoss's and proceeded to fit it. It was made up in the usual way of discs of rubber rollers cut and stamped out of recycled vehicle tyres, three inches in diameter with a one-and-a-quarter inch hole cut through the middle to pass a quarter-inch chain through. Then we had six-inch lengths of rubber hose pipe as a spacer between the rollers to make it lighter to keep the weight down. Eventually, we had it all back together, so it was taken back to the *Boat*, and we were keen to try it out. At the earliest opportunity we were out in the river. We went to our usual spot where we knew what the ground was like and had the same half-hour tow. Gone were the heaps of dead shell that we usually caught. Instead, fish, crabs, jellyfish, and the usual amount of seaweed, plus some dead shells, but nothing like the back-breaking netfulls as before. Now we could tow for an hour or more in between hauls.

Some early spring days in March and April used to be very cold in our open boat, so we thought some sort of shelter would be a good idea. On a cold, wet, breezy, wind-chill day, we would tie the tiller so the boat would steer herself, pulling the trawl. The three of us would sit and huddle side by side on the floorboards with our backs against the bow locker, hoping that the higher planking of the hull, where it joined the stem post, would afford us some form of protection from the biting wind, and it did to a degree. We had no means of heating water to make tea or coffee; we had to bring a drink and a bite to eat with us, but usually we didn't take anything. We would wait until when we came ashore and go into Fleetview Stores. As Swiggy used to say to Alf Parrish, "A cup of Choc-hot-late and a rake and Sydney pie, please". Alf looked at him quizzically for a second or two, trying to work out what he said. Then we would sit outside the shop scoffing the pies, drinking the hot chocolate as if we hadn't eaten for a week, then rolling and lighting up an Old Holborn fag; there was nothing better!

We found in our scavenging wanderings a three-section metal frame and hinges that would have been used as a fold down, canvas-covered cuddy on an open boat; exactly the same idea that would be used on a baby's pram. It was fractionally too wide but, with a little bit of alteration, it fitted from gunwale to gunwale perfectly. We screwed and fitted the hinges and framework, and with Swiggy's mum and uncle working at Gowens, the sailmakers, they had it measured, and the canvas cuddy was made very quickly. It also had a clear flexible plastic window in the front section. We took it up to Hoss's and spread it out on his lawn where we gave it two or three coats of green Danbolin, then let it dry in the sun. We brought the boat onto the hard and fitted our new shelter over the frame; it was perfect. The front of the cuddy was screwed to the bow thwart, then, as it was pulled up, it was secured into place by two 6-foot triangular sections of canvas wings tied amidships on either side of the boat by a cord and fixed to a small cleat. When the cuddy wasn't being used, it was laid flat on the forward thwart out of the way. Now on wet, windy, rough water days, when the waves came over the bow, we could lift the cuddy and at least two of the crew could take shelter; but the poor unfortunate on the tiller still had to get dressed up in oilskins and a sou'wester as he was showered all the way home as waves, rain, and cold spray came over the top. All through the summer we would be out as much as we could, enjoying being on the water using our brilliant little boat, and towing the net at all different locations where we thought we might do well.

7: The Winds of Change

As the summer months receded into September, our attention was drawn into the pursuit of wildfowl. Our *Boat* was used when a trip was planned at the furthest points of our range. We used to head quite often for the saltings in the Tollesbury channel areas; Flaxy was our first choice normally. The weather didn't worry us too much now and it would have to be blowing very hard from an easterly direction to stop us. We would motor up into the "leavings" and pick up a vacant mooring. If the tide was coming in, we would anchor her on the mud at the water's edge, knowing she would be afloat when we came back to her after flight. We would then separate and go to our favourite creeks and hopefully await the forthcoming magic. Flaxy was in a very good place in that it was well situated between Mell Hall and Old Hall. The Island picked up the two-way traffic of wildfowl which flew across the two wide channels that separated the freshwater marshes. It was covered in flashes of small areas of water that teal loved especially; lots of seed-bearing plants, especially samphire, grew all over the islands. It was a brilliant place for evening flight.

We would also take the little boat up into Old Hall Creek and flight the saltings at Brand's and Joice's Head where the different species of ducks that found their way into our game bags were quite noticeable. When we used her to flight Copthall, Abbots Hall and Old Hall saltings, with the flatty tied to the stern, the *Boat* was anchored in the middle of Salcott Channel; we would scull ashore and await flighttime in our favourite places and creeks somewhere on the big marshes. If one of us fancied their luck on the opposite side of the creek by Quince's corner on the Old Hall side, the *Boat* would be nosed into a small creek, if the tide allowed, and whoever wanted to shoot that side would slip over the gunwale onto the marsh and make his way to where his best chance of a shot would be. Then whoever was left in the boat would take it to the middle of the wide channel, anchor her, and then scull the dinghy to the saltings opposite at Copt or Abbots Hall.

The two areas of saltings on either side of the channel were very significant by the fact that they were in the direct flight line from Abberton reservoir, and into the fed areas of water and flight ponds of Old Hall. At dusk, quite often it would be a constant stream of ducks passing by and over you, but of course not all were in range. The anticipation, however, was thrilling. At morning flight, it wasn't a complete reversal of movement, but hopefully the wildfowl came and flew about the saltings and water-filled creeks before heading off to sleep and rest out the daylight hours. If the creeks in the saltings held water from an early tide, it offered you the chance of some exciting shooting as they came to your handful of decoys. After flight, the flatty would be pushed down the mud to the water, then to the *Boat*, and drop one of us off to start her. Then the one left in the flatty would scull across the channel to pick up the person who had, by then, walked down the soft mud to the low tide mark, wash the mud and filth from his thigh boots, put his bag and gun in the dinghy, and climb in after washing the rest of the mud from his boots. Sometimes, the pair of them would get into the *Boat* and motor off down Salcott Creek for home, leaving you standing up to your knees in the soft mud and pitch blackness trying to maintain your balance, and listening to the receding exhaust note as they motored for home away from you, only to then come back after 10-15 minutes with, "Oh sorry, mush; forgot about you", as they smirked in the darkness. Turkeys.

On other days, we would meet at Wyatt's hard at 1.30pm, scull the flatty across to Feldy, and anchor her on the high water by the wreck of the ADC. We would then go to the seawall and make up our minds to walk to either Abbots Hall, Copthall or Sampson's Creek for flight. Firstly, we would sneak up the seawall, peep over the top, and look along the borrow dykes, left and right, to see if any mallard were there; if there were, we would then hurry along the seaward side of the seawall opposite, hopefully to where the mallard still were, then walk up the seawall on our knees as quietly as possible. We would peep through the long grass to see if we were in the right place and then, as they flew away, have a shot at them as they tried to make their escape. Depending on what time high water was, if we didn't have a dog we would flight on Sampson's freshwater fleet inland, or a flooded fleet somewhere on Feldy, but if the tide was leaving Sampson's saltings then this would be the favoured location, especially if it was cold and with an easterly airstream. Teal would come to feed, and with the muddy creeks emptying, it was then that you could retrieve any shot ducks more easily.

I remember, it was Boxing Day, 1962; we were at evening flight at Sampson's.

Earlier that afternoon we had rowed on the last of a flood tide up to Ray Island; as we rowed and rounded Ray Point, three ducks swam out of the saltings very close to us and seemed very tame. We didn't recognise and identify them as they swam very close to the dinghy; then one of my mates described two of them as looking like a court jester with patchwork clothing. I agreed and kept the description in my mind as we carried on. Firstly, we were going to try to outwit the pheasants that were quite abundant amongst the thick undergrowth of blackthorn and long coarse grass, which is still a feature of the Island today. However, we tried in vain as we didn't have a dog; the pheasants were impossible to flush for a shot. We came back down the Ray Channel and anchored the flatty on the ebbing tide line high up the mud by Sampson's Creek, then walked up the muddy ooze and soft foreshore; we separated and went to our favourite places to await flightime in the saltings and creeks. The sun slowly dropped below the horizon; the sky was cloudless with a gorgeous orange colour. The visibility, I remember, was incredibly clear with hardly a breath of wind. The black silhouettes of flighting gulls heading south to the Blackwater to roost could be seen for miles as they passed. Also, I could see bunches of ducks flighting from Old Hall, some heading our way very high. As some of them got over the marsh, they would drop to zero altitude and flew about looking for somewhere to land and feed. The shooting was quite busy as they zipped about; it was brilliant sport, mostly at teal; then I spotted a pair of mallard heading our way. They circled round the marsh a couple of times, but luckily neither of my mates fired at them. They circled around one more time and passed, in range, in front of me; both hit the saltmarsh, my first right and left at mallard.

I picked up all my birds successfully, then as I was nearest to the dinghy, I went to it first and pushed it down the mud to the ebbing tide. As I walked about in the shallow water, with every step the black water lit up around my feet with luminescence. I could hear my mates talking and sploshing about in the mud and shallow water looking for their birds; one of them whistled to see where I was, so I gave a whistle back to let them know I was with the boat. It was then, as I was waiting for my mates, that I noticed my eartips were tingling from the freezing cold, frosty, northeast airstream; my fingers were aching with cold from when I had got them wet while picking and washing my birds, then sponging the mud from my thighboots. Eventually, my mates turned up; they put their guns and bags into the boat, washed their ducks and boots in the cold water of Ray Creek, and stepped into the flatty. I rowed as we recounted our hits and misses, proceeding on the ebbing tide of the dark creek. "Did you get a shot at those mallard?", Hoss asked and, in the same breath, "how many did you get?". "Both of them" I replied. It went quiet for a second or two. "Jammy bastard", they both muttered. But it was a good flight; we had all shot ducks, mostly teal, with the darkness beating us in the end as trilling and calling shadows flew close past us as they dropped into the marsh and creeks. As we rowed for home, the person on the oars would complain how his hands were freezing cold. We would take it in turns rowing so the moaner could blow and rub his hurting digits, then put them inside the tops of his thigh boots onto warm legs to thaw out. Phosphorescence dripped from the oar blades as they came out of the water, briefly and dimly lighting up our pale faces between each stroke; straight lines of brilliance rolled across the calm water on the boats bow wave, and in the turbulence of the dinghy's transom.

As we made our way home on the still, calm waters of the Ray Creek, we quietly drifted past the *Bluebell* smack on her mooring; the cabin hatch was slightly ajar showing a narrow orange light. Paraffin, the smell of cooking, and tobacco smoke wafted out and caught our senses on the freezing north-east light air as we crept past. We didn't want to meet the owner as rumour had it that he had bought Ray Island, and we had just been trying to outwit and shoot his pheasants that afternoon. We left it astern, somewhere far ahead in the darkness with the occasional cronking calls of Brent geese, laughing shelducks, bubbling curlews, shrieking redshanks, and twittering dunlin having been disturbed from the creek's muddy edge close by, the rollocks rattling and chattering as they flopped about in worn chocks as we proceeded back to our bikes at Wyatt's hard. It had been another memorable day with my two mates. We would get the pheasants on the Ray, but not during this season. After I got home, later that evening, I was watching television in front of a roaring fire when the three ducks that we had seen that afternoon came to mind. I reached across to the bookshelf and pulled out my bird book. I thumbed through the pages once again on wildfowl and found them: harlequin ducks, the patchwork feathers on the drakes matching exactly what we had seen that afternoon. Apparently, they are rare visitors to the UK.

That night it snowed and snowed and blew a gale from the east-northeast; all the following week there was heavy snowfall and blizzards. Roads were blocked with drifts. Then the sky cleared, and it froze – for weeks it froze; the Blackwater froze, and all the channels and creeks froze solid. It was a catastrophe for the birds that, particularly, used the tidal foreshore mud and saltings to feed and exist; waders, ducks and Brent geese suffered terribly. Shellfish, particularly the valuable native oyster stocks, were decimated from the unrelenting freezing weather that lasted for three months. Wildfowlers stopped shooting voluntarily as it was quite evident the wildlife was starving and suffering from the intensity of the conditions. On a field right next to

Bocking Hall Farm, where the wind had blown the snow off the apex of the field exposing the grass, two hundred European whitefronted geese and a lot of wigeon were sharing, and existing on, a tiny area; they were roosting and feeding in the same spot for weeks and weeks.

Just below where I lived, a massive snow drift filled Cross Lane; my sister and I were down there walking the dogs and, in the drift, we carved and wrote our names. The snow drift and our names remained and were still there in April. After the thaw, the high-water mark on the beaches and sea walls was banked up with dead and empty seashells, and with the corpses and sad remains of fore-shore birds that had died, having been entombed and trapped in the ice, only to be released as the thaw set in. How many, I wonder, perished during that winter of 1962-63? I never want to see another like it. The *Bluebell* was left abandoned in the Ray channel, which was full of thick ice from one side to the other; huge icebergs scrunched back and forth on every tide, and eventually she broke up to sink on her mooring. We never saw the smack again, nor her owner!

When we met at Wyatt's hard, and if it was high tide and the flatty was out of reach at anchor, one of us would wade out in the tide up to the top of his thigh boots, and, with the long sculling oar, try to reach the dingy and bring it to shore. If you still couldn't reach it then you would borrow any available boat or dinghy nearby and use that to reach yours, then bring them both ashore and anchor the dinghy you had borrowed back where you had found it. We arrived at the hard and we could see that the flatty was out of reach, so I volunteered to get it. The nearest boat available was Doodle Whiting's punt; it was floating in about two or three feet of water as I waded out to it. Hoss and Swiggy had their backs to me, looking at something or someone far more interesting on the causeway and not paying any attention to me behind them. Doodle's punt, by reputation, was probably the narrowest, most tippy, unseaworthy coffin that ever floated in Punt Bay. I swung a leg over the side, then the other, and as I did the punt promptly capsized, flinging me out the other side into the water onto my back. I clambered to my feet, soaked from head to foot. I looked over to my mates who were still not paying any attention to me; one of them must have heard the splash, or me cursing. It was Hoss; I can still remember and visualise his face, looking at me with an expressionist gaze and just a tiny smile. He tapped Swiggy on the shoulder, saying at the same time, "Look at this useless ******". Swiggy turned round and both of them just stood there smiling and thinking, "You w****r", then falling over themselves in fits as I waded out to the flatty with all my shooting gear on and fetched it ashore for them. I could see the funny side of my misfortune and we laughed till our sides ached. I tipped out the water from my thigh boots, wrung out my socks, and then rode my bike back home to get out of my wet clothes. I didn't come back, I left them to it. They didn't mention it ever again. Not much!

Another afternoon, we were shooting up at Sampson's area; it was a still day, probably in November when often, in the afternoon, it becomes misty and foggy, as it was on this day.

We split up to go individually to our places to flight. As it got darker, so the fog got much thicker; you virtually couldn't see more than ten yards in front of you, so I decided to pack up and find my mates. After a few whistles we found each other by the sluice at Sampson's Creek; none of us had shot anything and I don't think we even saw a bird! We then walked along the inside of the seawall on the grassy folding for half a mile or more back to the dinghy where we had left it anchored near the ADC. We came over the seawall by the right-hand sharp bend, our landmark, and it took us a few minutes before we stumbled across the flatty in the nil visibility; the boat was afloat as it was nearing high water and still coming in. We put our gear aboard and looked out across the sea to where we thought Mersea should be; there wasn't a breath of wind, nor could we hear a sound that would have given us half a clue of the direction in which we should head. Furthermore, we didn't have a compass between us to help us to navigate back. We knew that in the middle of Thornfleet there would be boats moored and also mooring buoys. There were also whithies that marked an oyster laying; that would be the first indicator of our position. We set off, straining our eyes and ears; if the tide had been low, it would have been easy finding our way back, just by following the mud edges of the creeks that we knew off by heart. Over fifty-five years ago, there weren't as many boats moored in the channels as there are today; the few yachts back then would have been taken out and stored for the winter. A lot of the moorings, the rising scopes, and buoys would have been taken ashore, and the only boats left afloat were those fishing, together with the oyster smacks and skiffs.

The ADC smack wreck is on the Feldy shore, abandoned and left in a creek in the saltings more or less right opposite the Gut. We rowed, as we thought, in a straight line heading for the Gut, or at least perhaps the flooding tide might take us to the other side of the Thornfleet to land up on the saltings of Ray Island, then strike off across the Strood channel and come ashore by the Nothe. We rowed out into the creek, after a while we saw land; we got out only to find we had rowed in a complete circle and were back on the Feldy shore. We cast off again, and rowed out into the blackness where we found a mooring buoy and held on that for a while as we tried to work out our position. The tide was still coming in so the stem of the dinghy should be pointing up the channel towards the Blackwater; Mersea should be on our port, or left-hand, side. We cast off again, the buoy disappearing in the darkness as we rowed away from it. Then, in the gloom, we could see a boat moored. We went to her and recognized her straight away; we knew where she was in relation to the creek. We hung on to her and had a good look to see if we could see another, but we didn't, so we cast off again and after a while found another that we knew lay near the Gut. Eventually, by going from boat to boat that we recognized, we came ashore, very relieved. I have always hated being on the water in thick fog and darkness; you think it is going to last for the rest of your life, never finding your way home.

I remember just a few years ago, fast forwarding fifty or more years, in the gunning punt rowing for home and coming out of the Walton channel with Julian Novorol ("J.N."). It had been, and was, as they say "as thick as guts"; from the first thing at dawn when I left Mersea in my car for Little Oakley, and as we rowed and paddled the punt down the long creek to the estuary, then crossed over from the northern to the southern shore before heading east out to sea, visibility was less than 50 yards. We cautiously polled along an edge in shallow water. As it was so foggy, we were lying flat in the punt as J.N. had heard some wigeon some-where in front of us, and not knowing how far they were, we wanted to see them before they saw us. The first group of ducks we came across were six mallard and a few wigeon, but they were all on the water spread about, not worth trying for a shot. We lay there for several minutes watching the ducks, very close to us now as the ebb tide was taking the low punt nearer to them. Suddenly, a head went up on a long neck; we had been spotted. A few anxious quacks and calls and then they lifted and flew away without any panic. We carried on for several hundred yards, still lying flat. Looking through the fog and gloom with my binoculars, as it had cleared slightly, I could make out a group of birds on a gravelly shore 150 yards away: wigeon.

They sat in two groups; the further lot were better, but we had no option but to go for the closer birds. The punt stole forward into long range; we managed another 30 yards closer. I saw a couple of heads suddenly lift; we were being eyeballed and scrutinised. I noticed from their movement that they didn't like this low, strange object suddenly coming towards them out of nowhere, and so were about to fly. I pulled hard on the trigger lanyard and fired; a cloud of grey-white smoke was blown forward from out of the big gun's muzzle for about twenty feet, then slowly it drifted back towards us in the practically non-existent easterly air stream. The smoke stayed in the freezing, still air all around the punt; it seemed like an age to clear as it slowly drifted back past us in the thick atmos-phere. We could then see that we had a few birds; after a quick chase for one or two cripples, we picked them all: one drake tufted duck and twenty-two wigeon. I stowed the birds under the side decking as J.N. cleaned and rodded out the gun, reloaded, got things shipshape, and then carried on rowing east, wanting to look at another area further away to see if it was worth planning a trip for the next day. It was!

By now it was about 2:30 pm; too late in the afternoon to try for another shot, even if one presented itself, as it was getting increasingly darker. We turned the punt for home. It was by now very dark and still very foggy as we came out of the channel into the wide estuary and headed west with a now flooding tide under us to help find our home creek miles away. Visibility was zero as I pulled on the oars. "Any idea where we are, mate?", I enquired. "Yep, of course I do", he replied. "Do you mind if I try the GPS on my phone and see how accurate it is?", I asked. "You don't need that, I know exactly where we are", he said, and I didn't doubt him. I proceeded to set up my phone anyway; I placed the phone on the floorboards in between my legs and our GPS position immediately came up on the screen. I rowed the punt in the zero-visibility using the phone right up to the mooring two or three miles away.

The Victory public house was our usual meeting place in the evening with some of the other lads who went out wildfowling. There was always a sense of rivalry and competition between us, such as who had got what, attempts to find out where they had shot them, and if someone had had a good flight. It was all tight-lipped stuff, and a good spot wasn't revealed readily only to be shot out by all and sundry. The boy who was building his punt in his front garden was starting to find his feet; he was first taken out by his older brother and mate during the previous season, but he was now using it and going out by himself. The punt was overbuilt; it was strong, but as the wood planking soaked in water it turned out to be very heavy. Basky and Doodle Whiting rowed the punt to Pennyhole one evening for flight, leaving it anchored in a creek. The tide ebbed away from the creek leaving it on the mud in the bottom, but trapped, so that neither of them could shift or move it. They were marooned. Basky's mum and dad were now getting concerned that he was late getting home, so Terry, Basky's older brother, was sent on a mission to find them both. He guessed they had gone to Pennyhole. As he turned up on the Mersea hard, he heard shots from Old Hall point; he guessed it was a help signal from the two of them, so he borrowed a dinghy and found an oar under Gowens' sail loft, then sculled all the way out to Pennyhole to rescue the very relieved pair, getting home at midnight. As for the punt, the three of them still couldn't move it; they had to go back at high water the next day and rescue it as the tide lifted it from the creek. Basky built another punt, a lighter one, soon after that, selling the heavy one to Mac (I think!).

I was beating for the shoot over at Feldy every other Saturday with my fellow beaters and relatives, but on the days that I was beating, I couldn't go for morning flight. I was going fowling very often now, every weekend and evenings if I wasn't ferreting or working. I didn't want to miss morning flight on the day that I was beating; I knew Basky would be going out somewhere, so I would arrange to meet him early on the Saturday morning at Punt Bay. He would then row me across from Mersea and drop me off the on the Feldy shore by the ADC. I would then walk the mile or more along the seawall to Copthall or Abbots Hall and flight the saltings. Then, after morning flight, I would go to Newhall or Copthall Farms and join my fellow beaters, walking all day in my thigh boots to the waiting guns. At the end of the day, I would get a lift down to the hard where I had left my bike that morning and ride it back home.

Basky and I were now shooting and wildfowling very often together; I would go and see him at home mid-week, and we would make plans as to where we should go at the weekend for morning flight. A lot of the time we would go to Pennyhole and, depending how good it was at dawn flight, we would go back again in the afternoon and stay until after dark.

As the 1,100 acres of Old Hall marsh flooded during the winter months, the population of wildfowl increased as the migratory population passed through or stayed and over-wintered locally. It was still being fed and shot by the owners and at times there were thousands of birds using the freshwater ponds, fleets and disused decoys. On an area what we used to call "The Lagoon", was the last piece of low-lying fleet of several acres to flood; during the spring and summer, after it had dried out, a weed called fat hen would grow, and the ducks loved to tear and feed on the seed heads that were now floating in water. As the dawn broke, birds that had been out all-night feeding would come back to Old Hall to digest, rest and sleep on the water- filled ponds and fleets; on some days it was alive. Teal would flight back in and if they had a gale of wind behind them from out of the west, they would overshoot the lagoon and Marsh, coming over the seawall and turning in a wide "U" over Pennyhole saltings to head the wind back.

We would find our favourite creeks, hopefully to intercept them, perhaps put half a dozen decoys out if there was water, and then flight them as they headed the wind back into Old Hall. On some mornings it was a non-stop as they came in and out in singles, pairs, big bunches, and little bunches as they gave us the best of sport, of only what wildfowling can offer. Often, the flight would stop abruptly for some reason or another, or sadly we would be flooded out of our creeks with a rising tide and with nowhere to find cover, or if we had simply run out of cartridges as they continued to flight into us; they were fabulous red-letter days. Several mallard always flighted back in, coming from Mersea, Bradwell, Dengie or Cobmarsh Island, or even further, to spend the day resting, and if the wind was particularly strong as they flew and headed into it there was more of a chance they were bought down out of the clouds into the range of us hiding in the creeks. They were always the first to flight. It used to be still quite dark as they flew in or out back to a favourite resting place for the day, but not all the time as sometimes it would be quite late in the morning before they moved. That is the appeal and beauty of wildfowling: it is so unpredictable, with one day being totally different from another.

I remember one particular morning, having just dropped into my favourite creek, when I would normally face the lighter sky to the east until I could see clearer to the west so as to spot any birds just that little bit sooner. Perhaps I just hadn't sorted myself out; I had only just taken my gun out of its cover and had just slipped two cartridges into the breech. I was facing the dark sky to the west when I spotted six ducks just skimming the saltings as teal would do; it was still very dark. How I saw them, I don't know. They were in a tight group as they passed to my right; I instinctively swung through them and fired one shot. Four of the six fell out of the bunch and went into the saltings; my first thoughts were that they were teal and should be about 25 yards from my creek, all laying in a neat line a few yards apart. I got to where I thought they should be; nothing could I find. I searched for several minutes in the deep marsh, vegetation and creeks; nothing. I couldn't work it out, where were they? It was still quite dark and anything lying in the thick, deep vegetation would be well hidden. Then, as I continued searching, I spotted some more heading my way. I ran forward to gain cover of another creek and shot one out of the bunch as they passed in front of me. I went to find the teal where I had marked it down, but I was amazed to see, also lying on the mud, the four ducks I had shot earlier; not teal as I had thought, but mallard. In the dark I thought they were teal at 25 yards, but in fact they were mallard at 45 yards.

We now had a new beater in the line who had joined us (1959-60) a couple of years previous. Doug Sawkins had moved to Mersea from Abberton after marrying a Mersea girl, Eadie Webb, and he was very quickly accepted as a very good friend. He also owned, and drove, a 1950s Bedford Dormobile van which had a side door, windows all round, and slatted wooden seats; an early people carrier. So now Doug would pick up dad and me from our home together with Swiggy and, at times, David ("Pud") Garrard, Pinky Hewes, Steve Green, Billy Jowers, Pat Clark and Doodle. He would also help Din with the pheasant rearing, gamekeeping and ferreting so, in repayment, he used to accompany Din and Hoss shooting on Feldy quite often.

Changes were now happening in the farming industry; more land was bought into crop production and encouraged by the government and the quangos from

MAFF, the destruction of the countryside as I knew it at the time was being undertaken. Feldy and Copthall marshes were flattened, then drained, ploughed up, and set with wheat or barley. Hedges were dug out to make fields bigger as farming machinery now increased in size. Toxic chemicals were sprayed on the land, killing everything apart from the plant and crop it was designed to help. Firstly, it was light aircraft dropping its lethal poison from altitude, the breeze blowing the yellow mist onto houses, gardens, drying laundry, and allotments without any thought of its consequence as it settled. I can remember the first shoot of the season that winter after the destruction of Feldy; as we sloshed and dragged heavy boots through a sea of yellow clinging clay and mud, which was once a pristine organic environment, we held the forlorn hope that there might be a covey of grey partridges or a cock pheasant or two to push over the waiting guns. Not a cat in hells chance!

As I walked beside my father in the beating line, Din was on the right-hand flank and track; he shouted across to the line of beaters to keep in a straight line and anyone behind the line to catch up. I can honestly say, before that day and every day afterwards that I spent with my father, I never heard him once use an expletive, but he did that day. I am sure it was just pure anger, sadness, and frustration at seeing his world that he had spent countless days enjoying and then fighting for, was now a lifeless, muddy, clay prairie. His brother got a full tirade back at him, but knowing Din, he was just as sad, frustrated and angry as my father and all the rest of us who understood what had been lost to us and the wildlife from that day. The little shoot was basically finished; a pristine, wonderful area of natural habitat was systematically destroyed just to gain a few more acres of wheat that weren't required. You can't lay all of the blame at the feet of the farmers; they were struggling and were just coming out of a post-war Britain. The government and the relevant Ministries encouraged the farming community with monetary and, probably, blackmailing incentives to destroy the habitat, just for the sake of a few more tons of wheat! Din didn't live very long after that. He died a few years later with gullet cancer, after smoking and sucking all his life on that bloody pipe! Just 57 years old. My grandfather had died just a few months before Din.

Back on Mersea, the same thing was happening: hedges ripped out, and acres of marshes were drained and flattened. On the neighbouring farm, the freshwater marsh where me and my father often went to flight, was now a sea of featureless wheat or barley. I do recall that same marsh after it was destroyed; the wheat or barley waiting to be harvested that autumn was standing in acres of floodwater. I had never seen so many wild mallard raiding a crop; hundreds and hundreds came to it. We never got one even though we spent many evenings in the vain hope that some might come in range.

At about this time, a wonderful, powerful, hard-hitting book was written and published about our vanishing farmland, birds, butterflies and insects. Rachel Carson's book, "Silent Spring", was an eye-opener as to what was happening to our native flora and fauna. For us in our small, nature-watchful group in the beating line, we were probably one of the first to witness and take note of the disappearing coveys of grey partridges and other birds, nature and creatures that had been such a common and regular sight before, as we walked through the countryside. The book was a revelation and it made governments and chemical companies more accountable to the devastating damage, which was happening to, and the poisons being sprayed and spread over, the environment and countryside. It has been a slow and very depressing, painful episode over the past sixty years. Now, people are protesting and throwing up their arms in horror as we have the rainwater runoff from this abuse; our estuaries and rivers are polluted, and our saltwater creeks and channels are dying right in front of our eyes. They are victims of sewage, a host of toxic pollutants, and, dare I say it, our freshwater drinking! Companies are pumping out millions of gallons of untreated sewage into our estuaries and waterways somewhere every day. When is it going to end? As I have mentioned a few pages before, nature has to be treated with respect as someday it will bite back!

8: Becoming Mobile

THE THREE OF us were still using our little boat a lot, but we noticed that as the temperatures dropped, and on cold damp days during the winter, the Thetis got harder to start; sometimes it would take twenty minutes on the starting handle to eventually get it going, often resulting in water-filled blisters across your hand, as you called it every name under the sun. A painful hand dipped into cold seawater brought some relief, and I am sure a glove or a can of Easystart spray would have helped, but I am not sure if it was on the market back then. We decided another engine was required, not petrol this time but diesel. We enquired locally at all the marine workshops, engineers and boatyards for something second hand that might be for sale, but nothing was available. We made it known locally that we were looking for an engine – anything would be considered. I can't remember now who told us, but they had seen an engine at the entrance of a scrap yard on the quay at Rowhedge, at the bottom of Rectory Road.

By this time Hoss and I had a driving licence, I think, so we drove over to Rowhedge on a Saturday morning and, sure enough, sitting up on a brick wall was the engine. We parked up and went to the yard and found the owner; it was for sale. It was a twin-cylinder, Petter stationary engine; it was fitted previously to an agricultural piece of machinery that would be used to convey bales of straw, hay or even stooks of wheat or barley onto the top of a stack, or even on a tractor-pulled combine harvester. How old it was, the owner had no idea. We asked for the handle to try and get it running; it had lots of compression, but we couldn't get it to start. Under all the dirt, grease and diesel it was a maroon colour, the same as that used on Massey Harris machines. The airways around the cylinders and flywheel that pushed the cooling air through were clogged with mainly barley ables and straw; I am fairly sure it hadn't been touched or serviced from new. The other problem was that it didn't have a gear box and one would have to be fitted, but how?

We left it with the owner, saying that we were interested but would have to find out if a gearbox could be fitted. Then we drove back home and went to seek advice from the experts straight away; it could be done, and we could even use the gearbox from the Thetis, but would have to get a steel plate machined and lathed with a bearing and oil seal in the centre to take the drive shaft and to keep the gearbox oil in. It entailed quite a bit of precision engineering. We decided to buy the Petter. How much we paid for it, I can't now remember. We bundled it in Hoss's Ford Anglia van and brought it back to Mersea; we bought a tin of Gunk, liberally brushed it all over the engine, gave it time to work its magic, and then washed off years of oily dirt with buckets of water. It came up spotless. We checked the engine oil. It was still okay; we drained the fuel tank and cleaned the filters, then filled it with clean diesel, primed the fuel lines, bled the ejectors, and turned the engine over. Within a few minutes we had it running, as sweet as a nut.

Hoss went to see the wonderful engineer Fred Hayward in his large shed-cum-workshop in Rainbow Road, and he couldn't see a problem with machining and lathing the sealing plate. Our boat was once again stationed on the land between Pinky's and Jim Gladwell's; we set to getting the Thetis out and putting it in the boatshed to work on. We removed the gearbox and took it down to Fred's workshop for him to assess the work required and to give us a list of materials so he could make a start. While the boat was out of the water, we gave her another paint up and did other essential jobs on her while we waited for Fred. Roger Butcher welded sections onto the new sealing plate; as he and Fred worked for the same engineering company, they would see each other at work, with Fred letting Roger know what he wanted and required before we even knew. After what seemed like weeks, the plate and work were finished. Roger made, and welded, fixing brackets on a heavy steel metal plate to drop in between the existing oak wooden engine beds. We manhandled the heavy diesel engine over the gunwales and laid it into its new home, fitted and lined the engine and gearbox to the prop shaft and coupling, marked the engine beds and plate, then drilled and bolted down the Petter. We had to make another box to cover our new engine. When that was all finished, we were ready for sea once again.

We launched our *Boat* at the hard, started up the Petter, tied the flatty to the stern, put it into gear, and went on our usual test-run route up the Strood Channel and back without any problems. We then put her back on her mooring and sculled ashore. The starting handle fitted straight onto the crankshaft with approximately three inches of clear shaft left from the engine cowling to the starting handle; hopefully there was enough room to fit a double "V" pulley with a belt to another larger diameter pulley fitted to a capstan which would haul in our trawl. We obtained a pulley, had the centre hole lathed and enlarged by Fred to fit onto the engine crankshaft, and also a grub screw, threaded, that held it tightly onto the shaft without it spinning under driveload. Then we had to find a

Triumph Herald back axle differential; after spending hours going around scrap yards, we eventually found one in Mersea. Then the gearing inside the box had to be welded together so both half shafts turned as one. On the coupling where the car prop shaft would normally be fitted, another ten-inch double Vee belt pulley was bolted on. We decided on a position where the capstan was to be installed, brought the boat ashore onto the hard, and our good friend Roger was entrusted with the job of making the fixing brackets to hold it securely in place onto a large floor bearer. Then Fred turned up a wooden dolly capstan head on his lathe that, in turn, was secured to a short shaft which also bolted to the differential. Then a bearing, with its housing, was slid over the shaft and screwed and fixed to the middle thwart which secured the capstan securely in position. We then bought enough Brammer Vee belt sections to connect the capstan to the pulley on the engine crankshaft. Roger made a stainless steel, slightly domed, cover to fit on the top of the wooden capstan which would keep out the rain and weather.

We were keen to try out our new engine. We sea-trialled and ran our new acquisition for several evenings and weekends before we fitted the Brammer belts to drive our winch. Once we were confident of our new fit-up, we were up by Tollesbury pier the next weekend once again. We shot the net and beam and did our favourite usual tow east towards the Nass beacon; on the Sampson post up in the bow we had shackled another single block pulley, then passed the trawl warp through the block that reached back to the dolly. When we reached the end of our tow, Hoss wound a couple of turns around the capstan. He then put a little bit of pressure on the free end of the warp to tighten it onto the dolly, and it started to pull and drag the trawl to the boat; it worked brilliantly. The Petter didn't even change its engine note as it took the extra strain. The boat was also still in gear going ahead; as the trawl got close to the boat, the warp was lifted out and clear of the fairlead by the person on the tiller. It would then pull and turn the boat to port with the beam and net laying alongside, ready to haul over the rail.

In 1954, a new bird protection law was passed in parliament, and several birds that were on the quarry list were now protected: the Brent goose, shelduck, Green plover, and other waders. The new duck-shooting season now started on the 1st of September instead of the 12th of August. The muzzle diameter of a punt gun could be no bigger than an inch and three-quarters, not that that mattered too much, but it did make several bigger guns obsolete.

It was about this time that some enlightened people saw this as a direct threat to our traditional wildfowling way of life, and with guidance, in some cases from W.A.G.B.I. (The Wildfowlers' Association of Great Britain and Ireland), wild-fowling clubs were being formed all around the coast with a view to protect that which we all had once taken for granted. There was no argument that, in most cases, saltmarsh was owned by someone, but where it was covered at high tide, it was free for anyone to shoot so long as you abided by the unwritten rule and didn't stray inland over the seawall to poach! The new 1954 Act didn't affect me in any way, as it was my first year of wildfowling; what you didn't have, you didn't miss, but to the older generation like my father, his brothers, and my grandfather, it was a bitter pill to swallow. It took a couple of seasons for it to sink in. So, for now, I was very lucky that my wildfowling apprenticeship wasn't knocked off course in any shape or form.

In those early years, in the late fifties and early sixties, talking to the older generation of fowlers at Mersea, they never gave it one thought that their lifetime rights and traditions could be under threat, so we, as 14-,15- and 16-year old kids, thought that the older generation knew better in safeguarding our shooting as it was then, and took some comfort from that. How wrong we all were! But things were happening, and not very far away; the writing was on the wall, a red light was flashing over it, and we still didn't read it here at Mersea (or perhaps we just didn't want to!). Lennox Leavett, as I have mentioned before, was a keen, active wildfowler, living just a few miles away, as the duck flies, at Tollesbury. The gunners there were doing exactly what we were doing here at Mersea: enjoying their free shooting. However, unknown to them, a large area of saltmarsh that they had always used was sold right under their noses to another Essex wildfowling club; it shook them to the core. Shortly afterwards, with a huge sense of urgency, they formed their own club in around 1962, and secured, with rents and leases, the shooting on the rest of the saltmarsh on and over which they had always shot. When we met Lennox in the Victory, the first thing he used to ask us was when were we going to form a club here at Mersea to protect our shooting; we just poo-pooed him, saying it will never happen here! Still to this very day at Tollesbury, they view an outsider wishing to join their organisation with mistrust and suspicion; you have to be very well-known before anybody is allowed to join their ranks. Once bitten, twice shy, and who can blame them?

With the motor car now becoming more common, the coast and its shooting attractions were within easy reach of a lot more people. In places, you could just park a vehicle and walk straight out onto a piece of salting with a shotgun, and this was happening with much more frequency. Hence, the local wildfowling communities got together to form clubs to control the "Townies", as they were often referred to. At the time here at Mersea, it was very much harder to get to the better places; a boat was required. An outsider would have to know someone living here with a punt or dingy to gain access to these places; light plastic or glass fibre boats that were towed behind a vehicle were still relatively unheard of, so the Mersea locals still enjoyed the shooting on their traditional grounds for themselves, in the naïve belief that we were isolated and secluded, and no one was going to take it away from us!

At about this time, in early 1964, an advert appeared in the Essex County Standard enquiring whether there was any interest in forming a wildfowling club in Colchester. When Graham McKillop ("Mac") placed the advert, he had a response from a few enthusiastic people who all met up in his grandmother's house where Mac was living at the time. Almost immediately the club was formed, and a committee was assembled. The Colchester Wildfowling and Conservation Club ("CWCC") was born. I remember at the time, John Knight, who lived at Brierley Hall, attended that meeting and was the first person from Mersea to enrol as a member. In those early days, the CWCC only had one piece of saltmarsh to legally shoot over. Ken Crawshaw, who was the newly formed club secretary, was also a founder member of the Essex Wildlife Trust ("EWT"), as it is now called, so he acquired Rat Island in the Colne estuary for the club to shoot. As wardens, back then there was a large nesting colony of black headed gulls which was monitored by the EWT; it was quite isolated and a boat was required to access it from Brightlingsea, quite a distance away, so visits weren't very common. Rat Island was ideally placed in the Geedon Channel; to the south of the island, across a wide tidal creek, was the Ministry of Defence ("MOD") firing range on Langenhoe marsh, with all of its freshwater fleets and large areas of shallow water, ideal for ducks. Across another wide creek to the north was a huge and extensive area of saltmarsh called the North and South Geedons, intersected by a very large creek, owned by the MOD and also part of the firing range. Further still, to the north, were extensive gravel pits and workings which all held a lot of ducks, mainly mallard. Seven miles to the west was Abberton Reservoir which is internationally famous for its large concentration of wildfowl.

Basky and I were very friendly with John Knight; we would meet up at the Victory public house on a Sunday lunchtime, and swap stories of what had found its way in the bag over the previous week. We used to talk about the CWCC, but I was sceptical in joining; Basky was fairly keen, so he applied to join and was accepted in April 1964. The club met up every Wednesday evening at a pub called the Blue Boar in Newtown, Colchester, and John and Basky used to go together, I believe. Whenever we used to meet, he would go on about how good it was and encouraged me to go along to see; so, I relented and went. And I did enjoy the company of so many keen and like-minded individuals, made up of mainly pigeon shooters and rough shooters. One or two had pieces of saltings and flight ponds to shoot, but they all did very little wildfowling in comparison to us here at Mersea.

In March 1964, I bought a Honda 50 motorbike from Dennis Osbourne in North Station Road, Colchester. I had also passed my driving test for a car the year before but couldn't afford to buy one, so the Honda would have to do until I had saved enough money to get a car. Basky, at the same time, also bought a Honda 90; these two machines made life so much easier to get to places for work and pleasure. So, every Wednesday evening it was off to the Blue Boar pub to enjoy the company of like-minded people, and they were all very keen shooters. I applied to join the CWCC, and, in August 1964, I was accepted. A few more people from here at Mersea started to join: John Green and Simon Cutts, to name but two. The club was growing in members but still only had Rat Island to shoot. Access to Rat Island was always a problem; the club had close contacts with members of the local garrison who mainly worked in a civilian occupation on the Ranges at Fingringhoe and at Middlewick on the Mersea Road, and at other military establishments in Colchester. One such was Ernie Holland who, I believe, ran the Musket Club, a military pub on one of the army housing estates; he was a very close shooting mate of Ron Pittock, a leading figure in the CWCC. They acquired permission to use a fairly large wooden shed that was once used by the Essex River Board for their seawall workers to shelter in, right at the far end on Langenhoe Point or the Sunken marsh, miles from anywhere. This dwelling was used as a base by a few hardy members to use and sleep overnight in order to access Rat Island for an early morning flight, or for the whole weekend.

Although the CWCC had very little wildfowling, it had the use of thousands of acres of farmland for pigeon shooting, the largest area being Strutt and Parker's farms adjacent to Lavenham in Suffolk where they grew acres and acres of peas: a magnet for wood pigeons. It would be very fair to say that the CWCC was one of the first shooting organisations to offer a service to farmers for crop protection, and it worked well for both parties for several years. One of the main reasons we used to go every Wednesday night to the club was to book, with one of the field secretaries, to go to a farm somewhere and shoot pigeons at weekends and evenings, especially when farmers were spring-drilling wheat and peas. The CWCC used to get fully stretched in getting enough shooters on the farms to cover the service, but the pigeon shooting was brilliant, especially at Lavenham, Monks Eleigh and the surrounding district; we had exclusive access to these farms, and we took full advantage of it. Two of the local club farms near Mersea were Peter Wormell's land at Langenhoe Hall, and Mr Archie Howie's at Battleswick Farm at Rowhedge, where me and Basky could easily access the farms on our motorbikes. The two field secretaries at the time were Ron Pittock and his assistant, Ray King. I was to work with Ray a few months later at the same plumbing and heating company where he was contracts manager, and he invited me over onto the fields and farmland belonging to Bill Bruton, adjacent to Abberton Reservoir, on a couple or three occasions to try and shoot some ducks; I was relatively lucky, but in those early days there were hardly any geese. l rented the farm in my own right a few years later, but now Pat Bruton has sold the farm, so that is probably the end.

In Johnny Hart's, (Terry and Basky's dad), the village barbers' shop, I would go to get my haircut every few weeks. In the magazine rack, apart from one or two risqué magazines, were also copies of the Shooting Times which I would read from cover to cover, if I had time, while awaiting my turn. In the 1950-60s, one of the journalists for the magazine was someone called A.E.B.Johnson, who was a very good writer and storyteller of his forays in wildfowling on the fore-shore, or on this particular farm inland where he flighted wildfowl coming and going to a large reservoir, mostly at morning flight. He had cut and lowered a section in a high hedge, 6 feet high by 60 yards wide, that he had removed with a bow saw and axe; teal particularly, coming back to the reservoir at dawn, would be magnetically drawn to pass through and over the cut-down hedge. He called it "teal gap" as he positioned himself to try to intercept them with some success. At the time, I had no idea where this high hedge and reservoir were, but I was enthralled as he recounted the stories of teal zipping like bullets, flying through the man-made gap, passing him by in the early dawn. Thirty or forty years later on, I found out that A.E.B.had also rented the shooting on the same farm in the 1950s-and early 60s, and that, unbeknown to me, he also lived in Colchester; if I had known that I most certainly would have tried to make contact and meet him. You could still see where the "teal gap" was, although it has now grown back. I have one of his books on pigeon shooting.

Hoss and Swiggy were still riding their bikes, while I was using the brilliant Honda; it would get me down to Hoss's in no time at all from where I was living up by the Fox, saving miles of pedalling on my bike. I used to tow them up Firs Chase hill and Victory Road hill, both either side of me holding on to a shoulder as it pulled them effortlessly along. Also, when we went pigeon shooting over to New Hall in the Grove at Wigborough, I would tow them there and back to Mersea, keeping a watchful eye out for the local constabulary, as they crept about on their ultra-quiet Velocette Noddy bikes! We were stopped one evening coming back over the Strood, but the policeman was spotted a long way back behind us, so the boys had let go by the time he was anywhere near us. When the Rowhedge-based policeman caught up with us, he asked me, "Were you towing these two?". "No, of course I wasn't", I lied through my teeth. They peddled the rest of the way home, just in case he was hiding on route somewhere, ready to pounce.

I remember, one time, being pulled up Victory Road hill on my pushbike after leaving the Victory; I was holding onto Rod Hayward's shoulder with my left hand. Basky, not wanting to be left out, held on to the sidecar of Rod's combination motor bike; somehow his bike pedal went into the spokes of the sidecar wheel. As the wheel turned, it lifted Basky and his bike up and down quite vigorously as it rotated; it was as if he was riding a bucking bronco. As he tried to stay on the mad bike, it looked hilarious; Basky thrashing up and down, ending up crashing into the grass verge. Hoss and Swiggy were behind, following on their bikes in fits as Bask was rolling about in the dirt. Luckily, just his reputation was dented!

Now that I had the Honda, I had a quicker and easier journey to the places where I used to shoot. On a shoot day over on Feldy, I would occasionally ride the motorbike for an early morning flight over to Copthall Farm, make up my mind as I walked down the track to either flight Abbots Hall saltings or Copthall saltings depending on wind and tide, then after, walking back to the farm, taking my place in the beating line for the shooting syndicate for the rest of the day. I would ride to places like Jack Marriage's at Barrow Hill or Alan Gray's at Bocking Hall, if it wasn't too wet and muddy. Across the fields I went, as close as it was possible to where I would do an evening flight, instead of having to pedal, walk, or run to be in time before it was too dark to see a duck. The only problem was, you couldn't expect a dog to run and keep up with the motorbike!

Otto.

9: An Irish Adventure

SOME OF THE members of the CWCC had arranged a duck and goose shooting holiday in Southern Ireland at Roscommon, close to a huge lough some 25 miles long. They had booked the trip through a sporting agent in the UK called, I believe, "Fur, Feather and Fin", and they were going to stay with a duck and goose guide called Tommy O'Connor. He lived with his wife and two daughters in quite a large chalet-type house called "Skein View" in the tiny village of Lisgobbin. In the summer months he would guide and take out fishing parties on the nearby Lough Ree which was reputed to hold huge pike and other big freshwater fish. During the winter months, of course, the lough and surrounding bog, and low-lying land, held thousands of ducks, particularly pochard and tufted ducks, using the very deep water of the lough to feed – their ideal habitat. The geese that overwintered there were primarily Greenland whitefronts which used the bogs to feed and graze the sphagnum moss that was so abundant then.

I can remember that I was fascinated by the thought of going to a different place to shoot wildfowl, and particularly geese, so I read up on all that I could to find out about shooting in Ireland. At about this time John Knight, David Lord, and a couple of farming friends had a week's shooting at Strokestown in the county of Roscommon; they had a very good week's shooting in pursuit of ducks and geese, but also the area is very good for woodcock which is one of the main reasons that they went. The building company I was working for was going through a bit of upheaval; it was being taken over by a larger firm and we heard through the grapevine of rumours that redundancies were going to be inevitable. Tony Weavers, the plumber I was working with learning my trade, immediately went to another plumbing and heating company and found himself another job. He asked me what I was going to do and in the same breath said, "Do you want to come with me and join this new firm?". Technically, I was still a bound apprentice, so I had to get a legal transfer. I handed in my notice, got my cards, and started with the new firm very shortly afterwards. I left Joseph Moss and Son who I had started working for in February 1961; they had given me an apprenticeship and a good start in my working career, and I have always felt indebted to them. They taught me my trade and independence, and learning of the big, wider world, and I had worked alongside a lot of brilliant tradesmen and hardworking men.

I joined Tony working for the Colchester Heating Centre; they had a shop and office opposite St. Botolph's railway station in Colchester. Stuart Murray was the owner and Ray King was his right-hand man. I was told to start work at a new housing estate in Berechurch Road. Farrans were building hundreds of homes for military families and soldiers; at the start there were just four of us plumbers working on site, but as the contract quickened pace, at least ten of us towards the end were trying to keep up with progress as the houses and flats sprung up. David ("Joey") Dawson, a carpenter from Mersea, and his working partner had acquired the contract on the same site to do the plywood shuttering for the concrete stairs and floors to the blocks of flats; it was very labour inten-sive, so several carpenters and labourers were required. Hoss left G.A Cock and Sons, and Swiggy did the same, packing in his job at Wyatts, and both of them went to work for David. Also, Doodle Whiting joined them, so at times we were all working together on the same buildings but there wasn't much time to chat. We were all flat out trying to keep ahead.

At the time "Joey" Dawson was converting a ship's lifeboat into a fishing boat, mainly for trawling, drifting, and long lining. She was about 35 feet long, very beamy and constructed in the double diagonal fashion. She was laid beside the causeway on the high-water mark, and that is where he worked on her, so Hoss got involved into helping David get her ready for sea, together with me and Swiggy at times. Joe Dawson, David and Peter's dad, had recently bought Fleetview Stores from Alf Parrish. Joe and his wife Anne lived next door to the shop, so when we were thirsty and hungry, it was all round to his mum and dads for a drink and something to eat. She was a diamond; she always made us very welcome, plying us all with lots to eat and drink but poor Anne, at about that time, had a very bad cold or influenza and it had left her completely deaf. Joe had a small menagerie in his back garden where he kept chimpanzees and a few South American birds called trumpeters, plus parrots and cockatoos.

The CWCC members who had booked to shoot in Ireland were travelling by car to Holyhead on Anglesey, then catching the British rail and car ferry to Dun Laoghaire near Dublin; they were going for a week in November 1965. I think four of them went, but at the moment I can only remember the names of two: Ken Harlock and Frank Fenning. Could it have been Peter Moss, one of the others? They couldn't have picked a better week; it blew a hurricane from start to finish, and they shot a lot of ducks and geese. The highlight of the week was when Tommy O'Connor placed Frank on the shore of Lough Ree for an early morning flight in the pitch black of a nascent dawn, and in the half-light, Frank was shooting and dropping ducks all around him. As it got lighter, he looked about him trying to see his floating shot ducks. As he did so, he noticed in some reeds a few yards away what looked like a pair of ivory-coloured feet bobbing about in the waves on the stormy shore. He carried on shooting for a while but couldn't hold his concentration; as it got lighter, he could now see much clearer. He plucked up some courage and went to investigate, and sure enough it was a body floating and washed up in the reeds and vegetation.

Frank couldn't believe his eyes. He left his dead ducks where they were, gathered up his gear, and got out of there as quickly as possible. He went and found Tommy and told him what he had found. Tommy just looked at Frank in disbelief, so he went and had a look for himself. Tommy gathered all of his guests together, firstly sending in his gundog Sox into the lough to retrieve Frank's ducks, and then they drove to the nearest Police (Garda) station and reported their find. The Garda, in their wonderful Irish laid-back attitude, took all the details and then asked them all to come back to show them exactly where Frank had found the body, which they did. The Garda then radioed for support and after a while a Volkswagen two-door Beetle turned up with two policemen in waders and with a canvas fold-up stretcher; they went into the reeds and water and retrieved the body. The poor dead unfortunate was laid and strapped onto the stretcher, as stiff as a board with rigor mortis, and was taken to the Volkswagen police car. However, as he was so stiff, they couldn't bend him to get him in so one of the policemen had to sit on the backseat of the Beetle and support and hold the stretcher and body. It was laid on the backrest of the passenger seat, the passenger window wound down fully open, with the legs and bare, ivory-white coloured feet of the corpse projecting out of the window as it was driven away. Frank had to sign a statement, and when he was at the station a couple of days later, one of the Garda officers explained to Frank that the poor unfortunate was an inmate of a nearby asylum who had thrown himself into the water from a nearby bridge. At the club the following week, their exploits were retold of how exciting their trip had been, and Frank's deadpan facial expressions as he recounted the saga of the ivory-coloured feet kept us in fits of laughter.

Mac booked our trip with Fur, Feather and Fin, and we set off on our journey to Roscommon on the Friday 29th December 1966. We would have to be at Holyhead on Anglesey in North Wales to catch the midnight ferry boat to Dun

Loaghaire, Dublin that day. For some weeks prior to our trip, it was a matter of sorting out the necessary equipment and gear that we needed. I was using the sixteen bore; getting large size shot for geese wasn't easy so it was a trip into Colchester to see if K D Radcliffe, the gun makers, could help. They didn't have any in stock but would make some enquiries; they told me to come back in a few days. I left it a week and went back on the following Saturday. Pat Dennis, who worked in the shop, told me that he didn't have much luck in obtaining some, but they had some large B.B. shot in stock and could load me some cartridges; how many did I want? "Could you load me 75 please?", then, as I paused, "I would think that should be enough! What do you think, and can you also get me 250 x 5 shot Winchester rangers please?" "Okay", replied Pat, "I will ask Peter if he can fetch them back to Mersea for you; that will save you having to come in especially to pick them up."

I had a disaster with the sixteen at the end of the previous shooting season in, I think, January 1966. I had been to evening flight at Jack Marriage's on Barrow Hill saltings and hadn't had a shot. I was walking back across the saltings to the seawall; it was quite dark, my gun was over my arm in the usual fashion, but still loaded, just in case something flew past or over me. Suddenly, a roosting cock pheasant jumped up right at my feet, startling me and making me jump out of my skin; in a panic, I threw the sixteen into my shoulder and fired at the quickly departing bird in the darkness, but the gun felt wobbly and strange as I bought into my shoulder. In the panic and haste of the moment, the heel of the stock had caught my shooting coat before it was properly into my shoulder; the stock had snapped in exactly the place where I hadn't spotted a crack when I had bought the gun five years previously. The stock was now just being held onto the rest of the gun by the horn trigger guard and was precariously flopping about. I found my gun slip on the seawall where I had left it earlier, and gently put my precious sixteen in it.

I got home and showed my dad. "Bloody hell boy, you have buggered that", was his comment; I grimaced and quietly nodded in agreement. However, by a stroke of good fortune and luck, a husband and wife had, about the same time, bought and moved into one of the cottages behind the Fox pub. Jim and Heather Spalding used the Fox to have a drink and socialise with their new neighbours, and Jim, as he still is today, was one of the best woodworkers and gun stock craftsmen in the country. Hallelujah! I went to see Jim as soon as I could, (probably the next day), and asked him if there was anything he could do to fix it. "I'm sure it's a new stock mate", he replied. So, I left my broken gun with him. "I will start on it straight away", he said as I walked out of his workshop to my house, one hundred yards away.

In 1965 I bought my first car, a one-year-old Mini, registration ALL129B, and, just like my sixteen-bore, it was hard won; scrimping, saving and hard work getting the £375 together to pay for it. But just like the sweet sixteen, the Honda, and now the Mini, these were my most hard-won treasured possessions, plus our lovely little *Boat* that I shared with Hoss and Swiggy.

I saw Jim in the Fox a week or so later. He was doing the finishing touches to the stock and told me that he should be finished by the weekend, if I wanted to come around and pick it up.

On the Saturday at midday, when I came home from work, I went right away to see him; he was in his workshop polishing the brand-new stock. He assembled the gun and handed it to me. "Bloody hell mate, that is just brilliant", I gasped as I absorbed the workmanship of what I was looking at. "Cheers, Jim, that is just fabulous. How much do I owe you?", I enquired. "£25 mate, if that is okay?" I paid him and walked home with the treasured gun. What I noticed more with Jim's expert workmanship was the sharp pyramid-shaped chequering around the grip. It was just lovely to feel on the palm of your hand as you held it. Just after I wrote this, in March 2020, I unlocked the cabinet where the sixteen is kept; the chequering has worn right back to a smooth finish now, fifty-five years after Jim's workmanship, mainly from wildfowling, using and handling it often with mildly abrasive, muddy, wet hands, and, in cold frosty weather, with damp string or cord-palmed "miller mitt" fingerless gloves.

A few days later, Peter Radcliffe dropped the cartridges off my mum and dad's house with the bill and a note to say he could only get seven-eighths of an ounce of BBs into the cases, whereas the Winchester rangers were loaded with one ounce of number five shot. We were getting close to the date when our adventure started. Lists of items required were written and checked a dozen times. I borrowed a roof rack from someone and clamped that to the Mini. We loaded up the Mini and roof rack, and set off on our journey, stopping to pick up Mac from his house in Colchester, plus all of his gear, and headed across the country to North Wales and the ferry at Holyhead. I had never driven any great distance before; it just seemed an age before we eventually arrived at the ferry. I think it was probably about 9pm and the boat left Holyhead at midnight for Ireland. Mac went to the booking office to get us and the car on board; he was asked, "Sorry, sir, but did you previously book yourselves and the car for the crossing?" On receiving a negative response, the clerk said, "I'm sorry, but you will have to wait until tomorrow to catch the next available ferry". We couldn't believe our ears. We had a cup of tea in the waiting room cafe and dwelt on what we were going to do while waiting for the next boat; we were totally deflated. At about 11pm, a British Rail chap found us and said, "Get your car beside the ship; we will take you tonight". Mac paid for the tickets and all three of us went aboard. I had to leave the keys in the car for a crew member to move it; the next thing I saw was the Mini swinging about on the end of a crane and being placed on the deck. I think it was strapped down; I couldn't believe what I was seeing! "Don't bloody drop it!", I thought to myself. So, we settled in for a sleepless night but at least we were on our way. I had left a brand new 2 oz packet of tobacco in the front of the car which I couldn't get to as it was out of bounds to passengers, so I was smoking Basky's fags all night!

We arrived at Dun Laoghaire, disembarked, and waited for the Mini to be craned off. Eventually it was, so we climbed in and found our route through Dublin, then across Ireland to Tommy O'Connor's place. Basky went to roll a fag, so I said to him, "No mate, use my tobacco in the glove box and roll me one please". He searched the car but there was no tobacco; one of the bastards who worked for British Rail had nicked my tobacco! I have never forgiven the Welsh light-fingered bastard to this day. After a couple of hours of travelling, we were getting close to Tommy's address in Lisgobbin. At an entrance on the right-hand side of the road, suddenly there it was, "SKIEN VIEW", a name board on a post, and just a short drive down a made-up track to Tommy's bungalow. I stopped the Mini just as the front door of Tommy's house opened. A short, stocky 45-year-old man stood there dressed in a green roll-neck pullover, brown corduroy trousers, slippers and with a pair of white waterboot socks over his trousers pulled up to his knees, and a thick head of black hair. He gave us a pleasant smile as we got out of the car; he had a missing tooth which was quite noticeable as he smiled. He vigorously shook our hands as he introduced himself, and we did the same. "Come in, come in", he said, "you must be gasping for a cup of tea after your journey," speaking with a quiet Irish lilt. We entered his house, went through to a big lounge, and he told us to make ourselves comfortable in front of a peat burning open fire. He disappeared as we sank into comfy armchairs. After a few minutes, he reappeared with his wife who was carrying a tray with a huge teapot, cups, saucers and sandwiches. He introduced his wife, sat down, and spoke to us, as his wife handed us our cups of tea and a plate for sandwiches.

We were full of questions, asking about the ducks and geese. Then, after a while, he said, "I will show you your rooms; empty your car and then we will try our luck this evening. Somewhere for some ducks and maybe a goose". As it was still about midday, we had a couple of hours of much-needed sleep, got dressed in our shooting clothes, and came back down to the lounge in front of the peat burning fire. We crammed into the Mini, Bask and Mac in the back, Tommy and his lovely setter-looking dog, Sox, who sat on the floor in between Tommy's knees. After a while, we arrived at our destination where we were going to have a walk round for a cock pheasant, woodcock and then later try for a duck. Mac shot a hare while Basky was in the hot spot and picked up three mallards, but where I was shooting, I didn't get anything.

I can't remember if we went on the Sunday morning, but we were certainly up early on the Monday for an early morning flight on one of the loughs. Tommy had a large currach tied up to a tree and he rowed us out to some tiny islands. We had

L to R: Jack Hoy, Tommy O'Connor, Trevor Hart, Graham McKillop.

Lisgobbin, Roscommon, Ireland – 30 Dec 1966 to 5 Jan 1967.

one each to shoot from; they were tree-covered so it was easy to find cover and form a hide. The shooting was brilliant at, mostly, mallard, but a lot of tufted and pochard flighted through and over us. I could hear geese in the distance, but I never saw one. After a couple or three hours, Tommy came and picked us up, then rowed around picking up our birds. We went back to Tommy's home and his wife had cooked us an excellent breakfast. We then got back into the car; we were going to do a recce to find some geese for the next morning. We drove for miles looking for geese which mainly fed on the very extensive bogs, and we did find a quite a number feeding on the grassy fields and bogs in the area.

On Tuesday morning we were back out trying our luck once again for a goose. Tommy dropped me off first, Basky having to drive the mini somewhere else to another location. Tommy had given me instructions as to where to watch. I could hear geese in front of me, a long way off; I could only imagine they were on a lough somewhere and were thinking about coming off to feed. Ducks were flying over me towards the geese, but very high up and not offering me a shot; perhaps just as well. As it got fractionally lighter, so the goose music increased. Suddenly, there was a clamour; I could make out birds passing to my left-hand

99

side, and I thought I heard a shot, but perhaps not. I kept peering ahead in the hope that something might come my way. There was just a single bird heading straight for me; as it got closer, it started to veer to my right-hand side. It might have seen me, but it was still in range when I fired. I missed! I was well behind it, it was so quick, but the second shot absolutely nailed it, and it crashed onto the bog track and didn't move. I sprinted to where it fell, picked it up, and was surprised just how small it was as I handled it. It was about the size of a large Brent goose, but what a lovely, iconic bird: my first-ever grey goose, a Greenland Whitefront. Sometime later, I saw my mini a long way off in the distance coming over the undulating bog track towards me. As they all got out, Tommy asked me how I had got on; I pointed to the goose lying by my gun. Basky had also shot one, but Mac was unlucky. I drove us all back home to Tommy's for the usual full Irish breakfast, then a quick sleep before venturing out again somewhere to try our luck.

The next morning, we were up early and out after the geese once again, but it was going to be a sorrowful, sad morning for us and Tommy. We were positioned by a stream that ran into the lough and which had overflown its banks, spreading out and making a very large area of shallow water. It had several ducks using it, mostly shoveller and teal, and we all had a lot of shooting, getting several ducks. Quite close to where I had parked the car was a small bridge that crossed the stream; it didn't have a fence or wall to show the sides and was at eye level height. We were all together walking back to the car, chatting away to each other, when a shoveller passed over which was shot at and hit; it then went into a glide, falling the other side of the road and bridge. Immediately, Tommy's dog, Sox, was on his way, crossing the road, then after a few minutes finding the duck, before making his way back to us. We all heard, then saw, the single-decker bus coming down the road from the left. It was like slow motion; we all knew what was going to happen before it did. As the dog was crossing the road back to us, the bus, not braking or slowing down, just ploughed straight into him. I can remember it so clearly, we all stared open mouthed in horror and disbelief, watching and seeing the gorgeous dog rolling and being dragged along under the vehicle for 50 yards; then the lifeless, broken body lying in the middle of the road on the bridge. The bus carried on as if nothing had happened, disappearing in a cloud of dust as it continued its journey. Tommy shouted at the bus and driver in astonishment and rage as we all ran to the lifeless body of Tommy's pride and joy lying motionless on the road. We were stunned. Tommy lifted up the limp body, tears streaming down his face, as he carried and then laid the dog in the boot of the Mini; it was a very quiet, sombre drive back to Skien View. The next day, we all went to Tommy's solicitor to sign a witness statement as to the incident.

We had two more days shooting before we packed all the spoils and our shooting gear and equipment back into the Mini. We thanked Tommy and his family for his hospitality and made a provisional booking for next season, to which he nodded. We shook his hand, climbed into the Mini, and gave him a wave as he stood on the doorstep of his house before the long drive home. Just recently, I searched through an album looking for some photos recording our trip; all I could find was one which was taken of the bag, and the lower half of Tommy's legs standing outside his front door. Looking at the photo and trying to count the bag on a small dark picture, we hadn't actually shot that many: two geese, ten mallard, seven shoveller, ten teal, two pheasants, one woodcock, and one hare. Thinking back, I can remember Tommy as he sat beside me in the passenger seat of the Mini, his lovely dog clamped tightly between his knees sitting in the footwell. I heard Tommy sucking and squeezing air past his tongue, pushing it into the gap where his missing tooth should be; the faster and quicker I drove the car to get to our destination, the harder Tommy sucked, almost as if he was in fear of his life or something!

10: Bigger Fish to Fry

I **HAD SHOT** at a few clay pigeon targets from 1960 up until 1966. The three of us – me, Hoss and Swiggy – would get on our bikes and ride with our guns to the Peldon flower show where someone would set up a clay pigeon stand, a single manually operated clay trap throwing out ten individual targets and just one prize for high gun, usually a bottle of whisky. One year, I was high gun, so I had to bike all the way back to Peldon to claim my prize. I can remember another year seeing an O/U being used; the chap shooting didn't miss a target. When he went back to his car, I spoke to him and asked if I could hold, and look at, his

The author enjoying a spot of clay pigeon shooting.

102

two guns. "Yes, of course mate, do you want to shoot with one?", he asked. "Yes, please, that would be great", I said. I didn't have any 12 bore cartridges, so he gave me 10 to try and use, it felt very strange sighting the gun, looking down a single barrel, and just the one trigger to fire the other cartridge. I was enthralled.

The chap's name was Sid Basham from somewhere near Maldon. Over the next thirty or forty years I would see him and his son, Spencer, on a clay shoot somewhere, both very good shots. John Green and Simon Cutts suggested that we should drive into Suffolk and shoot at the Bentwaters U.S. Air Force base near Woodbridge where they have two or three Skeet ranges. You could buy cartridges and use one of their collections of club guns for the day, all incredibly cheap being subsidised by the American Government for their personnel. You had to join the club at the base, I seem to remember, called "The Bentwaters Rod and Gun Club". Membership costs were a pittance. We would buy a hundred cartridges and shoot the lot in a couple or three hours. It seemed so extravagant; a hundred or so cartridges wildfowling would normally last a whole season, let alone just two hours! In the gun rack at the club was a Miroku 800 Skeet gun: twenty-six-inch-long barrels, a joy to shoot and very quick. I loved that gun. If someone else was shooting on the range with it, I would wait for it to be returned to use, though it would be another eight or nine years before I had my own.

However, all good things sadly come to an end. The goodwill and generosity of the Americans were abused; some shooters were buying subsidised guns and cartridges from the club, minus the purchase tax, and reselling to other people very cheaply. Word had got back to the base and all non-American Air Force personnel were barred; a great shame as it was good, cheap shooting. I loved it, competing with my friends and mates

You can't win them all, Jack. The look of disappointment says it all. Better luck next time!

103

and the other people at a shoot somewhere and, of course, meeting other like-minded people.

The CWCC had just recently acquired permission to form a clay shooting area on a farm near Marks Tey. Tony Thompson, who had recently joined the club, was a mate of the landowner's son, "Fussy" Porter, so Tony, with several other keen members, set up the newly formed clay pigeon section of the CWCC. A few manual traps were acquired, either bought or borrowed, and the club shot clays there, in the first instance, for about five years up to 1970. It was very popular with the members and started to make a small profit, enough to buy new traps etc. I was still using the sixteen for all my shooting, including for my new passion, clay pigeon shooting, but to be fair, the sixteen was never a clay gun and I always felt I was being handicapped using it. I stuck with it for a few more years until I bought the new Miroku 800 Skeet gun in 1974, which I still own. Over the next few years my mates were changing their side-by-sides and getting over-and-unders; I personally think the standard of marksmanship increased dramatically with the change. Tony Thompson had just bought a new Browning A1 and he kindly used to let me shoot it occasionally. As for other kind people, God only knows what they thought when I used to beat them using their pride and joy!

David Dawson was getting on fast converting the ex-lifeboat into a fishing boat and by the summer of 1968-69 she was fit for sea trials. A few weeks later, a trawl net was bought. Roger Butcher made a pair of otter boards; these were fitted to the net and to the steel cable trawl warps, then to a winch situated in front of the wheelhouse. She was ready to fish. In 1967, I had firstly lost my grandfather, which was a great shock and loss to me, but then, sadly, Din had been diagnosed with gullet cancer, probably from smoking that bloody pipe that never left his mouth. Just within a few months after losing my grandfather, Din, whom I had thought the world of, had also gone.

Hoss was seeing Jean Third, who lived with her parents at Maydays Farm; he announced one day that Jean was pregnant (although we all knew) and the pair of them were going to get married, after receiving a fair bit of flak from his mum, Gladys, who wielded the shotgun! So, in a hurried affair, the deed was done to save face. I personally think it was a big mistake. Jean moved in after the wedding and lived under the same roof with Gladys. Din had died; he never met his daughter-in-law or his granddaughter, Jane. It would be seven long years living with Gladys before Hoss and Jean bought a house in Churchfields, just up the road from me and Heather. Then eventually, they were alone. Swiggy was seeing Hazel, Jean's friend who lived at Brightlingsea, so he sometimes disappeared off the scene for weeks. So, it was an upheaval of normality when my mates weren't there. Then Swiggy announced he was also getting married, to Hazel, and Michelle followed a few months later. He then lived at Brightlingsea for quite some time, so he was off the scene until he moved back to Mersea a while later. Marriage didn't change Hoss one little bit, and in my opinion, he should never have been browbeaten by Gladys into marriage; it just wasn't Hoss, but Gladys was a strong-willed person! I felt really sorry for Jean at times.

Joey's boat was ready. For its first few fishing trips, we would leave at high water and fish the ebbing tide down river, prepare everything, and then, when we were somewhere off Waldegraves, the trawl was shot. A course was set to fish the muddy, sandy shore, passing the Molliette wreck beacon to port, then out to the bench-head buoy to haul. This procedure took about an hour, so in that time we would be working on the boat getting little jobs done that hadn't been completed before she was launched. The boat and set up worked brilliantly, the cod end would be be brimming with fish as it was dumped on deck to sort out the catch. While this was being done, Joey would motor across the Colne to the Colne Point buoy, then turn her in a wide circle to port as we shot the net for our next tow down the Wallet Channel towards Clacton and Walton. We could probably get in two or three tows before the tide turned at low water, then once again shoot the gear and fish the young flooding tide, bringing us back into the Blackwater and home to the mooring. When I think back, it was absolutely astonishing the number of fish we used to catch and land. When we had all taken a feed, Joey had enough to sell in order to pay for fuel and running expenses, and some pocket money.

In between shooting and hauling the net, which would be something like an hour, and after we had sorted out what we wanted to keep, gutting and boxing the fish, then swabbing down decks, we would sit on the foredeck with a mug of coffee and a fag, and play cards, either Knockout Whist or Brag, to while away the time as she steered herself out to sea, fishing as she went. On some of those really hot summer days, I would strip off all my clothes and dive into the cooling water, swimming alongside the boat as she fished, but even at a slow trawling speed, I found it tiring and difficult to stay alongside. When I wanted to climb and clamber back up, the boat had to practically stop as someone dragged me onboard. Luckily, Joey had his diving gear onboard so I would borrow his flippers and, using those, I could keep pace with the boat easily. When we trawled with the JBJ a few years later, I bought a pair of swimming flippers and used those to keep pace with our boat.

I remember one weekend when just me and Hoss took her out and trawled in the usual places. The weather changed and started to blow. We winched in the trawl, probably in a rush, up to the boat, when somehow the chain bridle got

Jack and Hoss Hoy trawling on David Dawson's boat 1968-9.

caught around the propeller and shaft which snapped; we were able to get the net and the otter boards onto the boat but when we put her in gear, a piece of the bridle which was still wrapped around prop and shaft would hit the boat with every revolution making a worrying noise. Down in the hold was Joey's scuba diving gear: air bottles, flippers, masks and wetsuit. It was decided that I would don all the equipment and jump over the side to see if I could free the chain from the shaft and prop. We had been with Joey (who was once a scuba diver in the Royal Navy) a few times when he had dived on plane and boat wrecks in the river, so I knew roughly what to do! After donning all the gear, I turned on the valve on top of the cylinder to let the air come through but did not hear the usual hiss! I jumped over the side into the sea and dived down to the propeller but found I couldn't breathe. I surfaced, gasping for breath. Hoss was laughing as I tore the empty cylinder off my back and passed it up to him. I went down again, just holding my breath; I could feel the chain but couldn't see it in the murky dark water under the boat. I was also amazed just how much of a current there was, so I tied a piece of rope around my waist to hold me near the boat; it appeared to be quite a short section of chain, what I could feel, about two feet in length. I couldn't free it, so I left it there. We steamed home at a very slow pace as the chain was still hitting the hull at every revolution. The tide was coming in, so it didn't take us that long to get home and we put her straight onto Wyatt's hard. When the water had ebbed from her, all was revealed; we unwrapped the chain from the shaft and prop in seconds. Why I couldn't remove it when I dived, I couldn't make out! There was no damage done to the boat and we shackled the piece of chain back onto the net, ready for the next adventure.

We still used our little lifeboat a lot, particularly for shooting, but we were spoiled by Joey's bigger boat to fish. If we were caught out suddenly by the weather, she was big enough to handle fairly comfortably, so, in the back of our three minds, we wanted a bigger boat. We had booked up to go back to Ireland with Tommy the following New Year in January 1967 but were thwarted at the 11th hour by a Foot and Mouth outbreak in the U.K. We even had the car packed and ready to go, but an hour before we were destined to drive for Holyhead, the Irish Government announced and banned all travel into Eire.

In March 1967 the oil tanker Torrey Canyon was swept onto the rocky shore of Cornwall, leaking its entire cargo onto the vulnerable shore, killing thousands of sea birds and causing an environmental disaster. The CWCC was spurred into trying, in some way, to help; money is what was wanted mainly, so an open clay pigeon shoot was organised with the help of Peter Radcliffe. We held it at his clay ground at Abberton. Clay pigeon and ordinary shooting folk wanted to help in some way and turned up to take part and shoot the course. After all of the expenses had been paid, several hundred pounds was donated to the relief fund. It had been a wonderful success, and the clay shoot was the first of several organised over the years.

One day, I was walking and shooting at Weir Farm with my dad's dog, when I thought I could hear the unmistakable sounds and calls of grey geese on the north side of the Island, either on Maydays or Reeves Hall marshes. I was walking the blind side of a high hedge. I ran as fast as I could to a clearing where I could see through, and there they were, about 50 circling and landing on Reeves Hall marsh. It was only the fact that I remembered hearing their musical calls that had stuck in my memory from when I was in Ireland 12 months previously; I probably wouldn't have taken much notice. More than likely, they were European Whitefronts that occasionally turned up some winters if it was cold on the continent. I never saw them again.

11: New Horizons

NOW THAT DIN or my grandfather weren't there, the shoot at Wigborough just didn't seem the same. Hoss was helped by Doug Sawkins and Graham ("Hank") Woods in organising the beating line, while the team of guns' captain was a young army officer who didn't seem to have a clue. I can't remember going much after that. At some point before the season finished, a vermin and coot shoot was organised by the Garrison game shoot over on the Fingringhoe army ranges. A few military personnel were members of the CWCC, and some of the club's members were beating and helping to run the Army game shoot; in return for payment, they would either go wildfowling on the Geedons saltings, or a pond or fleet within the fresh marsh.

We all mustered at the range control, allocated into teams to either beat or shoot, and then spread out across the marsh in as straight a line as possible, driving whatever was in front of us to the awaiting line of guns somewhere ahead. Someone would shout out "Fox!", as a glimpse of gingery red was spotted running from one dry reedy fleet to another; then another shout would erupt as another fox was driven from its hiding place towards the waiting guns. Little puffs of blue smoke and the sound of distant gunfire indicated that something was happening way ahead. So it continued, until the whole of the great marsh was driven and covered.

All the time we were walking and driving, parties of teal, mallard, and wigeon would leave the water-filled fleets, fly over the seawall, and head out to find a quieter place to doze for the day, or to line the wide saltwater channels and creek edges adjacent to the Geedons and Colne estuary until the danger had passed. I can remember shouting over to Basky as another pack left the fleets, "Look at that lot!". When we had reached the most easterly point, we gathered on the counter wall for a breather and a cup of tea. The spoils of the drive were laid out on the counter wall for the count up and recording of the day. Several foxes lay there, along with crows, magpies, coots, and woodpigeons that had been caught up between the two lines of guns, some paying the price of being in the wrong place at the wrong time. Neither Basky or I had seen Rat Island or the Geedons before that day, or even the watery point of Langenhoe Marsh; we could see it was duck heaven and we were already making mental plans as how to get around onto the Island next season from Mersea, on the other side of the wide Pyefleet Channel. We had to get a punt or boat down at East Mersea, permanently moored, and a place to leave a car or van parked when we were shooting, but out of the way so as not to cause aggro. We couldn't wait for the forthcoming prospect of somewhere new for us to shoot. While we were waiting on the counter wall to get a vehicle back to range control, little lots of teal were trying to land on the fresh water inside the point, and bunches of more cautious wigeon were flying over, and much higher, circling over the point before heading back out and passing over Rat Island to the Geedons and Colne estuary.

As we drove home, we discussed the prospect of where we could leave a punt for the best, and easiest, place to be moored permanently. We would have to go down to East Mersea and have a look. Our main problem was the fact that we only had the one punt and that was anchored during the shooting season in Punt Bay at Wyatt's hard, four or five miles away. A few weeks later, we drove down to East Mersea and parked by the little spinney right at the end of Shop Lane. We followed the footpath across the field to the seawall; a couple of hundred yards further along, the wide saltings came to an end but, fortunately, a creek came into the saltings which was just big enough to moor the punt and leave it out of sight at low water. We still didn't have another boat or punt to use, so it was probably another year before Basky luckily found a plywood, lightly constructed ten-foot boat that would push over soft mud easily, and light enough for one person to manhandle while wildfowling. Also, the person wanting to get rid of the boat had a Seagull outboard engine to go with it, so Basky acquired the two very cheaply. That would be our western-end boat.

In, probably, the August or September 1969/70 season, after a paint up, we set off from Wyatt's hard on a high, midday spring tide. We set off, heading for the Strood. We joined at the Strood causeway with the water covering the road; negotiating the railings, we walked the floating punt across the road and set off, rowing the four miles down the Mersea and Pyefleet channel, to the punt's new anchorage at East Mersea. The tide was still coming in and flooding the saltings, so we were able to take shortcuts, cutting off corners to straighten our journey. A mile further on, somewhere by Red Island, the tide turned to ebb; we caught it, and it swept us along as it surged back out into the North Sea. We made landfall

The punt laid up at East Mersea.

into the creek which was going to be the punt's new location. The water was still high enough to take her right into where she would be moored; we had rowed the four or five miles in forty minutes.

We were worried about her security, being so far away from home, so we had acquired a solid metal bar, about four feet long and one and a half inches thick. It had a shackle welded to it and was hammered deep into the mud on the fore-shore; then a chain was attached from the bar to the stern, just long enough so she would float on a spring tide. The punt's anchor and cable were taken over the foredeck, tied to the bow paynter, and pushed into the saltings in front of the bow. We made her secure, then walked back, carrying oars and tools across the field to the spinney and the vehicle which we had left earlier.

Coming back to East Mersea after a flight, either morning or afternoon at low tide, the push up the soft, muddy foreshore to our mooring was 150 yards from the low water edge after a hard row back, then, when pushing the punt uphill to its home creek, even with two persons pushing one either side, a stop was needed every fifty yards to get some air into burning lungs. A couple of years later, we withdrew the metal pole from the foreshore and hammered it into the saltings, had a plate welded to the top, and bolted a boat trailer winch to drag the punt close to the saltings, the last twenty-yard knackering push over shell and gravel when there wasn't enough water to float her over. But it was worth the effort, the wildfowling was brilliant. The area was relatively quiet as regards other wild-fowlers; the military used the ranges extensively, so the wildfowl had to contend

110

with the sound of rifle and machine guns firing. Also, with the large explosions of mortars, grenades and other ordnance that echoed across the saltings and creeks, the birds would lift as one, fly a few hundred yards to a quieter place, or fly to a local water-filled sand quarry. It didn't seem to worry them much.

Back safely after another successful session.

Looking back through my first written records, I can't identify our first trip to Rat Island; the CWCC had the shooting, so we would have had to book in with the club field Secretary. That was a strict rule; only four people at any one time could shoot on the island. In my early hit and miss records, I used to write down the different duck and other species shot and how many of each, but never the location. It wasn't until the CWCC insisted a few years later (bag returns) how many birds had been shot, the different species, and the location, that I had any idea of where my bag had been achieved. On our way to the club on a Wednesday evening, we would decide where we were going to flight at the weekend, study the tide table, and book in. If it was high water at dawn, the punt would be afloat when we got to it, and then, when we got to our chosen place, we could float the punt right into a creek to hide it, so the ever-wary wildfowl couldn't see it. Wild mallard, particularly, are notoriously watchful and distrustful when anything changes in their environment; if they spot anything that looks like danger, they will deviate their line of flight and pass by well out of range. They are full of self-preservation. If high water was at midday, and we were to leave early at dawn, firstly it was the long push down the muddy foreshore to the low water mark, clean the mud from off your boots, take your place in the punt, and then the longer row around points and spits uncovered by the tide to reach your destination. On arrival it was a case of hiding the punt, then separating to go to our favourite creeks, a few hundred yards apart, and await the dawn.

It took us a while to suss out our new area and the ways of the wildfowl using it, but after a while we were able to predict times, flight lines, and even different duck species according to what month of the season it was. Mallard were very

111

prevalent and were quite predictable in their comings and goings; we always kept a close eye on the time and usually right on cue at 7.30am, they would leave the freshwater marshes and mostly head our way. The majority of them would pass wide or high and go and rest and sleep on a quiet piece of water or gravelly foreshore edge somewhere. Then, perhaps an hour or so later, some would come back after being woken by a flooding tide to the saltings either singly or in pairs, threes or fours, see our decoys, and hopefully come in range for a shot. Wigeon, too, would spectacularly react to a few decoys and a well-timed judicious call, pulling them out of the clouds into range. Brilliant!

Around Christmas and into the new year, pintail, which were so uncommon at the west end of Mersea fowling grounds, just five or six miles away, adjacent to the Colne estuary, turned up in good numbers and figured in the bag quite regularly. The only pintail I had seen before, was when Hank Woods shot five (very unlucky ducks!) with two shots at Pennyhole, in 1961. What a spectacular duck to look at and handle. My first pintail, according to my notebook, was in fact a female, which I shot on Sunday 27th December 1970, and also four wigeon; it also records a pheasant. My second pintail was a drake and that was acquired in the following season on 11th December 1971.

We reached the punt in total darkness on that Saturday morning at East

Unloading the punt ready for some action.

112

Mersea, after walking across the field carrying oars, guns, bags etc. We loaded up the punt, then pushed it over the foreshore mud down to the low water edge of the Pyefleet Channel, washed our boots, and took up our usual positions with a pair of oars each, setting off against the tide. We rounded the muddy spit and point of Langenhoe, a mile or so east, and down into the Colne estuary towards Brightlingsea, then the long row back the other side helped by the young flooding tide taking us west to the north creek of the Rat. We chatted away as we pulled on the oars, watching the dawn and listening to the sounds of the estuary waking up. "My first duck this morning, Razor, is going to be a fine drake pintail, mate". I saw his head cock up as I was sitting behind him rowing; he laughed and muttered, "Do you reckon?"

Eventually, we entered into the virtually empty north creek looking for a thin pole on the edge of the Rat that marked our creek. We continued rowing for another 100 yards, then pulled into the edge after spotting the marker, and pushed the punt up the mud into its hiding creek, wishing each other luck. We then separated and settled into our usual creeks, a couple of hundred yards apart. After a while, as the light improved, I could see the single bird coming towards me from off the Geedons; as it got closer, I could see that it was a pintail, and, what's more, a drake. I lowered myself down into the creek. When it was directly overhead, I swung the sixteen through it and fired; it folded up instantly and fell stone dead 25 yards behind me. I found and picked it up quite easily. I held the bird aloft for Basky to see; he stuck his thumb and fist up in celebration, and in acknowledgment of my prophesy. I hadn't held a drake pintail since Hank's five in 1961; it was an absolute beauty as I admired its wonderful plumage, stretching and opening its wings, admiring its bronze speculum and vermiculated feathering, the incredible set of tail feathers that gives it its name, and the cream and Cadbury's chocolate coloured feathering covering its head. What a bird.

At about 8.30am, I noticed and watched a Land Rover heading down the range; the wardens, I assumed, were going to erect and fly the red danger flags which meant that the Army were practising, and firing on the range was about to commence. Over on Langenhoe marsh, at the extreme east end, is a small lookout building built into the seawall which was manned by a warden the whole time the range is being used and who suddenly appeared and raised a red danger flag to the top of a pole. He then went inside to make a cup of tea and light a fire; his job was to warn any boat or person straying into the danger area; they would be hailed and advised to stay clear.

Rat Island sits at the entrance of a wide channel off the Colne estuary, where it divides it into two as it passes north and south, then joining as one again at the western end. The wide channel carries on as one, then 500 yards further on

113

it divides again into two very wide creeks, one carrying straight on to the west and the other turning sharply to the north. They both drain, and practically dry out at low tide, just leaving the huge muddy foreshore; in this relatively warm and sheltered sanctuary all forms of waterfowl came to rest and feed. On some days thousands of birds use the area but mainly it is waders probing the food-rich ooze. At nine o-clock sharp, the peace was shattered. The loud reports from single and rapid staccato gunfire were carried with the prevailing air stream down the range, over the sea wall and saltings, and bouncing off the creek's edges. A black lift of everything that could fly took to the air, mostly waders but a lot of ducks, mainly teal and wigeon with a few pintail. I instinctively lowered myself into my creek as the birds poured out, passing us by, and neither of us getting a shot. Most of the teal landed in the water on the Brightlingsea side of the Colne, then, swimming and walking ashore, joined the Brent and several mallard on the hard gravely edge, while the wigeon and pintail favoured the salty flashes on top of the Geedons left by a spring tide.

After a while, I noticed that the waders were starting to move and fly back; a few more reports of gunfire sounded, the waders lifting their heads for a second or two, then carried on feeding, seemingly unperturbed. Imperceptibly, the ducks started to fly back as well; a pair of teal flew past out of range and just skimming the now flooding tide coming back in earnest up the wide creek. They totally ignored my decoys tethered by their lines; it was probably the rising tide moving the ducks as well as the trips of dunlin, redshanks, godwits, curlews and other waders passing by. More teal and wigeon started to move back up the creek, little lots I could see flying over the Geedons and also passing over Rat Island towards Langenhoe Point. I could hear Basky having a shot or two.

It was now about 9.45am, and I hadn't had a chance of a shot since I dropped the pintail an hour or so before, when I noticed about ten wigeon coming off the Geedons heading my way. They looked quite high as they came on to me; they were whistling and growling as they approached, but still at extreme range. I lowered myself down into my creek, gave them two or three calls on my whistle, and at that same moment they saw the decoys and dropped out of the sky into perfect range. On they came, straight at me. I raised up, picked a bird and fired; it dropped from the bunch and fell amongst the decoys with a splash, laying on its back paddling fresh air. The rest of them lifted at the sound of the shot. I chose another as they flared; it too fell stone dead to join its mate floating on the water. I watched as the rest of them flew back over the channel to the Geedons; I kept watching them, then I noticed one peel away from the others and went with the breeze into a glide. I kept watching as I know it was also hit; it carried on gliding away from me, then suddenly it cartwheeled out of the air and dropped

114

onto the saltings 300 yards or more away from me. I kept my vision on the spot where I last saw it go into the saltings, then I looked up slightly for something to mark its fall; it fell right in line with a building at the nature reserve, a mile or more further away. My two dead ducks, floating on the water, were now making rapid progress with the flooding tide up the channel away from me. I had to get the punt, which was a hundred yards towards Basky, then row and catch up with the wigeon which were by now a long way down the creek, but the breeze was slowly blowing them to the edge. I reached them, then scooped the birds across the shallow water using the oar blades, not having to get out of the punt onto the deep muddy ooze.

Before I left my hiding creek, I made a heap on the saltings of my shooting jacket, bag, and on the top of those I balanced my upright thermos flask, but I made sure I took my gun. As I rowed back down the channel, I looked across to Rat Island and could see my flask where it accurately showed the position of my shooting creek. I pulled into the side of the north channel, took the anchor, and dropped it onto the mud further up from the tide's edge before making my way to the Geedon cant edge. On reaching the saltings, I looked back to the ranges to see if the red flags were still flying but, to my surprise, they had been taken down; they had stopped firing and had gone. I could also see my flask. I walked a bit further along the muddy cant edge. I stopped when I thought I was in line with both the reserve shed and my flask. I got up onto the top of the salt-ings and strode off, in as straight a line as possible, having to jump small creeks, crossing and detouring larger ones, then getting back on my line, checking the flask behind me and heading for the building in the distance, and, hopefully, my duck. As I walked, I kept looking in the creeks and gullies; then fifty yards or so in front of me I could see a flash of white. Was it my wigeon? I pushed off the safety catch of the sixteen and cautiously walked forward, my gun ready in case it suddenly jumped into the air, but I needn't have worried – it wasn't going anywhere, except home with me.

I made my way back. The tide was now up to the punt's anchor, but the breeze had bought the floating boat to me. I washed my boots and stepped into the cockpit; I could see Basky standing on top of the saltings trying to catch my attention, pointing his arm and hand at something on my side of the Creek. I poled along the edge, then on the mud I noticed a trail of fresh footprints heading in towards the saltings. I got out of the punt and followed, noticing a few specks of blood; up by the salting edge, behind some mud lumps, I found Basky's teal. I held it up; he stuck his thumb up and waved before disappearing into the marsh once more.

I rowed back to my creek, stepped ashore, put my coat back on and had a welcome cup of coffee. I waited for another half an hour or so before the flooding tide forced me out. It was now about eleven thirty, high tide was about twelve thirty, and nothing much was on the move, so I gathered my gear together and stowed it into the punt then out into the channel to retrieve my decoys.

Basky was standing in the tide when I got to him; he was washing the mud from his thigh boots and muddy, bloody hands. He put his gun under the punt's foredeck with mine, gave his boots a last swish in the water, then swung a leg over the washboards and stepped on board. I took him out to his decoys, he wound the lines around the keel, put them in his bag and we then headed for home. But before we did, we rowed across to the Geedons to avoid the wash and bow wave of two coasters that were steaming and passing quite close and fast, coming down the Colne from Colchester. We crossed the wide, now water-full, breezy south channel to a more sheltered shore, and also to get out of the still quite strong tidal current that we were hugging. We crept along against the tide, but we were making good progress close to the edge of the sunken marsh sea wall and Langenhoe saltings. As we got closer to the saltings point where we would have to round and turn sharply to starboard, the sky was suddenly full of lapwings and other waders but mixed in with them twenty-five or more mallard; they were all standing on the top of the saltings and in the salt water-filled flashes having been earlier forced off the mudflats by the flooding tide. They couldn't see us, and we couldn't see them, as they were all out of sight behind a shell and shingle bank; we must have really surprised them when we suddenly came into full view, very close.

We rounded the point and caught the last of the flooding tide as we angled across the Pyefleet to where we had moored the punt. We anchored and secured her, then loaded ourselves up with oars, guns, bags and birds, and walked along the sea wall and across the field to the vehicle and home. I can't remember now how many shots I had that morning, or how many more ducks I missed. I am sure I wouldn't have picked up four ducks with three shots, but I don't know; I could have done! But we both made a mental note of the mallard!

Rowing back to our launch that morning, we passed close to Langenhoe Point and the sunken marsh with its sea wall that surrounds it. We noticed that the sea wall was eroding on the north-east corner from the wash and wave action made by the very frequent small coasters going to and from the Hythe docks, and also on a spring high tide with a strong north-easterly wind, it would flood into the freshwater point quite alarmingly. We both raised our concerns to the CWCC, and they in turn informed the MOD, but nothing was done. We even organised our own club members and, together with help from the Garrison Game shoot, filled and transported hundreds of sandbags, filling the gaps to hold back the seawater; but it was a fruitless task. We complained bitterly to the MOD for years, but nothing was done. Then, twenty-five to thirty years later, the incredible habitat was recognised as a priority; the breach, which was now 80 yards long, was repaired. Ironically, a newly arrived marsh harrier turned up on the scene, using it as a roost and then later to breed; now, coincidentally, it was deemed important!

Packing up after a successful session.

12: A Close Shave

AFTER OUR DISAPPOINTMENT of not going back to Ireland because of the foot and mouth outbreak in 1967, we had paid our initial deposit, so we had another week booked from 16th until the 23rd of November, 1968 but this time, instead of just the three of us, it was six, and taking two cars. Me and Basky were in Ken Wright's Ford Consul and, in the other car, were Ron Pittock, Mac and Kevin Benner, all sharing Ron's Vauxhall estate car with two labradors, Mason and Jasper. Those two dogs hated each other from the second Jasper jumped into the back of Ron's car. Both owners blamed each other's dog for the growling and snarling that lasted all week; then with Ron and Kevin arguing and defending their precious charges, it was mayhem. But it was Mason: he was a miserable bastard. Ron wouldn't have it.

But, apart from that, we had a good week of shooting and lots of laughs at the expense of mainly Kevin who couldn't see the funny and hilarious side of our warped sense of humour and pisstaking; he was a very serious man. Everything had to be just so, with no leeway for good fun and a good laugh; silly things, like when we swapped his pyjamas with Ken's one evening just at bedtime. Kevin was five feet nothing, Ken was six feet two. We were waiting downstairs in the lounge for the fireworks; Wrighty burst through the door into the lounge wearing Kevin's jama's, where the bottoms of the legs were halfway up his calves and the sleeves were up near his elbows. "Whose f*****g things are these?" he bellowed, as he paraded around the room in his tiny jimjams; we all fell about dying, watching Wrighty. Then Kevin walked in the room, his face full of anger, holding up Wrighty's jamas. "These aren't mine," he bleated, "who's been in my room and going through my stuff? I don't like it, so please leave my gear alone". It was like a red rag to a bull; the more he carried on, the more we laughed.

Then, another time, we were all going for evening flight on Lough Ree. We got out of the vehicles, the two dogs, Mason and Jasper, having another go at each other, then Ron blaming Kevin for Jasper's bad temper, Kevin retorting and blaming Ron's dog, Mason. We had to cross a deep water-filled ditch where Tommy was over first: a single plank, six-foot long bridge which was level with the water. Kevin, storming off, went next. Then, all of a sudden, there was a mighty splash when he went headfirst straight into the dark water. He had tripped and caught his foot under a piece of wire that was stretched across the bridge, joining and supporting the top of the posts that held up the plank. It was an accident waiting to happen. Ron had his back to us, holding onto his car, his shoulders and body shaking, stifling himself from bursting out laughing. Poor old Kevin!

Tommy would row us out onto the islands to flight the geese that would roost on the huge piece of water of Lough Ree for morning flight; he suggested not to shoot at ducks until all of the geese had flighted through. Suddenly, there was shooting from one of the islands. In the half-light of dawn, the big gulls flighted and Kevin, thinking the gulls were geese, was shooting at them. After the flight, with Tommy quizzing us as to which one of us it could be, we drove back home for breakfast.

On another day, Mac, Basky, Ken and I, after morning flight and breakfast, asked Tommy if we could go off somewhere and try for a duck on one of the smaller loughs. He gave us directions to a lough where he had a boat tied up to a tree, telling us to then row out to the small islands and try our luck. We found the boat just where he said and pulled up in the reeds; the four of us had just got in when we suspiciously noticed a Marley Lino floor tile stuck to the hull inside the boat alongside the keel. We had rowed offshore about fifty yards when we saw the floor tile had lifted and was floating about in the bilge; brown, peaty water came in through a large hole in the hull at an alarming rate, and, with nothing to bail it out, it was filling fast. I was rowing, Ken and Mac were sitting on the stern seat, with Basky in the bow. I turned the boat and headed back to shore rowing as hard as I could. Ken was trying to stop the water by covering the hole with his hands, the tile, and his boots, but it was of no use; it poured in. Basky was standing on the bow seat with one foot on the stem, ready to jump, screaming "Don't panic, don't panic", just like Corporal Jones from the television programme, Dad's Army. When we were a couple of yards offshore, he launched himself towards the reedy edge, his forward momentum pushing off the stem, and stopping the boat in its tracks, me with my legs and feet up in the air stopping myself, somehow, from landing in the watery bilge on my back. Basky landed with a splash into the water, not knowing how deep it was, and waded ashore, topping his thigh boots as he made his way to dry land. We that were left behind just creased up at Basky landing in the deep water, deserting the sinking ship, and leaving his shipmates to perish in the dark peaty water – he wasn't allowed to forget it in a hurry.

But we did shoot geese and ducks; I can't remember what the others shot, but the entry in my notebook records that I bagged two Greenland Whitefronts and six teal. We had a very enjoyable week with Tommy and his family. We bid our farewells and then made the long drive home. Driving across north Wales, we had a very close encounter with death; we had been up early all week for morning flight after geese, then rough shooting for cock pheasants, woodcock, snipe, ducks etc. during the day. We were then out again for evening flight for more ducks and geese, so we were all pretty tired. Our ferry left Dun Laoghaire at 6pm, arriving at Holyhead about midnight; then, having to wait for the cars to be unloaded, it was probably after 1am before we could start driving for home. I was in the front passenger seat, Basky was in the back, and Ken was driving. Basky was soon fast asleep in the back while I kept awake talking to Ken, asking him on a few occasions if he wanted a rest from driving, but, no, he was fine, so, I also fell asleep.

I don't know how long it was, but I was suddenly awakened by a loud bang. Ken had dropped off to sleep at the wheel and had hit and bounced off a line of wooden fence posts and strands of wire that marked the left-hand side of the road. He stopped a short distance further on, exclaiming, "Bloody hell! I must have fallen asleep", or words to that effect. We clambered out in the complete darkness just as the lads in the other car turned up, and we all surveyed the damage to the near side of Ken's car; it was dented and scored from the front wing, the two doors, and even the rear wing. A chrome metal strip from the front nearside wing was missing. Someone found a torch, we walked back, and located the point of impact; we found the strip in one of the wooden posts. Ken couldn't pull it out, so he had to snap it off leaving two inches still embedded, like an arrow!

As we stood there in the darkness, we could hear rapid water passing over rocks in a deep ravine in front and below us. The torch beam didn't reach the bottom; if we had gone through the fence, we would have ended up God only knows how far down. We stood there thinking and reflecting on what might have been; it really shook us up. A flimsy wire and post fence, six feet of grass verge, then a plunge into the black unknown. We walked back to the car and Ken insisted that I drove, which I did as the three of us quietly pondered on our fortunate escape. They both went back to sleep while I carried on driving until I was having trouble keeping my eyes open; I pulled off the road, where the three of us slept until the chilly dawn awoke us. Sadly, we never went back to Ireland again to shoot with Tommy.

It was soon after we came back from our second trip to Ireland, when, on a Saturday morning at 5.30am, I met Basky as arranged at Wyatt's hard. I was the first to arrive and swept the car headlights across the water and located the punt. Keeping the headlights on it, I quickly pulled on my boots and waded into the water out to it, Basky turning up just as I got it ashore.

Jack and "Basky" Hart rowing the punt to East Mersea.

I parked, got the rest of my gear, put it aboard, and we were soon away, rowing with an oar each against a strong wind heading down the long creek to our destination. High tide must have been about 6.30am, so we were able to row up Pennyhole Creek and pull into the saltings near to the far end. The sky was clear of clouds and bright starlight shone, faintly lighting up the creeks and saltings as we made our way in. We anchored, grabbed our gear, wished each other a good flight as we always did, then separated and went to our favoured creeks to await.

It wasn't particularly cold, but the wind soon took the heat generated from the long row from your body as we stood on top of the saltings in the blackness, waiting for the water to recede out of the creeks so we could gain a bit of cover.

Behind us to the east, the dawn was breaking far out over the North Sea. It was getting lighter by degrees, the tide was now leaving the saltings and creeks, and as the crab holes emptied, they popped and gurgled, sounding as if someone had pulled the plug on a bathtub. I slid into the emptying creek; the water came up over knees. My feet found the wide piece of driftwood that I had stamped into the creek bottom at some time previously, a firm footing. I slipped a couple of cartridges into the sixteen. Someone right up the top end of Tollesbury opened up with a couple of shots, then a couple more. The wind was certainly increasing as the light improved. Basky had the first shot, but I didn't see him move. A few more minutes passed when he had two more; I heard something hit the water behind and to the side of me, then I saw him leave his creek and go to the punt, push it thirty yards over the soft mud and into the tide. He carried on rowing out of the creek, leaving the punt anchored at the east end by Pennyhole Point.

He had a fair walk back, having to pass me to get to his creek. He said he had dropped a pair of teal, one dead that I had heard near me, and the other had carried on, winged, near to where he had now left the punt, and which he had also found. It was shortly after, as it was getting lighter, that I noticed a steady flight of teal heading into the wind coming out of the eastern sky, flying up the Blackwater estuary, and going into Old Hall. The ducks nearer to us were mostly flying up the middle of the very wide Pennyhole Creek, so out of range for us in the saltings to one side. Basky had also seen them, and it wasn't long before we were gathering up our gear and moving.

The seawall had been built across the creek some four hundred years previously, damming its flow, and to this we headed. We positioned ourselves sixty yards apart at the seawall base to, hopefully, get under the flight line, but to hide oneself was virtually impossible; the birds would see us and fall back, then give us a wide detour. We had one or two impossible shots; we had to conceal ourselves, somehow. At the base of the seawall, where the concrete seawall blocks met the muddy creek, tons of Kentish ragstone had been deposited, which in turn was covered in bladderwrack seaweed. This structure was being used as a breakwater to defuse the constant eroding wave action when the tide was at its base. We both set to work, erecting screens made from the stones, then covering the front and top with flotsam and seaweed. It was surprising how quickly we had them built; ten minutes and we were back in action. We had to shoot kneeling and crouching tight into a ball shape, just peering over the ragstone, then, at the critical moment, rise up, pick a bird, and shoot. The rocks were just high enough to give us enough concealment and for the teal not to see us until they were well in range.

The flighting birds continued, but in a wide front, some passing by well out of range to the right and left of us, but not all of them. Bunches large and small, pairs and singles, kept coming and flying over the seawall into the freshwater marsh; we had several birds laying on the mud of the creek and over the seawall which we left for the time being. The wind was still very strong and gusting as it passed over us, sheltering in our snug positions. Also, there were birds coming out from Old Hall and quite often caught you looking the wrong way. Basky would shout out to me, or me to him, as they passed over with the strong wind behind them at incredible speeds, and we did have several spectacular shots, and several spectacular misses; a single duck, or sometimes a pair, being carried on the wind quite dead, only to hit the mud and half bury itself, or slide across it for yards. The night before, I had filled my cartridge belt and probably had another ten in my coat pocket. I kept replenishing my pocket with cartridges from the belt under my coat. I felt around the belt for more; it was empty. I had two cartridges loaded in the gun and a few more left in my pocket.

A successful conclusion to a satisfying day.

Securing the cover for weather protection.

As the morning progressed, the number of teal got less, so we went up towards the top of the seawall and knelt on a worn sheep track some four or five feet down from the top and looked into Old Hall; a large area of flood, which was named locally as the Lagoon, was covered with hundreds of ducks. Just beyond the lagoon was a large eight pipe unused decoy pond; teal, mainly, but also a lot of wigeon were swirling over the pond. Occasionally, a few would lift from the lagoon, catch the wind, and head out towards us behind the seawall. We would bury our faces in the sparse sheep- and cattle-eaten vegetation, and, at the critical moment, rise up and try to get a bead on the fast wind-driven birds. Once or twice, I was just about to squeeze the trigger when Basky would shoot a split second before me at another bird over him, making your chosen target flare and turn. But, still pulling the trigger, the charge of shot would miss by a mile, so you pulled yourself together and succeeded with a spectacular second barrel shot.

As we were peering over the seawall, I could see birds lifting a long way away beyond the old marsh brick building near Joice's Head. The bright sunshine which we had enjoyed all morning reflected off something moving, a vehicle windscreen. We decided it was time to go and find, and pick up, the rest of our birds, but firstly we pushed our stone screens back into the holes we had formed for hides. We had another look to see where the vehicle was; it was now heading back up the central track to the farm, probably a stockman checking his cattle and sheep. We had picked up some of the birds as we had shot them, when they fell near to us; some fell on the short grass on the other side of the seawall, easy to see and pick, but out on the soft mud of the creek there were at least eight to pick, and also in the saltings and creeks behind us. Basky searched the saltings to the south of Penny Hole creek, while I searched on the north, and then to pick up the teal scattered about on the soft ooze and mud. I walked back across the saltings, searching and jumping numerous creeks to the punt anchored on the mud at Pennyhole Point. I had reached the punt first. Basky was on the other side of the wide, soft creek, which he had to cross to get to me sitting on the punt's long foredeck, having a drink and a breather. He slogged across, stopping every now and then to get his breath back, as he pulled each of his booted feet out of the clinging mud. He reached the punt and sat his backside down hard on the foredeck. "Are you alright, mate?", I laughed, as he gulped in draughts of cold air into his burning lungs. "FFS, it's bloody soft across there". He had finished his flask hours ago, so I gave him the rest of mine.

After a rest and a chat about the flight, we pushed the punt down the muddy foreshore to the water's edge, washed hands and boots, then the ducks, and laid them on the foredeck for a count up: 28, and all teal, but we reckoned there were one or two more to find. As we put the birds back in our bags, we searched the ducks for leg rings. One of the ducks had been rung, and it was a Dutch leg ring: "Vogeltrek station Arnhem". Were all those teal fresh birds in? From the direction they came, and following the Blackwater estuary that morning, they probably were. We went back again that afternoon to try and find the lost birds that we thought might float out of the saltings as the flooding tide lifted

Manoeuvering the punt across the glistening mud at East Mersea.

them, but we didn't find anything. We stopped for flight but hardly saw a bird.

It was at this point that, sadly, both my grandfather, 84, and, not that long after, Din, 57, had died. The shoot over on Feldy and Copthall finished, probably a season or two later, and with it the ferreting. However, I had several other places and farms to use. I had four ferrets, three jill's and one big hob, so on a Sunday morning Dad and I would load up the mini and go to one of the farms on Mersea. It was something that we loved doing. Sometimes, Basky would join us, and we would spend a few hours ferreting and netting up until lunchtime. If we got ten or a dozen, we were very satisfied and happy. There was always someone who wanted clean killed rabbits; we could never get enough of them. They were never a problem to sell, just like the ducks and game birds, even pigeons. They would sell like hot cakes. It was a different generation of people we supplied; most had been brought up when money was scarce and hard earned, and, with food rationed, people rightly never forgot those times.

125

13: Highland Fling

ON SATURDAY 25TH October 1969, according to my diary, I was off to Scotland with Peter Moss, Ken Siford, and Tim Stepenson, who were all CWCC members. I was surprised when Peter asked me, but I was very friendly with Kenny Siford who, at that time, was a range warden at Fingringhoe Ranges; it was the ideal job for him, as the duck shooting on the range marshes was fabulous. We used to shoot clay pigeons a fair bit together and he was a brilliant natural shot. I didn't really know Tim Stepenson at all; his parents owned Spring Lane Farm. He was another very good shot, as it turned out, and a very nice young man about the same age as me. Peter Moss, I am sure, organised the trip and we were going to stay at, and were booked into, a former Air Sea Rescue base, owned by a Mr. Muscatti, on the shore of the Dornoch Firth, very close to Tain, of Glenmorangie whisky fame.

We travelled up in Peter's VW camper van. I remember him telling me at the time the engine size; it was only 1200cc! We left Horkesley, where he lived, at some time that morning, on the long slow journey to the Scottish Highlands, mountains and loughs. I was spellbound by its wildness, beauty, and isolation as we ventured north, all the time watching for geese feeding on the fields or skeins flying in formation, criss-crossing in front of us. And it was slow; the VW seemed to labour along at 50mph at best. When we drove over the hills and mountains, I seriously thought we were going to have to get out and push, so underpowered was it. However, we laboured on, driving through the day and night. Twenty-three hours later, we arrived at Dingwall for the last leg of our journey along the A9 north to Tain and Meikle. Today, of course, a road bridge crosses the Firth at that point. We arrived at our destination, at Meikle peninsula: a collection of arched corrugated iron Nissen huts and sheds. On the point was the main building, which I assume was where the aircraft recovery crew lived and worked when it was operational but was now the home of Mr. Muscatti.

We met the owner, and he showed us to our accommodation, one of the Nissen huts; he pushed open the front door into a corridor, with a door on each side leading into two tiny bedrooms with two single beds in each. It carried on to a sitting room, which was the full width, then through another door which brought you into the kitchen and bathroom, then a back door to outside. In the kitchen was a solid fuel Rayburn, a sink, a few units, and a table with four chairs. We unloaded the VW and the first thing we did was light the Rayburn and filled it up with coal from a bunker outside. Someone filled the kettle and put it on the Rayburn; things were starting to warm up, and it felt more like home every minute! We came outside drinking our tea and took in the view across the Loch and all around: it was stunning. Peter produced an ordnance survey map, spread it out on the table, and we studied it to look for areas that might be productive in terms of shooting. As it was Sunday and no shooting, we thought we would have a drive about to see what we could see.

We headed south to look at Lough Eye. I remember it held lots of ducks but mainly divers and also some greylag geese; we carried on driving to Inver which had a lovely saltmarsh, then to Nigg Bay on the Cromarty Firth. We were hoping to see some pink-footed geese, but I can't recall seeing one all week. We headed back to Meikle and, as we were self-catering, we set to and soon had the pots and pans, and a steak and kidney pie bought from home, heating on and in the Rayburn. The living room had an open fire that was soon lit and roaring away. We were in our sleeping bags early that night for a start on Monday morning.

We spaced out along the Dornoch shore hoping to catch some geese coming off the sands to feed inland and ducks going the other way. We didn't see a goose, but we had a couple of wigeon and teal in the bag. We came home for breakfast of eggs and bacon, then out once again looking for geese. Someone had told us to take a look on the Black Isle, so it was back down the A9 in the VW. In an hour or so we were looking over every field alongside the road and in the sky as we searched, then we saw our first skien: greylags, crossing over the road to our right in front of us, then flying over the top of a small fir plantation, setting their wings, circling a couple of times, then gliding down onto a field somewhere. We carried on up to the plantation; a field on our right-hand side held several grazing and feeding geese. We watched them for quite a while. On the opposite side, up a track, was a farmhouse and buildings so Peter turned the VW up the track to the farm; he went to the house and knocked on the door. The door opened and we could see Peter talking to the farmer, pointing towards the geese. Then, with a handshake, came beaming back to us; as it turned out he was the landowner, and we were more than welcome to try for a goose. "We will come back early tomorrow morning, if that is okay?"

The farmer owned the fields opposite and he had seen lots of geese flying over his house; they had been using his fields for several days. We carried on further along the road; some more greys were grazing another field, and Peter, using his binoculars, could see through a wide gap in the hedge. There were more on the other side. We came home and got our gear ready for the next morning, Peter handing me the 12 bore that I was going to use instead of the sixteen! I put the gun up to my shoulder to see how it fitted. The stock seemed to be very short, but I thought that, with a thick jumper and my coat, it would be alright; also, it appeared to be very light, and the safety catch was very stiff!

We were up early the next morning and on our way back to the Black Isle, Peter pulled into a gateway and parked the VW. We loaded ourselves and trudged off down the road fifty yards, then through a gateway into a field on our right-hand side; we followed a post and wire fence for three hundred yards, ending at a high hedge that ran across our front from right to left. The field on our left-hand side was where we first saw the geese fly over yesterday. On the far side was the fir plantation, and on the other side of the plantation was the field that some geese were feeding on. We climbed over the fence and stood in the field looking towards the plantation and decided what to do; we didn't have any geese decoys! Thinking back, I don't believe they even made them then; I had never seen one, and I can never remember seeing any being advertised in the Shooting Times for sale. They weren't even discussed by us at all.

I remember reading about the pursuit of geese from the doyens of the past, and even then, at the present time, there was a perfectly good chance that BB, the wonderful storyteller and writer of his safaris to Scotland chasing pinks and others, could have been sharing that very same week with us, and somewhere not too far away. Was he using decoys? The only way was to space out and hopefully get a shot as they flew over someone, and hopefully in range.

Ken and Tim decided to walk to the plantation and go to the field on the other side, while Peter and I would stay in this one. The two of them walked off in the dark, while Peter and I stopped where we were for the time being and waited for it to get a fraction lighter. After a while, we could see the firs more clearly on the other side of the field 300 yards away. We could suddenly hear geese calling somewhere in front of us, then passing and going over the high hedge to our right, their calls getting fainter; but after a short while they started to get louder as they came back towards us. They circled over our field, wide of us and also out of range, then set their wings and landed the other side of the high hedge: greylags. As the light improved, we could see and hear many more, but towards the plantation where Ken and Tim were. There was no shot – had they gone too far? All the geese that we saw were feeding on the other side of the hedge. I said to Peter that I was going to go nearer to the plantation and hopefully get under some of them.

I left him and walked towards the pines; suddenly, there was a skien heading straight for me, coming from my left-hand side. I bit the dirt and lay prone, not moving a muscle as they passed over me. I was sure they were in range, but didn't shoot, mainly for the reason that I didn't want to mess things up for my mates. They landed on the grass on the other side of the hedge with the others. I got up and found a small gap in hedge that I could look through but not be seen by the geese; the area where they were feeding looked like it could have been ancient moorland with its undulating terrain but without any heather. It had probably been grazed by sheep and cattle, but the geese loved it. I had never been this close to wild greylag geese; I can recall as I watched them happily feeding away that they were making a strange buzzing noise, probably of contentment. Little did they know that danger and, perhaps, death lurked just the other side of the high hedge!

I watched the small skein pass low over the pines; they reached the bottom end where Ken and Tim should be somewhere. Suddenly, two geese dropped dead out of the bunch and the sound of the two shots came to me very quickly, ruining the peace and tranquility of the morning. Instead of the contented buzzing, it was now a cacophony of frantic calls and shouts as the geese erupted and were heading straight for me. I pushed the safety catch forward; it didn't move. I could hear the geese getting closer, making a hell of a din as they approached. I had to get what was left of my eaten and chewed-off thumbnail and hook it behind the catch to push it forward. Suddenly, the geese were in my face as they came over the covering hedge; they saw me and flared, just like teal or grey partridges. I was amazed. I lifted the gun up to take the shot; I didn't panic, I had time to pick a goose. The stock came up into my shoulder as I thought and as I tried to line and sight along the barrel and top rib with my eye. I found it impossible; the gun was so short that when it should have been properly into my shoulder, it was still about an inch away, or so it seemed when I fired. The recoil was horrendous from the powerful goose cartridge; it whacked the light, ill-fitting gun into my shoulder and face. The goose kept flying. I fired again, the recoil driving me onto my back foot; I missed again. I watched and scrutinised them; surely one will drop out dead in a second or two, but nothing did. How the ****? I couldn't believe it! I rubbed my stinging face and shoulder as I watched them; not one wobbled as they flew off in the direction they had come from. I was distraught.

Peter had witnessed the whole tawdry embarrassing episode. He came up to me with a half-smile on his face, but also thinking, I'm sure, "you useless bastard". He was holding a greylag; he must have fired at exactly the same instant as me. Well done, Peter.

The miss at that goose is something I have never forgotten from that morning in 1969 to this very day; it still haunts me as I write this story and event in 2021. I can still see that one particular goose that I had singled out to kill; I can still see the two beady dark eyes as it looked at me and I looked back at him/her as it climbed and flared in panic, showing off its wide pale and black flecked-breasted body and the huge thrashing wings and pinions as it powered, climbed and stood on its tail, trying to gain height over me. In theory there should have been only one outcome. No excuse, but it lived another day, and hopefully several days and years after. But we have all had those Victor Meldrew moments when you stand open-mouthed in utter astonishment; I can think of several over the last nearly 70 years and I hope, yes, I hope, to have perhaps one or two more in the future.

Ken and Tim came out of the corner off the fir wood, Ken holding a pair of greys, a right and left, but, like me, Tim had had a miss. It was still quite early, so Peter and Ken thought that, as they had got their geese, we should wait a bit longer to see if any more came to give me and Tim another chance to get one. Certainly, the fir plantation seemed to be a landmark for the birds to aim for, so Peter and Ken stayed by the hedge where I had missed while Tim and I went back towards the firs; Tim went through and back to the other side, and I stayed this side. Nothing happened for quite a while, at least an hour or so. I walked out into the field to see how much the field had been used by the geese: it was covered in droppings. As we waited, I kept mounting and shouldering the 12-bore, trying to get it to fit somehow, and also pushing the safety catch back and forth to try to loosen it; it was a pig, bloody horrible thing!

While I was out in the open field, I could hear geese. I looked over the farm and could see some at a distance, coming from the north. I sprinted back to the edge of the wood. I was standing about halfway up towards the road when I could hear some calling in front and to my left, over the top of the trees. I came out a few yards from the edge of the wood to get a clearer view when, suddenly, they were over me; I swung the pig and fired two shots. The goose I had fired at fell dead with my first shot, but I missed with the second. The gun whacked me once again in the face and shoulder, but I had my first greylag goose. We stayed a while longer for Tim to get a chance, but no more came.

When we got back to the Nissen hut, we discussed the morning over breakfast. I spoke to Peter about how short the stock of the gun was and how it kicked me. He got up from the table, walked out of the kitchen, and came back with his gun. "Try this and see if it fits you", he said. I put the gun to my shoulder; it was just the same as the one I had been using that morning, incredibly short in the stock. I must have given him a questioning look. Peter then went on to explain that, several years before, while at work, he was crushed between a vehicle and a wall, smashing his ribs and shoulder and disabling him. As for using and shooting a normal-fitting shotgun, he had to have the stock cut down and bent to be able to fit him, and to use it effectively. He had owned the shotgun that he was using for years, and he used it for all the years I knew him afterwards; it was a SxS Westley Richards sidelock ejector, a gun especially designed for shooting live pigeons in competitions. It was a very heavy gun with thick barrel walls, especially at the breech, and Magnum-chambered for three-inch cartridges, normally fully choked; but Peter had had the chokes opened up. I was to shoot with Peter a lot over the next twenty or more years; he was a very fine and competitive shot, plus a very nice man.

We planned to give the fields a rest for a couple of days and hopefully the geese would still be using them. Behind our Nissen hut was a large bay on the Dornoch shore called Cambuscurie Bay, and we had seen a few wigeon using it at all states of the tide over the last couple of days. We thought it might be worthwhile trying a flight that evening. The bay was covered in wigeon grass (Zostera). I hope it still is now. We walked out onto the firm, sandy shore, then spaced ourselves out and waited for the darkness to hide us. I could hear wigeon as they flew over us, but nothing yet was shot at. Then, as it got much darker, someone had a shot; it was by then extremely dark, and when a small lot flew over, they passed by me quite low. I shot into the brown with the 16g, and an unlucky wigeon dropped out and hit the hard sand. The others had a shot or two, but mostly at shadows. I seem to remember that we didn't get many, but it was exciting hearing wing beats and the wigeon whistling and growling somewhere above us in the darkness. We were guided back to the Nissen hut by a light at the old base, so, as soon as we got back, the pots and pans were put on the Rayburn; then we had a traditional Scottish drink distilled from just down the road and made plans for the morning. We had been to look at a lovely piece of salting at the tiny hamlet of Inver, and I mentioned that I would like to try there in the morning. Tim said, "If you don't mind, I would too". Peter and Ken elected to have a look, and flight, Nigg Bay on the Cromarty Firth.

We could afford another hour in bed the next morning, Inver being much closer to our HQ, but we were still up early as Peter and Ken had a longish walk out onto the shore at Nigg Bay. Peter dropped me and Tim off at a gateway and field that took us down to the saltings and creek at Inver. We had never been down there before, so it was a bit of touch and feel as we made our way across a grassy field. After a while we came to some saltings; we decided to wait for a bit, so sat in the long grass for a half an hour or so, waiting for some light to help get some idea of where to head. Behind us to the south-west somewhere was Loch Eye and we knew it held roosting greylags; if they decided to leave and fly out, there was a chance they would come our way, so we were quite keen to get into position somewhere. It was a bit lighter, so we went. I carried on straight out in front of us while Tim angled off and went to his left; I wished him luck as he disappeared in the darkness.

The saltings, I seem to remember, were quite hard: sandy and short grass to start with, then they started to take on a familiar look of Essex. I angled a bit more to the left and came to the creek edge. I thought this would do, so retraced my steps twenty yards and settled in. To my right I could make out a few lights which I thought must be Inver just waking up, and the dawn was breaking beyond the town to the east. In front of me to the north, across the channel, was a firing range owned by the M.O.D. which we didn't know about at the time and, apparently, it was excellent for ducks. Beyond that the Dornoch Firth. I heard a shot which I assumed was Tim; I had seen some teal flying to my left up the channel in front of me, heading to Loch Eye, I thought. More teal were on the move, heading on the same line. I heard some more shooting from Tim, then a small lot passed me which I shot at, and one fell out. I could hear geese on the move behind me, probably coming from off the Loch. Then I noticed a skein heading our way; they were heading where I thought Tim should be, then I saw them lift and flare, and one dropped out. Tim's first goose. More geese were on the move, all greylags by their calls and shouts, some heading our way, another lot near Tim; two shots and another bird fell out. But I was going to be unlucky this morning as regards geese, but it had been a fantastic morning, an incredible sunrise over an incredible country, that was where I was lucky.

I met Tim back at the long grass. He was grinning ear to ear as he came up to me. "Bloody hell, I wasn't expecting to get these" he exclaimed. "That's what we have come for, mate", as I congratulated him. He, too, had shot a teal.

We walked back to the road and waited for Peter and Ken to pick us up, which they did shortly afterwards. I now can't remember what Peter and Ken had shot, if anything. That morning Peter had taken out a four-bore which belonged to John Anderson, who also lived at Great Horkesley: they were good friends and shot together. As we came back along the road to our HQ, Peter noticed four wigeon bibling and feeding on the water's edge quite close to the shore. Peter then said, "I reckon the four-bore would get all of those", and in the same breath, "do you want to try, Jack?". "Well, I could do", I hesitated, "not too sure about firing that cannon though!". The railway line at that point ran very close to the beach. Peter reckoned, "If you keep close to this hedge down to the embankment, then cross over the railway line, then creep up the embankment the other side, and lay the four-bore on the top like an old bank gun, then give 'em one." He opened the side door of the VW and produced this huge single barrelled gun, then gave me two cartridges which I put in my pocket. I crept along, going downhill on the field, close to the hedge and keeping out of sight of the ducks. I reached the first embankment, went over the top, and cautiously listened and looked both ways for a train; I didn't want to meet a Scotsman, flying or otherwise, then hurried over the single, shiny railway track. I slipped one of the huge cartridges into the gun. I crept on my hands and knees, stalking up to the top of the next embankment, and peered through the long grass. I pushed the mighty gun up in front of me and lay down behind it; I looked for the wigeon – they were still there but they seemed a long way off. Behind me, I imagined three anticipating faces peering out through the windows of the VW watching. I pulled back the hammer (although it could have been hammerless); I pulled the stock tightly into my still-hurting shoulder and cheek, wincing like a woman. I took aim; I didn't know what to expect. I tentatively curled my finger around, and put some weight on the trigger, then pulled hard: a massive boom, a cloud of smoke and the recoil pushing me down the embankment, I'm sure. I immediately looked up to see how many I had got; three were flying away, but one was left on the water swimming about in circles. I left the gun and raced across the sand to get the duck; when I was about 10 yards away, it suddenly took to the air and flew off as if nothing was wrong with it! I came back to the VW, rubbing my shoulder and face.

We arrived back at HQ, cooked a welcome breakfast, and made a pot of tea. We conducted an inquest, then decided on another drive out to see if we could find some geese.

We came back down the A9, searching either side of the road onto fields and likely-looking places, and eventually we were back to the Black Isle. We arrived at the scene of our successful shoot the other morning; the fields were covered in greylags, and we sat and watched them for quite a while. The fir plantation still seemed to be the focal point of their entry as they flew into the fields. It was then we decided that another trip in the morning was on the cards. Back to HQ but stopping firstly in Tain to replenish the larder, and also to get a couple of bottles of whisky for our friendly Black Isle farmer.

Early on the Thursday morning we were once again heading for the Black Isle. Peter stopped and pulled over in the same gateway; we stayed in the vehicle for a while, peering into the inky blackness through the windscreen, sipping coffee from the everlasting communal flask, and cigarettes were then being lit. After a while, the smoke and fug were getting too much for the non-smoking Peter who, coughing and choking, clambered out of the VW to get some cold, fresh air. We loaded ourselves once again and walked for the last time down the fence to the high hedge, crossing our front at the bottom; once over the fence, we headed for the fir trees. We were going to use the trees for cover this morning. Ken and Tim went, once again, to the other side while Peter and I stayed on this side. Peter elected to stay at the bottom corner; his thinking was that if the geese flew over the end, he could shoot along towards Ken and Tim. I went back up the side of the trees, roughly to where I had shot the other morning. As we waited for the light to improve, I could hear geese on the move, but couldn't see them; they seemed to be flying to the east and away from us.

We kept waiting. One or two high lots came over the fields and plantation but not stopping to feed; we hung on in high hopes then, after a while, I saw a low skein heading our way from out of the north. I gave Peter a wave and an indication that some were coming; he waved back, and the geese disappeared behind the trees. I came out from the edge ten yards into the field, just as I did the other day. The leading edge of birds must have just cleared the bottom of the plantation when shots rang out; just behind them there must have been some more, calling and shouting. They turned towards me. Over they came; I picked a bird and I hit it hard, having to give it another barrel which killed it, falling behind me on the field. I looked back towards Peter. He was just emerging from the high hedge with a goose that fell to the other side. We waited an hour or so, but nothing more came, so we walked up to the road and back to the VW. We drove up to the farmhouse to thank the farmer and to give him his bottles; he was surprised when we gave him the whisky. "They are only geese that keep eating my grass, glad to to see the back of them," he said. We shook his hand and thanked him, saying that we were leaving for home and won't be able to come back this year, but maybe next. He gave us a friendly wave with the bottle of whisky in one hand as the VW headed back to Tain.

We soon had the frying pan sizzling away on the Rayburn, with bacon, black pudding fried bread, and eggs. Then, wiping our plates clean with a couple of slices of bread, we mopped up the HP sauce, egg yolks and grease, and downed copious cups of tea while discussing the mornings events and our plans for the evening. We had time for one more flight on the Thursday evening and it was decided we would flight Nigg Bay. Peter and Ken had shot there but Tim and I had not. The tide had gone by the time we got there, so we walked out together for the first few hundred yards, then separated. I wasn't very hopeful but then, having settled in, and as it got darker, we listened; it surprised me, the number of duck calls and whistling wings that passed over me as I knelt on a black area of seaweed. I had a couple of hopeful shots but didn't get anything.

Ken, I remember, shot a pintail and Peter, a wigeon. Tim had a shot but didn't get anything either. We had a sleep-in on the Friday morning. Breakfast, a bit of housework, loading the VW, then paying the rest of our rent to Mr. Muscatti before making the long drive home.

The lovely Tim used to smoke like a chimney; he virtually chain-smoked tailor-made fags. We both shot clay pigeons at the Colchester Gun Club together. He got married a few years after me and shortly afterwards, his wife gave him a son. Sadly, Tim contracted lung cancer and died at a very young age. Ken Siford moved to Hampshire, I believe, to be a gamekeeper on a large estate, a job he was born for, in about 1974; I never saw him again until the 50th anniversary of the CWCC in June 2014, when he turned up with his brother Roy. Peter Moss passed away several years ago.

14: Scotland Revisited

DURING THE SPRING of 1970, I wrote to Mr Muscatti to book a Nissen hut for the first week in November of that year. I was asked to book the trip by Basky, Ken Wright and Tony Thompson; we had to find a vehicle to hire, when someone told me a chap from Peldon had a VW camper van which he hired out. I went to see him, and I arranged to hire the VW for that week for the sum of £40.

When the time finally arrived, we set off up the A604 to link up with the A1, the Great North Road. When we left that Friday afternoon it was blowing quite hard, but as we got further up the A1 it was storm-force gales; the VW was buffeted and blown as we proceeded. I was driving, when suddenly the radio aerial snapped off close to its body fitting, it being so violently shaken and weakened by moving side to side in the strong wind, but the radio still worked! We stopped for some drink and a fry-up somewhere, then carried on through the night, arriving at Tain on the Saturday morning.

Unknown to us at the time, Peter Moss and John Anderson were also there. We had a bite to eat and a couple of hours sleep. We came outside just as Peter and John were coming ashore in a punt with a punt gun laying on the deck. I couldn't see any ducks in the punt so I can only assume that they didn't have shot, but what annoys me is why I didn't speak and ask them then, and at any other time afterwards for all the years I knew them both, of how they got on that particular week punting, or at any other time out in the punt in the past or future. I can remember being interested in both punt and gun when I saw them. The gun, which was owned by Peter, was, I think, a 1.08 inch diameter barrel with a Snyder action breech loading system; also, the punt belonging to Peter, which I remember him building. In about 1995, Peter asked me one day if I was interested in buying the gun which, at the time, I wasn't. I seem to remember it being sold and ending up in Kent. Then, in about 2015, I was a

136

gun in the Horkesley shoot that Peter and John were both members of back in the sixties and much later. I was a standing on my peg, in amongst a group of disused greenhouses, and, through the glass of one I was standing quite close to, I could see a punt at the end of the drive. I went into the greenhouse to have a closer look; I thought I recognised it by its distinctive slatted floorboards. After the drive I spoke to Adrian Golding, Peter's son-in-law, and asked him about it. Sure enough, it was Peter's punt, the same one that I saw floating on the Dornoch Firth all those years ago. As for John, I know he came from somewhere on the Suffolk coast and used to puntgun on the river Alde before he moved to Colchester.

It wasn't a very successful week in regards shooting geese; not one of us even had a shot at one. Our favourite farm on the Black Isle didn't have any geese; I saw our farmer friend and reminded him that I had shot a few geese there in the previous year, which he remembered, but luckily, he had some more land further up the road which we could walk about and have a shot. I thanked him and we went to have a look. The farm was nearly all fir plantation and bracken; it was right on the coast overlooking the Moray Firth somewhere near Eathie. We had a walk about without our guns; we put up several coveys of grey partridges, with hares and pigeons in the fir plantations. It really was a bad week for shooting. We saw a few flocks of geese feeding on various fields and farms, but when we enquired if we could try for some, we were greeted with a degree of hostility! It put us off a bit.

We flighted in the same locations as the previous year on the shore, but it was hopeless. However, one morning after we had had breakfast, we were looking at the OS map when one of us noticed an indentation on the shore not far away from a village called Ardmore. The tide was out, so we walked across the sands of Cambuscurie Bay, then headed along the beach towards Ardmore. When we got there, we were surprised at what we had discovered: a burn ran across the beach in front of us from our left; it meandered into this wide, quite muddy bay or indentation, about three hundred yards deep and, probably, two hundred yards wide. Surrounding it was a cliff edge of perhaps fifteen feet; it looked a good place for ducks at flightime.

We came back to our HQ, got into the VW, and drove up the road to see if we could access it from a road or a track somewhere close by. We came to a farm and buildings. I went to the house and knocked on the door; when the door opened, this older woman stood there. I explained that we were shooting locally, and would she mind if we crossed her field to try for a duck on the shore this evening? "That's absolutely fine", she said. "Help yourselves". I thanked her and went back to the VW.

That afternoon we were back just as the daylight was fading. We made our way across the field and past some grazing cattle; just a short distance away was Ardmore Creek, according to the OS map. We negotiated our way and spaced ourselves out, settling in some washed-up trees and roots dotted about which had been left stuck in the mud, and which made good ready-made hides on the quite firm, muddy shore. As it got darker, ducks started to flight into us: mallard and teal. We were quite busy. Suddenly, there was a shout and a torch being flashed at us from the shore. I was the last one back as I was the furthest away. When I got back to them, there was a policeman and a man standing there who turned out to be the farmer and the son of the old woman. He started to go on a bit about not shooting here, and all the rest of it, but the first thing I noticed, which made me smile, was that the policeman was only wearing a pair of shoes. As he stood there talking to us and lifting his feet every now and then, marking time, he was slowly sinking into the mud which went over the tops of his shiny shoes. How he didn't leave his shoes there when we left, I'll never know. We had to help him get back to terra firma.

So that was flight over. I think what the farmer was concerned about, mainly, was his cattle: they had come right up to the cliff edge, and he thought that we might accidentally shoot them in the dark. When we got back to the VW, the policeman explained, while he was wiping and cleaning the mud from off his shoes on the grass, that there was nothing the farmer could do to stop us shooting there, as it was the tidal foreshore, but he was worried about his cattle

A good example of the fine art of milking a goat. (Scotland 1970).

138

getting shot. He then asked us to turn up at Tain police station in the morning with our gun licences! But we did get a couple of mallard and teal. We were going back; f*** the farmer!!

We went back to HQ, put the pots and pans on the Rayburn, and decided what to do on the following day. We sat around the table eating our meal and having a drink, chatting and smoking, when we thought we heard the front door of the Nissan hut open. We all looked at each other, mouthing "who the hell can that be?". Quite loud, slow footsteps sounded on the wooden boarded flooring, coming down the passageway towards the kitchen. We all watched the door to see what our fate awaited. Slowly, the kitchen door opened a couple of inches; we sat there in silence, not knowing who or what it was. The door moved again. Suddenly, it opened, and a urine-soaked, stinking billy goat walked in. The anti-climax was brilliant! We couldn't believe what we were seeing; we cracked up. Somebody grabbed it by its horns and led the stinking animal out through the back door.

The next morning, after breakfast, we were heading back to the Black Isle to try our luck at Eathie for a walk around, but before that we had a flight out on Cambuscurrie Bay shoreline for a goose or duck, but we didn't have a shot between us. We pulled the VW off the road into a plantation at Eathie and onto a track. We spaced ourselves out and walked in a line through the plantation of firs to the far end. I was surprised by the number of hares there were, and we shot one or two that tried to break back, but it was difficult sporting-wise; as they ran through the trees, we tried to get a bead on them, but we missed a few. Then the trees gave way to more open terrain but with waist-deep bracken which, surprisingly, wasn't that hard to walk through, and it was here we found the grey partridges that would get up and fly forward in a covey or ones and twos, and of lots of woodpigeons that were either flying over the trees or clattering out of them. The land went right to the edge of a very high rock face and cliffs; hundreds of feet below us were cormorants flying about. Basky had a shot at one, but it was strange aiming and shooting down on a bird instead of being under it.

As we were walking and shooting, a bird suddenly flapped out of in front of us with an injured wing and tried to fly. Me and Basky went after it; when we caught it, I thought it was a peregrine, but on closer inspection it turned out to be a male sparrowhawk. Basky put it in his pocket and bought it back to HQ, then tried to fix its wing; he found a cardboard box to keep it in and fed it fresh ducks or partridges for the rest of the week. It came home with him, and he kept it in a run with a Canada goose, mallard, and some chickens; it lived happily for several years afterwards. The barber's shop owned by Basky's dad was next door to the butchers in the village, so if he couldn't get anything with his gun for the hawk, his dad would bring home some fresh minced meat; it was fed well, that bird, but sadly it never flew again.

Our plan before we left to come home was to go back to Ardmore for another evening flight, where we had the encounter with the police constable and the farmer. It was a wet and windy walk along the shore to Ardmore Creek, but once within the confines of the bay it was reasonably sheltered, so we settled in on our tree root hides once more. I looked back to where we had the encounter with the farmer and the policeman, and on the field above the cliffs I could see one or two silhouetted cattle grazing, but they were safe from us. As it got darker, so the ducks came, mostly mallard but some teal. The tide was slowly ebbing back out into the Firth, but as the fast, fresh water came down the creek, the tide slowed its progress and backed it up, so covering the mud around us with a couple of inches of water until it eventually drained away. If a duck fell into the creek, it would be swept down the fast-running water, then out into the Firth and impossible to retrieve; we lost a couple that way. But the flight was excellent. We all got bags full of ducks, but it soon got too dark to see them, so we packed up and came home to our digs.

When we got back, there was a light on in one of the other huts and a vehicle parked up. We had plucked some partridges and teal earlier and had left them in the Rayburn to roast before we had gone to Ardmore to flight. We soon had

Dogs primed and ready for action in Scotland (1970).

140

the veggies simmering and had a brilliant meal with a few beers and whiskies to follow, then crashed out in our beds and sleeping bags. We were driving home the next day, so after breakfast and a bit of housework, we loaded up the VW. As we did so, we noticed a couple of bunches of teal hanging on a nail outside the door of the occupied Nissen hut, a dozen at least. We were curious to say the least. We walked down to pay and thank Mr Muscatti; then, as we came back, one of the occupants was standing outside drinking a cup of tea. We introduced ourselves, then we mentioned the teal hanging on the nail and enquired as to where they had got them, and when. The two of them had come up from Newcastle and had shot the teal under the moon that night on the MOD-owned firing range. It is out of bounds during daylight hours, but at the end of the day it is left unattended, and apparently it was a brilliant place for ducks; we didn't have any idea!

We set off for home, stopping somewhere near Perth to do a bit of souvenir shopping. We found a shop and were all browsing around, buying a few things. I sorted through my wallet, separating the Scottish pound notes from the English, to pay for what I had bought. As I stood behind the counter, the owner, or whoever, was serving someone in front of me and Basky, when I looked up and nudged Bask and said, "Look at that painting, Bask, it's of the packing shed at Mersea." It was our turn to be served. She had heard us talking in our English Essex accent and it seemed as if she wanted to be confrontational before we spoke to her. "Good morning, ma'am", I said, as I put what I wanted on the counter. I then pointed to the picture and said, "That's amazing, that oil painting hanging there is where we both live". She looked at me disbelieving but didn't say a word. Then Basky could see in her face that she didn't believe me. "It is", he said. "That is a painting of where we both live". "Oh aye, oh aye", cocking her head as she answered back. I then paid her with the Scottish notes. She pressed the buttons on the till and went to give me my change back in Scottish currency. "Sorry", I said, "could I possibly have English money as, back home, our local shops don't take them?". It was like a red rag to a bull. She ranted on about it being legal tender and currency anywhere in the UK! She rummaged about in the till, then thrust the change in English money across the counter at me. Charming! We left Nicola Sturgeon's; it must have been the miserable, poisoned dwarf's grandmother standing there. Then, the long drive home. I had to explain to the sceptical owner of the VW about his snapped-off radio aerial. But it was a good few days, although not very productive.

At some point at the end of that season the punt went missing from its creek at East Mersea; it was deliberately stolen from its padlocked chain mooring and fastenings (I wonder if the key to the padlock is still hanging from its nail fixed to the tree where we parked our vehicle?) and we had no idea where to search.

Months later, Basky was looking through the Essex County Standard and came across an advertisement: "Punt for Sale, Brightlingsea, Essex" with a phone number which he rang and made an appointment to view. He went with his older brother and, of course, it was Basky's punt. After a bit of heated conversation, the chap selling it insisted that he had found it washed up on the Brightlingsea shore. I can't remember now how we got it back to Mersea, but back it came. It went missing again a couple or three years later; I found it anchored on the Pyefleet saltings, on the north side of Mersea Island, a mile or so away. Again, it did a runner but this time we never found it. Well, I say that. I did some work on a Mersea farm in approximately 2003 and in one of the farm barns, just above my head, sitting on two beams, was a punt; was it ours? It certainly looked familiar. We had to find another punt. I was talking to Peter Dawson in the Victory pub at some point after, and he had rescued one floating down the Blackwater a couple of years previously, going out to sea on an ebb tide, so we came to a deal, and I bought it from him (see page 53). So, we used that for several years after.

Using Joey's boat spoiled us into dreaming of acquiring something larger and longer. Ex-ship's lifeboats were the most common and more readily available to acquire, so we put out a feeler to purchase one, but when you want something badly and quickly it doesn't happen. I seem to remember Peterborough was the place to find one; we had contacted all of the people we knew who were in the know, but without any joy. One weekend, we decided to drive to Southampton docks to see what we could find; we drove there in Hoss's Ford Consul, had a good look round at the boatyards, scoured advertising boards, but found nothing. Hoss said, "Before we drive back to Mersea, I will just check the engine for oil." He lifted the bonnet and pulled out the dipstick: it didn't show a drop. We found the nearest garage, pooled what cash we had on us, and bought a gallon. When he tipped in the oil, it took the lot; it was dry! Nothing at all turned up in the following weeks but we were collecting items that we knew would be needed so that, when we did find a hull, we were getting gear together to fit it.

Word came back to us that an engine and gearbox was coming up for sale. Dr Fellowes was replacing two engines in the "Riis" – a 70-foot motor cruiser that was a well-known boat in Mersea, and her claim to fame was that she had been one of the fleet of little ships that went to Dunkirk in 1940. We went to see Dr Fellowes and said that we might be interested in one of the engines. We had a chat with Mick Lungley, and he thought that the price of £150 was very reasonable, so we chose what we thought was the better of the two and did the deal with the good Doctor; now all we needed was a boat. Terry Hart and I had got the job of re- plumbing and heating the Fox pub next door to where I lived.

David Dawson was doing some of the new building work for Ronnie Garriock, a local fisherman, and a newcomer from London, David Cocket, who had bought the Fox between them. A few months later, David Cocket bought the unused railway station at Heybridge and was converting that into a pub which he later named the Great Eastern.

On my journeys to and fro, from Mersea to Heybridge while plumbing the Great Eastern, I was working alone one day when I thought I would go and have a look at nearby Heybridge basin at lunchtime. I parked by the lock gates and, immediately, I caught sight of a boat laying on top of the saltings in what looked like in an abandoned state; her bow and stern were hanging over two creeks, so she was bending under the strain with no support. I thought that I would go and have a look. I crossed the canal lock gates and walked along the seawall nearer to where she lay. I only had my working boots on my feet, but with a few athletic jumps and leaps across creeks, I was soon next to her. She was clinker planked, over thirty feet in length, a transom stern, and quite narrow in the beam, but overall, she didn't look that bad, except for the excuse of a cabin and a wheelhouse that the three of us named, when we first saw it, the "chicken shed".

As I said, she was aground on a narrow piece of saltings, her bow and stern were overhanging two creeks by six or seven feet, and she was, in fact, bending. There wasn't much water in her, and she didn't appear to leak, unless the water had run out of her when the tide left her! I was quite excited by my find and couldn't wait to tell my mates. We drove over that same evening; they both agreed that she wasn't that bad, so we made the decision that we would try and buy her. The first place to ask was the nearby pub, The Old Ship. The barman shouted across the room to a couple of people, "Oi Bill, do you know who owns that boat on top of the marsh over there?". "What, you mean the Humpty-back camel?", came the response. We all laughed at his apt description. "Yeah, that's probably the one", we answered back.

He knew the owner and he knew also where he lived, so he explained the route which was only down the road. We found the address, knocked on the door, and a youngish chap stood there looking inquiringly at us. We explained that we were interested in his boat and wondered whether it could be for sale. He asked how we had found his address. We told him about his mate in the pub calling it the "Humpty-back camel". He laughed. "The cheeky bastard, I know exactly who that is; well, actually I do want to sell it", he said. "If not, she is going to break up." We did the deal there and then he wanted £105 for her; we didn't quibble, so we agreed and shook hands. We said that we would come back at the weekend to pay him, and then get her into a safer, and better, place so we could tow her back to Mersea.

We came back home and went straight down to the Victory pub to see Mick and Ashley; we told them what we had bought and asked if they could tow her back at the weekend, which they could, on Sunday. Fortunately, there were high spring tides that weekend, enough to float her off the saltings and to get her into the creek. We drove over to Heybridge on Saturday with buckets, ropes and anchors, found the owner, paid him and told him our plans for Sunday. We parked by the lock gates, then out over the marsh to the "Humpty", still in exactly the same position on top of the saltings. One of the creeks over which she was hanging ran out to the main channel; if we could float her into the creek, we could leave her tied and anchored nearer the edge, ready to take her back home. The tide started to come up the foreshore and into the creeks; we were ready to pull and push her as soon as she floated. The water came over the saltings and she started to rock as the tide lifted her. Then she floated. We manipulated her into the creek just as the tide turned to ebb away; we pulled her down the creek, nearer to the salting's edge and, as the tide ebbed, she positioned herself in the creek ready for the following day. We noticed that she leaked a bit, and that she was very whippy and flexible; we would somehow have to strengthen and tighten her up.

We met Mick and Ash down at the waterfront hard the next morning. They rowed out to their boat and then picked us up from the causeway for our voyage upriver to Heybridge Basin near Maldon. I can't remember now exactly what month of the year it was, probably April, but I do remember that it was a sunny, warm, clear day with an easterly, quite strong, breeze as we came out of the sheltering creeks of Mersea into the Quarters, crossing over the Nass spit, then out into the Blackwater. We then headed west to our destination. Bradwell power station was receding behind us as we passed the Thurslet beacon on our starboard side; up ahead, on our starboard bow, Osea Island, with all of its saltings and marshes, slid passed us. We caught a glimpse of the big house and outbuildings between the trees and bushes before the boat rounded the west end of the island, following the river as it meandered to the north, then back to the west. We could see Maldon in the far distance; the church, buildings, and houses up on the higher ground stood out in the sunshine. On our port side was Northey Island, so much different to Osea, being very low with some tall elm trees, I assumed, in the centre. Heybridge Basin loomed ahead with a forest of masts showing exactly where it was and, within a few minutes, we were motoring through the boats looking for Humpty.

Mick nudged his boat up to our new purchase. We jumped ashore, lifted anchors and untied her, clambered aboard, and found a strong fitting to attach the tow rope. Then Mick pulled us clear of the saltings out into the river. She had quite a bit of water laying in the bilge which we soon bailed out, then Mick and Ash headed for Mersea with all three of us in the "Humpty" on a now ebbing tide. When Mick was clear of boats and moorings, he opened up his engine; the "Humpty" rode and slid about in his wake as she surfed along. As we headed back down Collier's Reach, we rounded Osea Island, and then left its sheltering presence; the easterly, quite strong, breeze had roughened up the ebbing tide and large waves hit us as we headed into them. Mick didn't slow down but ploughed into them, flat out as he naturally did every day of his working life for C&C. Our boat bent, twisted and pounded quite alarmingly as she was dragged through, and into, the rough waters. We signalled to Ashley, who was standing on the aft deck of Mick's boat, to slow down as we were concerned that she was going to break up and sink. Mick slowed down, but often a large wave hit us which made her twist like a propeller! We had claw hammers, a saw, and crowbars on board, and it wasn't long before we started to dismantle the onboard chicken shed. The structure was thrown over the side in pieces to float away out of sight and mind, so, within half an hour, she was just an empty, bare hull; but now, as she didn't have any supporting timbers going across from gunnel to gunnel, she started to twist flex and bend worryingly. We had a couple of ropes with us. We signalled to Mick to slow to a crawl. Hoss and Swiggy went up to the bow, one either side with the rope, and dropped it down the stem while I pushed it as far as I could under the boat with a piece of timber. Then they worked it along, under the boat and keel, towards the stern for about two-thirds of her length. Hoss made a loop in his end and Swiggy passed the free end through the loop, then pulled and tightened it up and made it fast; we did the same with the other rope, a third of the way back from the stem. It temporarily strengthened her. Mick opened his boat engine up and he bought her onto the Mersea hard without mishap where we tied and moored her up.

Mick organised a boat trolley from C&C and, with the next convenient tide that week, we floated her on. Then she was towed up Firs Chase and was put on the piece of land between the council houses, next to Pinky. Over the next few days, we jacked her up from the trolley and dropped her down onto wooden blocks. Mick came with the tractor and took the trolley back. We were keen to get started. She had several broken timbers; we removed these, plus others that looked bad. Thinking back, I'm sure we renewed the lot. We ordered enough two-inch by one-inch American elm and ash planks from Wyatts, plus copper nails and roves to fix them; then we had to make a steaming box and boiler to make the timbers flexible enough to bend them to the shape of the hull. Gas and paraffin blowlamps were fired up; we burned and cleaned off every scrap of paint from her hull, then sandpapered the woodwork smooth, followed by a couple of coats of red oxide primer. Every day, while at work, pieces of timber that were going to be discarded and that were either going to be burned or scrapped, we kept. Anything that we thought could be of use, we hoarded; all of our mates, and us included, called it "The Beg, Steal or Borrow". It really was!

Where the planking was nailed and fixed to the transom, it was very chaffed, worn, and damaged, so we made the decision to fit a new transom nine inches further into the hull, which we left for Hoss to do. When it was finished, and fitting like a glove, the damaged planking and old transom was cut off, so she was now 31 feet, 3 inches long, whereas before she was 32 feet exactly; her overall width was 9 feet, 3 inches, but we felt she wanted to take a more open shape. We removed the pieces of baton holding her at 9 feet, 3 inches, and let her go out to 10 feet; she looked much better to the eye. All of the cracked, split, damaged planking was renewed and replaced but she still had a Humpty-back camel appearance. The three of us would stand in Pinky's garden at a distance and try to visualise a better bulwark shape. We would temporarily fix, and bend, a long piece of baton from the stem to the stern, stand again in Pinky's garden, then someone would go aboard, move and clamp the baton up and down until we were all agreed on a more eye-pleasing shape. We measured the shape, then cut and fitted a new spruce top plank on both sides from stem to stern, and a wide mahogany gunnel capping. Gone was the hog-backed shape, and no longer was she the Humpty-backed camel!

Having measured her original length and breadth at thirty-two feet by nine-feet, three inches, the experts reckoned she was an ex-naval rowing and sailing cutter; the kelson and keel had a nine-foot slot where a centreboard and box was once fitted. We also bolted an eight-foot, three-inch keel to the existing one, and ten-foot by eight-foot, three-inch bilge keels; it was incredible how these pieces of timber strengthened and straightened her up. We were starting to run out of money, so it was decided we would have to sell our precious little lifeboat that had given us so much fun and pleasure over the last ten years. While we were waiting to sell her, I negotiated a £300 loan from North Central Finance, an H.P. company in Colchester and the same firm that I had used to finance the Honda 50. My credit rating must have been good. I remember that they paid me out in cash, as not one of us had a bank account.

Hoss was working with a bricklaying gang on the same job. We had known Dick West from years before; he had heard our boat was for sale, so asked Hoss how much we wanted for it. "Well, three hundred quid, mate". The response was, "I'll give you two hundred and eighty", so the deal was done, and our little boat was sold to Dick; we even transported it over to Layer-de-la-Haye for him.

We never saw it again. I have often thought, and wondered, over the years what eventually happened to that brilliant little boat; she was well-loved.

We now had some cash in the pot and, over the next several months, we worked on her nonstop. Dr. Fellowes' Dorman engine was fitted and lined up to a 1.5-inch bronze shaft and 18-inch four-bladed propeller; deck beams and decking were laid, cabin and wheelhouse constructed, steering gear and wheel were wired to electrics and lighting, and then she was painted and the bottom varnished black. We paid Mick Lungley £70 for a winch and £28 to Nigel Mills for a five-metre Otter trawl. Roger Butcher came to the rescue, once again, and made a set of S/S navigation and masthead lights, and also a set of trawl boards; we were getting closer to her launch every day. I was buying my first house in Churchfields, and getting married to the lovely Heather on 1st September 1973, so, paying to equip and work on our new boat, and also working on our new house, spending money, redecorating, and getting it how we wanted, together with a mortgage, I was practically skint.

15: Living the Dream

CHANGES WERE HAPPENING to our freedom as to where we normally went wildfowling; a new gamekeeper was appointed at Old Hall, and with the recent armed trespass law being passed in 1968, some of the saltmarsh that we shot over was owned by Brigadier Colvin. Now we were poaching, full stop. It all came to a head in the 1970-71 season. One Saturday afternoon, we decided that we wanted to go to Rat Island to flight. Basky's brother, Terry, who I was working for, decided he also wanted to come; we tried unsuccessfully to book in with the CWCC field secretary but after several attempts we couldn't, but still went without booking, a capital offence in the club's eyes. Terry had built a dingy which was also moored at East Mersea, so the three of us motored to the Rat in that. As we were heading up the Colne to Rat Island, I looked across to Langenhoe Point and, by the lookout post, I noticed two figures on the other side of the seawall looking our way. As it transpired, one of the people was Ernie Holland, a mate of Ron Pittock who was the field secretary of the CWCC, so as soon as he got to a telephone, he was on the phone to Ron and checking us out. Also, in the meantime, Ken Salmon, the new gamekeeper on Old Hall, had been in touch with the club complaining that members of said club were poaching on his owner's land and wanted something done about it.

It didn't take very long for the club to contact all three of us and we were duly accused of breaking the club's strict rules; firstly, not booking in, and secondly, me and Basky shooting on Old Hall where we were never seen or caught but assumed to be guilty. In due course, we were contacted and summoned before the CWCC committee to defend ourselves and await a verdict. The club was using the Prince of Wales pub at Marks Tey at the time, so it was there that we turned up one evening. It was quite a friendly affair except for the new broom, Kevin, who read the Riot Act and carried on a bit, but he didn't really have a clue of how things were in the past and how traditions and freedoms take time to adjust to; he was an out and out club man and wanted us to be made an example of, so we came back out into the bar to await their decision which didn't take them long. At the interview we got the impression fairly quickly that we were going to be kicked out, so as we stood there awaiting sentence, I said to the committee before they said anything that to save any doubts we would resign from the club. With that, Kevin stood up and ranted, "You needn't worry, we were going to chuck you out anyway!" We were also blacklisted by WAGBI, for God's sake!

Unaware to the three of us, even before we were caught, negotiations were happening between the CWCC and the landowners of Old Hall and Abbots Hall. The landowners knew the land was being shot by other CWCC members, not just me and Basky, so when we were caught for not booking out for Rat Island, it was then a convenient excuse to get us before the committee and to throw the book at us. We were then made a scapegoat and an example of, so the CWCC could go back to the landowners and tell them that justice had been administered. But things did happen fairly quickly in favour of the CWCC after that; Ken Salmon joined the club as a free member, and he arranged for the CWCC to shoot the saltmarsh from Pennyhole all the way to Salcott.

On the north side of Salcott Channel was Abbots Hall and its acres of salt-ings where I had my first flight on all those years ago. A mate of Ken Salmon from Little Clacton, Phill Gunfield, had just started working on the farm for the new owner, Sir Leonard Crossland. The club acquired the saltmarsh and the pigeon shooting with the help of Phill, shortly after he joined the CWCC as a free member. But I haven't an axe to grind; both Ken and Phill were to become good friends in the near future and in the following years. Ray Island had recently been sold to the National Trust ("NT"), and the Essex Wildlife Trust ("EWT") were asked to manage it on behalf of the NT, so Ken Crawshaw, being a committee member of the EWT, arranged for the CWCC to warden and shoot over it. At about the same time, or just after, we were kicked out of the CWCC, Terry and I were working at a house at Bromans Lane in East Mersea; John Farthing was also working there, digging a trench for Terry, so when we stopped at 1 o'clock for a sandwich, Terry brought up the idea of forming a wild-fowling club in Mersea. We agreed that it was a good idea and that we would put the word about; if there was enough interest, we would arrange a meeting.

Shortly afterwards, a meeting was arranged and held at The Fountain public house, in its function hall, and several interested people turned up; so it was that the Mersea Island Wildfowling and Conservation Association ("MIWFCA") was formed. Joe Lewis, who was The Fountain's landlord at the time, wanted the word "association" in the title because he owned a pub in Walton before he came to Mersea, and "association" was in the title of the Walton Wildfowlers, of which he was a member. A committee was formed; Joe Lewis was elected as Chairman, Terry Hart was elected Secretary, and Colin Anstey as Treasurer. I was elected as a committee member, but working with Terry every day, I helped him as well in the role of Assistant Secretary. We did get our first piece of salt-marsh pretty quickly. John Benns and Colin Anstey both worked at Gowens, the sailmakers. Sammy Sampson, who owned Copthall Farm, proposed a lovely salt-marsh there; I think he was a director at Gowens, so the shooting was obtained for the MIWFCA on Copthall saltings. Mersea poachers, who had previously shot wherever they wanted, were now legally restricted to shooting at Copthall if they were not members of the CWCC, and if they didn't want to break the law. But we still had a few places to go which were still "free"!

As I mentioned a paragraph or two earlier, the right to shoot at the three marshes, Old Hall, Abbots Hall, and Ray Island, was in discussion with the owners, and was eventually obtained by the CWCC, although we, at Mersea, were also hoping to get it. The MIWFCA contacted the landowners at the same time, but we were turned down in favour of the CWCC. A foregone conclusion! Me and Basky were absolutely gutted. The thought of never being able to shoot at our favourite places, where we had previously enjoyed going, was something hard to bear. We could see it was a lost cause; the gunners here at Mersea had been a pain in the backside of the landowners for donkey's years and it was a chance for them to get back at us and even things up. All three marshes had been poached continuously, inside the seawall and out, and I had been one of them. An idea was muted and talked about, and it was proposed that, to save any hard feelings and problems between mates and friends in the two clubs, we should try and bury the hatchet. Many of our Mersea friends and mates who had joined the CWCC several years after me and Basky didn't come over to the newly formed MIWFCA, but, thinking back, why should they?

So, after a few months and with the forthcoming season looming, a meeting was arranged at The Fountain, and after a lively debate it was voted and agreed to try to get an amalgamation of the two clubs; but it wasn't that straightforward, some of the diehards at Mersea hated the CWCC. Were they not the reason the shooting had been lost? In no way could they be convinced it was otherwise (it is still the same today!). Discussions between the CWCC and MIWFCA went ahead, and a favourable agreement was reached between the two clubs; any person who was a member of MIWFCA would automatically be accepted into the CWCC, but that didn't include me, Terry or Basky. We would have to wait a few more months before the committee of the CWCC came to a decision to accept us back as members. After the decision to disband the MIWFCA, it was reformed straight away by some of the older diehard members and became the Mersea Island Wildfowling Club (the "MIWFC"), by which it is still known to this day, and Copthall is still the only piece of saltmarsh that they shoot. (N.B. now, in its 50th anniversary year, the wildfowling has been lost to the club on Copthall, with thanks to the NT and NE. Dipsticks!).

So, the three of us were left in limbo; we weren't members of the newly formed MIWFC, and we hadn't been accepted back into the CWCC. The first of September was looming, and we had nowhere legally to shoot. I actually persuaded Dave Conway, Hoss and Hank to become CWCC members, but I knew from the start it was a lost cause! The first of September arrived for the start of a new season; I went to shoot but can't remember where. It may have been on the Cobmarsh, I think. I couldn't have shot anything as there is not a record in my notebook. Where Basky went, I can't remember. Looking back through my notebook of that time, I can't recognize any deviation in entries and numbers as to ducks shot, so I must have been going out shooting somewhere. In due course we heard from the CWCC that we had to attend a committee meeting to see what our fate awaited. We were read the Riot Act (again!) as we stood there. We then had to leave the room as they discussed our wildfowling future and come to a verdict; we were then invited to come back in. The secretary, Kevin, informed us the vote was very close in our favour, and that we could rejoin. We were back in.

It was then that I realised just how much I needed to be out with the birds in the familiar wild places: the salt marshes and creeks that I loved, and that were so nearly lost to me by legislation and a wildfowling club. There was no way now that I was going to lose what I held so precious, and also the thought of constantly looking over your shoulder to see if someone was watching you and then confronting you was too much to bear; I couldn't put up with that, I wanted to enjoy what I hold so dear, and it was the same for my friend and fowling partner. Also, over the previous years, I had made a lot of good friends within the club, and I would have missed that friendship and comradery enormously. We had to knuckle down and abide by the club rules and accept the new legislation; if you are using a firearm on saltmarsh or private land without permission, you are poaching and committing armed trespass, a very serious offence. Today, if convicted, it means the loss of your guns and shotgun certificate.

We launched the J.B.J.in the autumn of 1972, Mick Lungley bringing the tractor and boat trailer one weekend, and taking her down Firs Chase to leave her on Clarke & Carters hard to await the tide; the water came up and over the trailer and she started to float. We started the Dorman and slowly reversed her off; when she was clear, Mick towed it away. The flatty was tied to the stern, and we motored on our usual trial run route up to the Strood and back; she was really fast, her cutter shape slicing through the water. We went down into the bilges, looking all around for water leaks, around the stern tube, keel bolts, and around the engine for oil and water leaks. Then we noticed a small trickle of water coming from under the head gasket, running down the engine block, and dripping into the bilge. We brought her back to the mooring and tied her up. Water was seeping through the lands on the planking quite quickly. We couldn't leave her on the mooring; she would have to be brought onto the hard by the high-water mark, so she was only floating for a short time. It was just about high water by now, and not a very big tide, so we untied her and brought her round, gently grounding onto Wyatt's hard.

On every tide, while she was afloat, we were in the bilge searching and trying to identify leaks that were quite numerous, including the leak on the head gasket; after tightening the head bolts, it still leaked. Mick and Ashley came aboard and diagnosed that the engine head was probably warped and would have to be skimmed; also, a new head gasket would have to be fitted. We moved her into a mud berth in the Victory dock and dismantled the head. It would have been taken to somewhere like Robinsons in Colchester to be machined, and they could also have found a gasket for us; it was all done fairly quickly and put back together, torqued up and tested. It was successful.

We had solved one problem, now we had to sort out another; the leaking hull was annoyingly persistent, so we made a decision that we would have to fix land cants to her outside planking. So, in January 1973, we brought her out of the water again. We went to see Mick and he arranged again for a trolley from Clarke & Carters; she was towed along the coast road and put on Douglas (the "Duke") Musset's forecourt, by his oyster shed. We spread a wonderful bitumen mastic called "Furatex" along each land, then a 3-inch strip of building paper stuck onto that. 2-inch by 1/2-inch by 12-foot lengths of pine, pushed up tight under the land of each plank, were then fixed with copper nails into the internal timbers, then a couple of liberal coats of black varnish were painted on her planking under the waterline. After a few days, we had it done. Mick hooked up the Fordson and towed her the short distance back to the hard; we waited once again for the tide to float her off the trolley, then the three of us crawled and lay about in the bilges, searching all over for leaks. She was watertight. We reversed her off the trailer and the J.B.J. went for her maiden trip with the flatty in tow, out into the Blackwater, around the Nass beacon, and back to her mooring.

Over the next few weeks, we were aboard her most weekends and evenings, working on her, and finishing off jobs that needed to be done in order to get her just as we wanted. On the first of May 1973, we went to see Nigel Mills as we had heard that he had a five-metre otter trawl for sale which had never been in the water; so, we did the deal and paid him £28 for it. Roger Butcher was, once again, kindly commissioned to make us a set of doors for the net, while the three of us made up, and fitted, a ground rope using all of the leftover rubbers and spacers that we had for the beam trawl all those years before. We had the trawl ready just as Roger finished the new doors, so everything was loaded in Hoss's van, then into the flatty and out to the J.B.J. We had it shackled up to the warps and were soon on our way, motoring down the Fleet to try out the new net and gear. We punched the flooding tide out to the Nass Beacon, towing the cod-end buoy, streaming astern. I steered a wide circle to port while Hoss and Swiggy shot the net over the side. I straightened up and headed west with the flooding tide, the net streaming astern. Then, with Hoss on one side of the winch and Swiggy on the other, they loosened the winch brakes; the new otter doors entered the water, swimming and pulling apart, opening up the mouth of the trawl as they sank to the bed of the river. Then they released and paid out 25 fathoms of warp wire, marked off at every five fathoms. I slowed the engine revolutions down to a fast tickover, locked the wheel, and joined the crew on deck as the J.B.J steered herself upriver.

We hauled after half an hour, mainly to see if the doors were running flat on the seabed; they were starting to shine on the rear corners, so the rope bridle was lengthened to drop the front of the doors, in order that they both ran its length on the seabed. The winch was released, and the trawl and doors sank once again to the riverbed, hopefully fishing. We carried on upriver, then, somewhere by Tollesbury pier, we hauled. The winch worked brilliantly, dragging the heavy gear up to the boat with the doors hanging from the gallows. I opened up the engine throttle and pulled the net fast, washing everything that had been caught, hopefully, down into the cod end. I then turned sharply to port and knocked it out of gear, ticking over the engine, the net hanging by her side ready to drag on deck. I joined my two mates on deck to haul it in.

We weren't totally disappointed for our trial tow; it appeared to be fishing judging by the amount of seabed debris caught: the usual crabs, five fingers, pissers, dead man's fingers, limpets, dead oyster shells, seaweed, small roker, a few dabs, and a few soles.

We shot the gear again, towing up towards the Thurslet Beacon. The tide started to ebb, so I turned a wide circle to starboard and towed back down with the ebb and, once again, hauled just west of the Nass beacon; this time we had half a bucket full of soles to keep. We came back to the mooring with just enough water to reach the rising scope. We securely tied her up and sculled the flatty back to punt bay and Wyatt's hard, very satisfied with our boat and hard work. Every other weekend, on a Saturday morning, we would leave the mooring at high tide, motor down the Blackwater, and shoot the gear after a couple of miles out towards the North Sea. We would tow, trawl and haul every hour or so going down the Wallet with the ebb tide, passing the mainland of St. Osyth, Clacton, and just about getting to Walton, when the flooding tide turned, before coming back to the Blackwater. It was then that we would haul, then tow the net streaming behind us, washing out the weed and rubbish caught in the meshes, as the deck hands swabbed the decks and flushed out the crabs hiding somewhere under the winch, or had walked up to the bow to hide. Then we would drag the net back on deck, laying the doors on top to hold it down. I would steer and head for home as the boys gutted, cleaned, sorted and boxed the catch. Congratulating ourselves, we were now living the dream.

16: Getting it out of my System

HEATHER AND I were still very busy on our house that we had bought in Churchfields, West Mersea; our wedding day, on the 1st of September, was getting closer, so we were both flat out paper hanging, painting and decorating, getting carpets laid, and all the usual things. However, I still found time to go trawling on a Saturday with my mates. We also went with Peter Dawson on his lovely Belgian beam trawler *Lorna*. I had got the fishing bug big time; I just had to do it as much as I could. I remember one day, in particular, we were towing out in the Black Deeps for soles and roker and we were having a very good run; the cod ends were full at every haul. We were all busy gutting and boxing the catch; we had hardly a moments break between each haul of an hour's tow, when Peter came out of the wheelhouse to tell us a force eight to nine storm was imminent within the next couple of hours. We had just enough time to finish this one tow, then we would have to make our way home. We hauled and Peter made the decision to have one more try; we went into the wheelhouse, I looked at the radar and at the green lit-up screen as it swept the horizon. Then Peter said, "Did you see it?". "What's that, mate?", I replied. "The weather front and storm", said Peter. I peered at the screen again and, at thirty miles range somewhere over the Essex mainland, the radar was picking up the mass. We had just dropped the two beam trawls for our last tow of the day when it suddenly hit us; we were heading into it bow on. *Lorna* stood on her stern, then plunged as she topped a huge wave crest, her bow dropping into the deep trough, then throwing hundreds of gallons of green sea over her stem head which then ran down her decks like a river, floating and washing everything that wasn't fixed in front of it, before discharging back into the tumultuous waters through the scuppers. Fish boxes, both full and empty, were floating and flying about as a continuous tsunami of water covered the decks, trying to wash you off your feet as it swilled about.

Peter made the decision to haul; the *Lorna* shook and vibrated as the powerful winch dragged the heavy trawl beams and nets across the seabed up to the boat's horizontal derricks. After a while, the two beams broke through the surface of the mad, rough sea; we took a bite around each net in turn, winched them over bulwarks, and opened the cod ends, dropping the contents onto the decks. Peter left the derricks lying horizontal, with the trawl beams hanging and trailing the nets, washing them through on each side of *Lorna* as they swung about on the warps. We motored slowly forward, heading through the rough, heavy sea for the spitway, our passageway through to our route into the Blackwater and calmer seas. As we approached closer to the south spitway buoy, Peter slowed *Lorna*, raised the derricks, and as gently as he could, expertly lowered the heavy, swinging beam trawls onto the decks alongside the bulwarks and gunnels. We arrived at the south spitway mark just as the tide was flooding to help our voyage home, but the *Lorna* required ten feet of water to float her through. We had to wait for the tide to give her enough depth; even then, as she steamed gently through, her keel occasionally hit the hard, sandy swatchway as she headed for the north spitway buoy a mile away.

We came slowly and cautiously through, passing the mark, and found deeper water. I kept peering through the rubber visor shading the radar. I switched it onto a five-mile range setting; it clarified our route to each navigational mark with incredible accuracy. I could see the storm and weather front as it quickly passed us by, our signposting, channel-marking buoys slipped astern as we came into the wide estuary of the Blackwater. As we passed the Knoll-marking buoy, the radar picked up the Nass beacon miles away, close by our route into the Mersea Quarters, the oyster bed withies along the shore of the wide River Blackwater with the channels and creeks that feed into it; what an incredible piece of technology.

The 1st of September arrived, the day I was getting married to my gorgeous, long-suffering fiancée, Heather; but firstly, it was also the opening day of the duck shooting season and a tradition had to be upheld. Basky picked me up for the last time from my mum and dad's house at 3.30am, and he drove his vehicle to the little spinney at the bottom of Shop Lane. The recently planted fir trees were now growing quite quickly and shading the once sunny lane where we parked. We loaded ourselves up and followed the footpath to the sea wall and to our punt. We were soon away down the Pyefleet, heading to Rat Island; it was going to be a quick trip this morning as I had an important appointment to uphold later that day. The guns over on the M.O.D. ranges sounded quite busy, but, according to my diary, all that I put in the bag was a shoveller; I can't remember what Basky had shot, if anything. I was back home by 10am, and a married man by 2pm. At the wedding reception later on that day, all of my shooting friends and guests disappeared; they weren't going to miss the opening day evening flight just for me!

Earlier that year I bought Swiggy's flatty; it was in a bit of a sorry state, so I gave him ten pounds, transported it up to my mum and dads, and repaired and repainted it. We still used it to get to J.B.J. but I could now use it for wildfowling more often by myself. Hoss and Swiggy found a slightly bigger 12-foot glass dinghy that they could use; with the upheaval of not being able to go where they always wanted to and being members of the CWCC for only one season, they had to be more discrete as to where they shot and to keep a watchful eye out. It was something that didn't worry Hoss in the slightest; he would go anywhere he fancied, but Swiggy was a bit more concerned. I was now married and back within the folds of the CWCC and both me and Basky had made a pledge to ourselves that our wildfowling was a very important part in our life, and we would now try to be model members of the club.

Over the course of the next few seasons, Swiggy stopped wildfowling altogether, but Hoss teamed up with Pinky Hewes, and the pair of them, individually or singly, would shoot just as much as they had done so in the past. They had their admirers within some of the local wildfowling community; also, working together, they would plan their escapades. But now, as I was a good boy trying to keep on the straight and narrow, I was an easy target for ridicule, jokingly or otherwise, as I was in their company working, fishing, and shooting nearly all of the time, but I didn't care; I was free to shoot wildfowl and did just that.

I worked on the house a lot that summer and autumn, but also found time to shoot, mostly at evening flight. It was still early in the season and morning flight would be a few weeks away, and well into October before rising out of bed at some unearthly hour; we usually ventured out on the weekend before the clocks went back. Looking at my notebook records, I had twenty-four successful trips, not counting the blank ones, up until January 12th, 1974, that season. I put a number of wildfowl into the bag, plus a few pheasants and rabbits, went ferreting with my father, the dogs, Basky and his fiancé Angela, and also Heather on a Sunday morning before when I went fishing full time, therefore missing the end of the season.

I was still working with Terry Hart flat out at P&H, but I still had the trawling and fishing bug. I had to get it out of my system. David Stoker was trawling for sprats and catching tons; I went to see him to see if he would take me on full time and he said he would, as long as the fishing lasted. I could start on the Monday if I wanted to, so as not to drop Terry in the lurch, which it probably did! Roger Butcher had a workshop in David's field behind his house. I just happened to be in the workshop when the VHF radio crackled and David's voice came through, "How are you getting on, are you still finding marks and catching fish?", Roger enquired. "No mate, it's gone bloody dead", came the reply. "If you see Jack, tell him he won't be able to start on Monday". I was gutted; I didn't hear the rest of the conversation, I was crestfallen. Bugger it!

I knew Trevor Mole was also doing the same thing, so with no more to do, I went and saw him to ask if he wanted a hand. He was going on the following day, Sunday, if I wanted to come along. I met him at the causeway and car park just after high water at 7am; his brother Alan also came, plus Gary Powell who must still have been at school. Also, Malcolm Cawdron was going trawling as well and could we give him a lift to his boat. We all got aboard the dingy and Gary sculled us out to Malcolm's and Trevor's boat. I kept out of the way as they readied the boat. Trevor and Alan both went down into the engine room through the hatch; I could hear them talking. Then the big engine roared into life, a cloud of black smoke came from the exhaust strapped and clipped to the wheelhouse, and a wonderful, powerful sound emitted as it ticked over ready for its day of toil. A stream of water discharged out from the side of the boat; after a while, a wisp of steam emitted from the engine-heated water and quickly disappeared in the chilly morning air.

The mooring ropes were dropped into the dingy, now tied to the mooring buoy, awaiting our return tonight. The *Janet Anne* caught the ebbing tide and proceeded down Thornfleet Creek with Malcolm following closely behind; in

Malcolm Cawdron's boat CK190.

gear, but still at tickover, she moved easily over the still water of the creek, making her way through moored yachts and boats out to the quarters and the open waters of the Blackwater. Trevor knocked her out of gear, came out of the wheelhouse, and went behind the winch. He came out holding a long piece of wood with a wire attached to a transducer at one end; he also had a claw hammer. He went to the side of the boat, pushed the transducer into the water to

158

a certain depth, and hammered and nailed it to the wooden hull of *Janet Anne*. He looked at me, smiling, as he stepped over the dangling wire, then went back to the wheelhouse muttering, "I must get the proper one mended!". He switched on the modified echo sounder in the wheelhouse, peering at it as it drew the shape of the flat seabed a few feet beneath us across the white paper in black ink.

Trawling on Trevor Mole's boat.

The ebb tide caught us, pulling us eastward as Trevor opened up the throttle. The big powerful engine responded as both boats made their way out into the North Sea. We gazed at the improvised fish-finding glass screen, searching for a black spike of sprats as it sent a rebounding electric signal to the sea floor. We glassed the flat, oily water looking for gull flocks fishing, and other birds that hope-fully might give us a clue as to the presence of a shoal. We zig-zagged this way and that as we steamed out to sea; each small flock of birds was investigated as we steered towards them in the hope that something might transpire on the hypnotising screen. Malcolm was further away from us now; the VHF would crackle into life as he spoke, either to Trevor or another fishing colleague somewhere out to sea. I remember it took me a couple or three days to understand the wavy, garbled speech as it was emitted from the VHF radio loudspeaker, and the quite loud click as the transmit button was pressed. There wasn't radar on the boat, but a navigational piece of equipment called a Decca that produced lanes of different coloured, intersecting lines, or corridors, of green, red and purple across a wide glass screen which depicted on a chart where we were in the North Sea. It picked up a signal from three transmitting high masts positioned somewhere across Europe that gave a fixing cross-reference signal and point onto the screen in the wheelhouse of the boat. We were somewhere near the Bench Head buoy when the sounder picked up a shoal of fish; very quickly, the experienced crew flew about getting the net ready to shoot. The net streamed over the stern rail, towing the long sleeve of the trawl behind the boat. Suddenly, the ropes and bridals attached to the huge net-opening trawl doors took the strain, and as it did, immediately the doors and net dropped below the water surface as the brakes on the winch released it. Trevor looked at his brother, remarking, "I wonder if we were quick enough?". We motored forward, turning in a very wide circle to starboard, all the time peering into the echo sounder; another black spike appeared on the screen as Trevor steered into it. We towed the net for the next twenty minutes and decided to haul.

The powerful winch was put into gear, increasing the engine speed slightly as it pulled the fishing gear up to the boat. The otter doors broke through the surface of the water. Trevor pulled up one door to the aft gallow, braking the winch as it hung, dripping, then operating the powerful winch, it pulled up the other door to the forward gallow on the other side of the boat, turning to starboard as he did so. The door rattled into its resting place hanging from the gallow; a hooked chain was attached to the otter doors and the winch was knocked out of gear. He released the two brakes, the chains taking the weight of the doors from off the winch.

The trawling boat owned by Malcolm Cawdron; trawling with Trevor Mole and Malcolm gave Jack many happy memories.

We looked over the side of the *Janet Anne* at the huge sprat net with its long, trailing sleeve ending at the cod end, 20-odd yards away, or further. It was floating on the water's surface, undulating, weaving, and moving from side to side like a massive eel as the wave action on the sea's surface made it move and act like a sea serpent. I couldn't believe my eyes at the huge number of fish caught and trapped, the combined numbers of thousands and thousands of tiny swim bladders making the whole sleeve float alongside, ready to be hauled on board. I was spellbound.

The sleeve, full of sprats, had to be divided into manageable weights, or bites, to winch onboard and drop into the fish hold. Eventually, we successfully achieved this. We carried on the search and shot the gear again, catching another net full of the tiny fish which almost filled the hold, but still with enough room for more. 'Never giving up' is the motto for these boys, so the search continued until we found another spike showing up on the finder. The net was shot again, but for a shorter period this time. Once again, the writhing, undulating sleeve of the trawl lay waiting to be hauled aboard; we peered into the hold, assessing what room we had left for another few tons of fish. "We will have to put the pounds in", Trevor exclaimed to his brother. A nod, then the 12-inch-wide pieces of timber slotted into purpose-made vertical slots; these went across the decks from the hold to the washboards of the boat's hull. The rest of the catch was released from the net slowly; it filled the hold, overflowing onto the deck and filling to the top of the pounds. We shovelled them forward to the bow, and slotted in two more pounds to hold them so as not to let the fish go back into the sea through the scuppers.

What the weight of fish was, I hadn't a clue; someone mentioned 14 tonnes. *Janet Anne's* bow dropped lower into the water, so now you could see forward over her stem head as you stood by the winch, the surface of the sea virtually up to the scuppers, so deep in the water was she, as we made ready for our voyage home. As we approached the Blackwater, we turned to starboard, rounding the sand bar-marking buoy into the Colne estuary, heading up towards the Hythe docks in Colchester. It seemed to be a bit of a race as two or three other boats were jockeying for position to get ahead of the competition. It was fascinating watching these other boats that were quite close by; all of them were former Belgian beam trawlers, probably having seen the best of their days, all with their bows deep in the water and the stern and aft end cocking up, looking like the propeller was just below the water's surface. The exhausts puffed out black smoke and throbbed as the boats seem to move easily, catching the flooding tide sweeping them, and us, before it. We were soon left trailing behind the faster, more powerful, boats as we followed them and the meandering, twisting Colne, past Rat Island and the Geedon saltings to our left that I know like the back of my wildfowling hands. To the right was Moverons Farm and its incredible flight pond. Also, we passed by Alresford Creek where one of my mates spends hours wildfowling in a muddy creek, hoping to bag a duck or two, and so on forward, past Wivenhoe and, a bit further, Rowhedge. I had never seen these villages from a watery perspective before. Eventually, the Hythe came into view; the faster boats were already tied up as we snuggled and squeezed into a spot against the concrete quay and tied up to wait.

Trevor walked to a phone box and rang someone to get a lift back to Mersea. There was four of us on board, so two of us cadged a lift from someone else; I can't remember now who it was. We arrived back in Colchester early the next morning. The elevator was emptying the catch of one of the boats and we were next. Large 20-ton lorries were lined up on the quay to transport the fish away. I asked Trevor where they were going, to which he replied, "They are all going for fish meal: fertiliser, in other words, to be spread on some farmer's land!". "That is terrible", I replied. I was horrified; what a waste of an incredible creature. I couldn't get my head around it.

We shovelled the fish to the elevator, firstly on deck then down into the hold, eventually scraping and shovelling the last remains of the catch onto, and up, the elevator into the waiting lorry. The high-pressure deck wash hose was passed down into the fish hold and the few remaining sprats, and whatever, were shovelled into a bucket and deposited into the Colne to be fed to hordes of, mainly, gulls that also feasted on the scraps and fishy remnants and morsels discharged from *Janet Anne*'s bilge pump. High tide had arrived, and we were nearly ready to go back to sea. Other boats were waiting for the ebb tide, then casting off their moorings and moving gently forward in tickover before turning to starboard, the bows catching the ebbing current of water which helped to gently turn them, but, with purpose, headed them back out down the winding river to try their skill and luck again. This we did for the next few days, but the sprats were getting fewer by the day, so early at dawn on the Saturday, after unloading, we steamed back to Mersea for a change of fishing gear. As we came back down the Colne (I was always looking for ducks) we passed by the Geedons and Rat Island. I unhooked the binoculars from inside the wheelhouse, stood outside on the stern deck, and glassed across to Rat Island. There, with just his head above the saltings top, was Basky, waiting for a chance and shot. In front of him, 6 mallard decoys floated; I gave him a loud whistle and wave, but he didn't hear or see me. I watched him until he went out of sight. I contacted him as soon as I could to see how he got on; he had shot some ducks, but I can't remember now what sort.

We came back to Mersea, moored, and tied up in the Thorn Fleet. We sculled the dingy to the causeway, met up with Malcolm, and went to get a herring midwater pair trawl that the two boats were going to tow. We dragged it out of a garden shed and stretched it out on Wyatt's hard to do a couple of minor repairs; this we soon did, put it in the dingy, sculled out again to the *Janet Anne*, and fitted one wing and side. Several other Mersea boats were catching herring, either pair trawling, single boat trawling, or, what the majority did, drift netting. We were soon away and back out in the Blackwater. Trevor was on the VHF radio, enquiring from the other boats as to what was being caught. Some didn't mind sharing information, but he wouldn't even speak to others. He called up Malcolm who came alongside and tied up to us; then, passing the other

Malcolm Cawdron's trawling boat CK190.

trawl wing of the net to Malcolm, he shackled it to his trawl warps. A long rope cable was made fast to the forward gallow on his boat; we untied him from us, and he steered away, taking up the slack on the connecting cable, which then held the two boats sixty or seventy yards apart. The trawl was then shot and lowered into the water from both boats to a certain distance astern; the winches were braked, the two boats pulling the trawl in a mid-water position, hopefully fishing. All eyes turned, once again, to the makeshift fish finder, the black ink marking pen jumping vertically on the paper when it sensed something passing by the transducer, but it didn't do it very often!

We had dropped the net into the water a couple of miles downriver; the Bench Head buoy was a rough marker to the start of the Blackwater, and it lay ahead, east of us two miles away. We altered course to give it a wide berth to the south and proceeded down the Wallet Channel to haul somewhere near Clacton-on-Sea; as we continued, black spikes appeared on the sounder which gave us more opportunism as we continued. We had been fishing for about an hour or so when it was decided to haul. Both winches started to pull in the net, the trawl broke through to the surface, then the two boats came together. We fixed the trawl from Malcolm's boat to the *Janet Anne* and proceeded to hand haul the net to us. Then, using a strop, a short rope with an eye spliced either end,

163

we passed it around the net as close as we could by the cod end and, using the derrick and winch, hauled it onto the boat. We emptied it onto the deck behind the pounds; we shot the gear again and continued on our way towards Clacton and Walton; turning in a wide circle, we headed back to the Blackwater.

We had a few fish on deck which I boxed and stacked as we headed west and into the Maldon river. We had to keep a sharp lookout for the dan buoys with their black flags denoting the position of a flotilla of herring drift nets attached; sometimes, the boat and owner would be drifting with the nets waiting and flocks of gulls would accompany the boats, waiting for an easy meal. As soon as someone started hauling, the screaming hordes would descend, diving and squabbling with each other if one of them had managed pick a floating fish, chasing the successful bird to try and make it give it up. The bigger herring and black-backed gulls were very successful and intimidating. This time, the haul was much more successful. We laid out the fish boxes under the hanging cod end and dribbled them out to fill the boxes. Once again, the net was cast over the stern and we continued on our way, Malcolm steering away from us to hold his side of the trawls, wide mouth open on his end of the tethering rope.

The radio was busy with chatter as we proceeded, music (always music, with the volume knob turned up to maximum) being broadcast from a nearby pirate radio station anchored just a couple of miles away. It blared out music of the pop stars of the day, as I sang, jigged and twisted on the wet, slippery deck to Chubby Checker or one of his contemporaries. I wielded a murderous-looking gutting knife in one hand and a writhing cod fish in the other. We proceeded as far west into the Blackwater as was practical. We dodged one or two rod fishers and anchored by the baffle wall as, once again, we hauled up the trawl for the last time that day. We winched it up and swung it aboard, opening the cod end; the herring dropped out and to everyone's surprise there was also one enormous cod. We had to guess its weight by picking it up by the gills and comparing it to other things, as we had no scales on board. It was at least four feet in length, and we reckoned it weighed fifty or sixty pounds. On its head, it had a couple of massive boils or lumps, and its huge mouth was stuffed full of Herrings. Neither Trevor nor Malcolm had ever seen a cod that big.

I boxed the herring while the two boats motored home to the moorings in the Thorn Fleet. When we had tied up, all the boxed fish aboard were stacked and put into the two dinghies. Malcolm gutted the now-dead cod, making it look a bit more presentable; before he did so, he held it up beside and against himself to compare its length and size. Its mouth was up to his shoulder, with its tail still on the deck; I just wish I had my camera with me that day. The dinghy was sculled back to the causeway with the herring, and somebody went to get a trolley which we loaded, pushed it up to the fish box and then iced the fish. I went home for a hot bath to rid myself of fish scales, a hot meal, and then crash out asleep, ready for the following day's adventure.

On one of the last herring trawling trips we did, we had several fish boxes, both wooden and aluminium, on board, full of fish, to bring back to the causeway. We were tied up to the mooring. Trevor was now in the dinghy, stacking the boxes as we passed them to him; he was trying to fit all of them in so we wouldn't have to make a return journey. As he stacked them, we noticed that the dinghy was getting lower and lower in the water with just a couple of inches of freeboard; the idea was that we would tow it back to the causeway using Malcolm's dingy, plus whatever boxes we could also get in Malcolm's. Trevor came back onboard, and we started to put boxes into Malcolm's boat; as we were doing that, somebody looked over the side to the first dinghy. It wasn't there: it had sunk out of sight with our hard-won catch onboard and was now floating down the Thorn Fleet on the fast-ebbing tide. We had to quickly take out the boxes of fish from Malcolm's dingy, scull, and rescue as much as we could. The wooden fish boxes floated, being buoyant, but the longer they were in the water, the herrings floated out and spread across the water and were lost. The aluminium boxes, of course, wouldn't float, so as soon the water came in and over them, they sank with the fish floating out and which were also lost. We zig-zagged about, sculling in the dark creek and trying to find and, hopefully, rescue and save as much of our catch as we could; but it was hopeless – a lost cause.

We came back to the sunken dingy which was still tied up to the *Janet Anne*. We had to lift it manually and bail her out. I seem to remember that a few of the metal boxes were still there, but now empty. We were gutted. We had lost at least half of our catch and came back to the shore in a very sombre and quiet but pissed-off mood. A hard and expensive lesson had been learned. All that week, and a few days more, we chased the herring until the numbers dwindled so low that hardly a fish was being caught by us, or the drift netters, so we had to try a different method to make our weekly wage. Malcolm was desperate to try out his brand-new midwater cod pair trawl, so it was sculled out to the two boats to fit; it was absolutely huge when it was fitted to the two boats. The two skippers spread out a chart and worked out a route where to tow the huge net for the greater effect that it was designed to do; so, back out into the Blackwater at high tide to catch the ebb tide and help us move the beast. The net was connected to the two boats and lowered, and shot, into the sea. Malcolm pulled away from us to take up the slack on the connecting cable, then held his position as both winches on each boat lowered the net to the required depth, Malcolm having to do all the work with his boat winching and steering, as he was alone.

I asked Trevor how long we had to tow the net for. "Well, normally for eight hours, but we will haul just off Walton pier to see how things are working", he replied. The ebbing current carried us to the east as we left the Bench Head buoy to our port side and made our way into the Wallet's wide channel. I could see the pier off Clacton in the haze, miles ahead over the bow, but not Walton; it must have been hidden by the curve of the mainland as it turned to the north. There was always something to do and look at, and observe, as the pulsating, rhythmic throbbing of the engine was heard out of the exhaust, and also felt on the soles of your feet, as it made the wooden deck vibrate with each revolution and stroke of a piston as it fired. Any metal loose object would rattle and irritate, so you moved or tightened up the offender to quieten it; but in time, you got used to the familiar noises and rattles, and when you didn't hear them, you wondered why.

In those very rare, uncommon occasions in between tows, I would go below and try to grab a quick forty winks sleep. If the sea wasn't particularly rough, the boat would rise and fall as every wave and trough passed under her, making her rise and fall, and rock from side to side. It was quite a comforting move-ment if it wasn't too violent; I would lay on the bunk with the underside of the deck about four feet above me, the after-gallow, which had the wire trawl warp passing through it, was attached and bolted to the wooden deck just above me. At every rise and fall of the boat, the wooden decking would move up and down on the beams, and if the seas were particularly rough, the water would come over the bow or gunnels and run down the decks and out through the scuppers as it should. But not all of it did; gallons would leak through the deck where it joined the hull, run and cascade down the planking inside the boat, and, concerningly, passed me by lying there in my waterproof oileys.

As we approached the pier at Walton, we made preparations to haul; slowly the two winches on each boat dragged the wide trawl up to the water's surface, then the cod end lifted with the aid of the winch and derrick, clearing the gunnels. The catch of fish was released from the net, the cod end was tied, and the two boats pulled away from each other motoring forward. The process started again, heading west this time, dropping the net beneath the water as we proceeded. It was quite a decent catch; mostly cod littered the deck as I started to gut and box them. Some were really big fish, "spraggs" Trevor called them, weighing at least twenty-five pounds and quite strong as they twisted and writhed while you tried to hold one to gut. I had them all boxed, then I washed down the deck just in time to haul again as the two boats came together somewhere in the Blackwater. It was now dark as the winches were put in gear and dragged the net up to the *Janet Anne*; again, it was a decent catch as the cod end was lowered, untied, and the catch spread onto the deck.

Malcolm's boat was untied, and his receding navigational lights faded into the distance as he headed for the flashing Nass beacon, and home. We both pulled the net onboard and stowed it, ready to shoot on the following day. Trevor went into the wheelhouse to bring us back to Mersea as I set about gutting and boxing the fish. I was still gutting the catch when we pulled up alongside Malcolm and tied both boats together on Trevor's mooring. Then the two of them gave me a hand. We soon had them gutted and boxed, placed in the dingy, and sculled ashore.

We were away the next morning at high tide, catching the ebb somewhere by the Nass beacon, the boats coming together and coupling up the trawl before proceeding east for the usual run to Walton. We turned in a wide circle and headed back to the Blackwater. The trawl was towed for eight hours, and the catch dropped onto the deck; it took me eight hours to gut and box up. Just as I had finished, it was time to haul again. We were fishing on 24-hour trips then coming home to crash out and sleep, before catching the ebb tide once again for another 24-hours. What Malcolm did alone on his boat, God only knows; keeping his side of the net open, making tea in his wheelhouse, and not having time to cook anything, he must have been bored out of his brains. There were no mobile phones back then.

We usually had 24-hour trips, but the skippers decided that this time we were going to fish for 36-hours as it was a good weather forecast and we were having a good run of fishing. It was my job of cooking a meal at some point in between tows, putting a tinned "Fray Bentos" steak and kidney pie in the oven and veggies on the burner rings to boil. Then, when the two boats came together to haul, I would pass Malcolm his dinner. The trawl was shot again, with the two boats pulling apart and carrying on fishing. It gave me and Trevor time to enjoy a hot meal at our leisure, before the task of gutting and boxing a cod end full of fish. All the time that we were afloat, we were always snacking on biscuits, chocolate bars, sweets, cups of tea, in fact anything to quell our hunger. 24-hours is one thing, but 36 is another; the food usually ran out at about 18-hours, so we were both famished by this time, always searching and scavenging through the lockers and hidey-holes for something to magically turn up to eat.

At some point during the week, I had put a "Fry's chocolate cream" into my coat pocket which I had forgotten about; I couldn't believe my luck as I felt its familiar shape in my hand, then came up on deck, snapping a section off and eating it. Then I heard a vigorous tapping on the wheelhouse window as Trevor was mouthing through the glass "Give us some", then running out of the wheelhouse and chasing me around the boat's deck like some hunger-mad black-backed gull. I ran this way and that, back and forth, keeping him the other side

167

The saviour from starvation.

of the winch and wheelhouse as I rammed the chocolate bar down my throat before Moley could catch me, then he wrestled me to the deck trying to wrench it out of my grasp. Hard luck – too late!

Trevor went back into the wheelhouse to steer his boat back on course and tighten up the bow line. I looked at him and grinned, licking and smacking my lips. He grinned back at me, and then mouthed some unprintable and unmentionable obscenity through the salt and sea spray- obscured glass window. But we were tired and hungry and survived on tea for the rest of the trip.

The cod lasted about three weeks; well, it was for us until Trevor decided that we should fish a bit further down past Walton pier. Not having a chart marking the wrecks and fasts, it wasn't long before the trawl caught one which stopped us dead and, bringing the two boats together and however hard we pulled on the net, it wouldn't budge. In the end we had to cut it and pull onboard as much as we could to free us. Malcolm's brand-new cod trawl was in pieces, he was absolutely distraught as he looked at the net in a tangled heap on the deck.

We came home back to the mooring with the boxed-up fish and Malcolm's smashed up net all placed into the dingy and sculled ashore.

It was certainly true that I was missing my shooting and wildfowling. I would see my mates and enquire as to what I had missed in the last three months. The season had finished regarding ducks and pheasants; now it was either clay pigeons or real live pigeons on the early drilled fields. The fishing lasted for about another month for me. The ground trawls were fitted and set up and we went after the soles and roker that came to the multitude of warm shallow channels and fishing grounds of the Thames estuary; but these soon came to a temporary end, so I bade farewell and left to take up my old lifestyle. But I left with no regrets; it was something that I just had to get out of my system, and I still had our boat to get out onto the water, trawling with Hoss and Swiggy on the warm evenings and weekends, which I loved.

168

17: The Apprenticeship – Part Two

IT HAS TAKEN me about five years to get to this stage in trying to remember milestones and most memorable moments over the two decades from 1954 to 1974. I have kept notebooks and diaries from 1965 right up to this present day, but my first five years of recording was a hit and miss affair, and several incidents were not noted down or written up. I still have another five decades of memories left to put into print; I don't think I have enough time and years left to finish. So, I will write this part in appreciation of the second part of my wildfowling apprenticeship, which happened on December 13th, 1994.

It clicked into place the season before, on 8th January 1994, on Abbots Hall saltings one afternoon while I was by myself shooting. As I settled into my muddy hiding creek, the tide was starting to cover the mudflats stretching away from me down towards Sunken Island and beyond me up to Salcott. It was very calm with hardly a breath of wind, so the water's surface was smooth and glass-like in appearance. Groups of mainly wigeon, which had been standing on the channel edge, were now being washed off their feet by the flooding tide and coming together to form a floating mass in front of me for hundreds of yards. Others were coming out of Old Hall and joining them; several hundred birds congregating in the wide channel. It was then that I said to myself, "I wish I had a punt and punt gun". As the afternoon wore on, the number of ducks slowly began to diminish, and hardly a bird was left in Salcott Channel. As I walked back to the farm, and my car, in the dark after a successful evening flight, I kept thinking about the wigeon on the water in front and beside me. A couple of months later, I was reading a Shooting Times, and spotted an advert where someone was selling a punt and punt gun up at Morecambe Bay in Lancashire. I telephoned the number, but I don't think I had any intention of buying it; I wanted to know how much I would have to pay if I did. The price he wanted was £1,200; I had no idea if that was good or bad.

At a clay pigeon shoot a few weeks later, the Colchester gun club, of which I was a member, had an interclub clay shoot against the Oakley wildfowlers at Radcliffes shooting ground on the Mersea Road. Then it was back to the Langenhoe Lion for a couple of beers, some food, and the scores for the evening shoot to be announced. I was sitting with a good friend of mine from Oakley, Albert Allcock, (R.I.P.), and I was telling him about the wigeon that I had seen that previous winter afternoon, and how I would have loved to punt to them for a shot; but I hadn't a clue of how to go about it and needed someone to show me what to do. "Well, Julian does it", he said. "When I next see him, I will ask him to take you out". I couldn't believe what I was hearing. "Cheers, Albert, that would be brilliant", I said.

A couple of months later, we had a return match but this time at Oakley, and Julian was on the desk taking cash and giving out score cards. I honestly didn't give it a second thought. Then he said, "I have been talking to Albert and I understand you want to go punt gunning at some time?". I replied, "That's great, I would love to". "OK, I will give you a ring at some point during the season to see what we can arrange and hopefully get a shot". Several months later, in December, the phone rang one evening. It was Julian ringing me to ask if I could make it on such and such a day next week. "Yes, yes, of course; I would love to. I can't wait."

I had not the faintest idea of what to wear, so I turned up at his house wearing a blue pair of overalls, my thigh boots, a blue jumper, and my camo wildfowling hat and coat; they were all the totally wrong colours and clothing. He had to lend me a pale-coloured fishing smock, a white coat, and a grey woollen hat. We drove down to the shore and punt in his Nissan patrol and parked over the sea wall. We loaded a wheelbarrow with our bags containing flasks and food, two guns for cripple stopping, the puntgun breech, and massive cartridges for the gun. We then made our way across the bridge to the steps and dinghy and the long, low punt on its mooring, with the gun projecting forward from under the cover laying on the foredeck, pointing towards the bow. I had never seen a gun and punt since I looked at Peter Moss's on the Dornoch Firth all those years ago, and it wasn't anything like this. What I was looking at, was sitting on the water, cunningly very low, with quite a pronounced curve on the foredeck for shedding water quickly. It was 24-feet long, with a long cockpit so two people can lay flat, and with quite high washboards to hide the occupants.

We put all the gear in a dinghy and rowed the short distance to her on her mooring. I stayed in the dinghy as he unhooked, and rolled up, the vinyl cover and passed it to me to put in the dinghy. I handed him all the bags etc., then I stepped into the punt for the very first time.

We set off down Barn Creek and then into Oakley Creek which took us out to the edge of the estuary. Julian rowed as I sat on the stern seat with the paddle, doing my bit to propel us along. Teal and wigeon kept leaving the saltings and creeks as we proceeded, going out into the estuary. The punt gently grounded on the muddy edge of Garnhams Point where Oakley Creek meets and empties into the Walton backwaters, where we could observe both east and west, and along the low water edges of Horsey Island and Skippers Island. He scanned both edges with his binoculars, something I didn't think to bring along but such an important part of the kit. He could see a small number of ducks, but they were not worth going for, so he decided to cross over the estuary to the south side; he said we could observe and view the north shore, and west up to the Moze and Hopgoods Creek.

I was full of questions, I remember, as I asked him this and that about the punt, the gun, how old they were, how long he had been punting, and what had inspired him to start, but nothing was too much trouble to explain, and answer my barrage of questions. We gently nosed her onto the quite firm, muddy shore of Horsey, then he carefully glassed the tide's edge as far as he could see. He gave me a running commentary on what was flying across the estuary, what he could see on the water or standing on the channel edges, what was worth going for, and what was not. Some groups were too far up the mud, so out of range; some sittings were too stretched out and gappy, thus not worth a stalk, and some had protected waders amongst them, and Brent geese, so we couldn't fire a shot. The list seemed endless as to when you could safely shoot, and then

A punt gun.

only when everything was right and in place.

Julian could see a little group of birds far away on the Moze Point, a couple of miles away. "They look like teal, or they could be redshanks, on the edge and in the water. Have a look with your glasses, what do you think?". I explained that I hadn't got any to use, so he handed me his to use and have a look. I looked at the group of birds and said, "I am not sure, they could be either". They were so far away! We crossed back to the northern shore and found a little shelter from the north-west chilly airstream. We

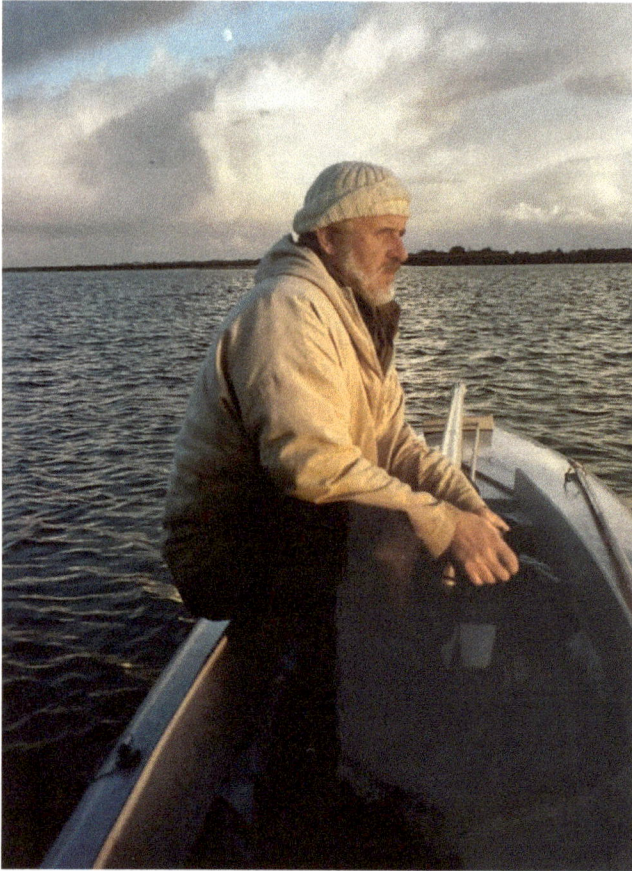

A contemplative Jack in the gun punt.

pulled into the edge again. He then put the oars onto the left-hand side decking, then opened a bag and removed the massive 1.75-inch breech. He opened up the ammunition box and brought out a huge cartridge loaded with BB lead shot that was used at the time, pushed it into the chamber of the gun, then screwed in the breech plug and then the action and stock. We changed places; I was then kneeling on the floorboards behind this huge gun. He selected a pole and started to push the punt forward along the edge towards the sitting of birds. As we got closer, still kneeling, he kept glassing at the sitting in front of us; when we were about six hundred yards away from them, he said, "We had better lay down so as not to be too obvious." He glassed them again and he said that they were teal.

I lay down, looking over the breech and sighting; this huge cannon of a gun that stretched out in front of me for nine feet, quite an impressive piece of ordnance. He selected a shorter pole from off the right-hand side deck, removed a section of coaming, then he also lay down, putting his arm through the gap onto the side deck and pushing us along using the short pole. We stalked towards the teal which were still hundreds of yards away from us. It was quite cloudy when we started off but after a while the sky cleared, and we were now bathed in brilliant sunshine. "Damn the bloody sun!", he muttered, as he pulled once again into the muddy creek edge to hold up. "We will stand out like a battleship. I'll hold up for a few minutes until we get some cloud cover." We waited, looking up at the sky to estimate how long it would be before we would be back in shade. Eventually, the sun disappeared, and we continued on our way. We were now getting closer to our goal; there looked to be about twenty teal in the sitting.

Quartering the saltings on the other side of Hamford over on Skippers Island, I could see a marsh harrier hunting, and at the same time Julian said, "What the bloody hell do we need next to bugger things up?". The harrier floated towards the edge of Skippers, came a little way across the estuary towards the teal, but then turned back; but of course, it made the teal lift. They flew low across the water into the Moze creek taking a couple of wigeon with them. Julian swore, but was now poling the punt again, kneeling, so we surged forward. As we drew closer to the point of the creek, he lay down again and the punt rounded the edge to view into, and open up, the creek; up on the left side of the Moze, two hundred yards away, sat our teal, but we had to cross the creek which had a fair amount of water in it from our side to the other. He had to use his longest six-foot pole, together with his hand and arm under the water, to reach the creek bed. He felt the bottom and poled and pushed us across into shallower water so we could continue to our goal.

"I should cock the gun, Jack, and keep as still as you can; keep your head down", he whispered. I hooked my finger through the ring on the cocking lever and pulled it back until I heard and felt a positive click. I put my left hand onto the stock and aimed, got hold of the trigger lanyard and, putting a little bit of tension on it, I moved the gun so it bore down onto the birds. The punt stole forward for another hundred yards, then, coming into long range, Julian whispered, "Aim at the bottom of the sitting; I will tell you when." We pulled into range and there was a pause for a few seconds before Julian murmured, "Now!".

I won't disclose the outcome as I have read about the end of the stalk and the event in Julian's extensive diaries and journals, which go to great lengths and details to remind you of that particular day, and all of the other days before and after. So, I think it is only right and proper that he should perhaps, one day, include that story and finish the outcome. It is also his memories, events and stories, after all.

And so, my first ever experience and shot with a punt gun was recorded in my own notebooks, the first of many over the past thirty years and seasons, mainly with Julian, but also with Peter Avery in his outfit and with my own. Also, taking other people who also had their first puntgun shot in the punt and gun that I built very shortly after. I owe a huge debt of gratitude to the chap who has pushed me countless miles with his bare, wet hand, holding a pushing pole on body-numbing, cold, frosty, snowy and wet, windswept days along an estuarine muddy edge with a skill that very few punters achieve. He is certainly a one-off. He imparted to me the chance, opportunity, and dedication to fulfil a new form of supreme special wildfowling, that I am still striving to achieve. If I did, I would never come anywhere near to being the incredible puntsman, naturalist, ornithologist, artist, author, and true countryman that he is.

There have been a lot of books written about other famous puntsmen in the past, and I know that Captain George Gould was a Victorian puntsman who was dedicated to the wonderful art of the pursuit of wildfowl afloat, and of whom my good friend is a great admirer. But even he, and all of the others, do not compare to the greatest wildfowler that ever lived, and still is as I write, thankfully. Also, there are fellow puntgunners that I have met over the years from that very first day, and his many punt-gunning friends that he has been afloat with at Hamford water and other places; he selflessly introduced them all to me. The wonderful trips to the BASC headquarters, where every two years there is an opportunity to listen, and to swop and share wonderful life stories of other legendary punt gunners, of their adventures afloat, on a wild, windswept estuary somewhere around the coast of Britain. Thanks, Julian.

Julian Novorol.

Acknowledgements

Saturday 22nd June 2024. Maydays sea wall point. 9.30am.

I AM SITTING on two pieces of plastic that were once the railings denoting the roadway or causeway that guided people and vehicles onto Mersea Island since it was first occupied; of which, only the Lord knows when. The Strood railings are of a more modern, recent time, broken from the posts that once held them, only for a very high gale-blown spring tide to remove them from their rusted fastenings, and to fall into the sea. They would float and drift on an ebb tide, to be washed up on the strand line at the base of a sea wall, very close to where I placed them as an observation position seat higher up the wall where I would take in the familiar 360-degree surroundings and views.

My first view is looking west, up and over the saltings and marshes and the wide channel or creek of the Pyefleet, with the occasional glimpse of the summer sun reflecting off a car or lorry on the Mersea road a couple of miles away, adjacent to Moor Farm at Peldon. My thoughts and memories are taken back to the first people I shared this watery idyllic landscape with. In my mind's eye, I can see Marshie Richardson standing close to his houseboat on the high-water mark close to the sea wall; also, my fowling mate, Pat Clark – just a glimpse of the top of his hatted head as he patiently waits in his favourite salting creek. I can also envisage the muddy narrow gutter where I positioned myself on those early mornings with Pat, being blasted at the time by the snowstorm and blizzard.

I turn my gaze slightly to the south, overlooking Bower Hall saltmarsh, and those school days being with J.J. and Stephen Rodwell. I can't remember us getting anything but came home with memories. Barrow Hill Farm: those other school day memories being with my father before and after I had a gun, following, watching, listening and learning from his fountain of countryside knowledge. Looking beyond Barrow Hill, over the Strood causeway to Ray Island, Feldy, Copthall, and Sampson's Creek, with Tollesbury and Tolleshunt D'Arcy in the far, far distance, and Old Hall acting as a stepping stone into those ancient villages. The wonderful times I spent with my close family, relatives and friends walking that incredible landscape is always captured in my heart and mind.

I can also visualise the creeks and channels close to Wyatt's hard and Punt Bay where me, Hoss, Swiggy, Basky, and a host of other boys, mates and friends have launched and come ashore with our spoils from a morning flight, or a long day's trawling in the Blackwater and beyond. Wonderful, nostalgic days. I remember the yearly ritual of scraping, scrubbing, anti-fouling, repairing, sandpapering and painting your precious boat or punt, all shared with my mates.

I turn on my improvised seat and look to the south towards the place where I shared the long freshwater fleet with my father. I learned so much from him. For example, how to encounter with some success, the fast-zipping shadows of jet-propelled teal as they passed us by in the failing light and darkening sky. Now, sadly, this fleet has been filled in and is a section of the levelled and flattened freshwater marsh. The same is true of the ditch full of nettles where we concealed ourselves as the wood pigeons battled against a gale-force wind flying towards the two of us over the sun ripening fields of wheat of Bocking Hall, Haycocks and Maydays farms.

Then looking towards East Mersea, across Reeves Hall to the lane where my original ancestor first moved to, and lived on, this glorious island, just as the 18-year-old Victoria ascended the British throne. At the end the lane is now a fifty-foot-high fir wood sheltering Fishponds stables, which was all part of the arable field where, close by, Basky and I parked a vehicle in the small spinney, then onto the footpath to access the sea wall and foreshore with our low fowling punt secured in the saltings creek.

Then I look north-west, north, then north-east towards the pristine M.O.D. firing ranges with its maze of freshwater reed-fringed fleets, and acres of rough, grassy areas grazed by both cattle and sheep, with brambles and blackthorn thickets making it a haven for nesting birds and breeding mammals. Then just beyond, over the sea wall, the acres of inter-tidal saltings of the Geedons, bordering the Colne estuary with its estuarine mudflats and with its wonderful wildlife and wilderness. Just 15 miles further east as the duck flies is another piece of the wild part of Essex: Hamford Water. I have been lucky enough to explore there with my good friend, excellent shot and wildfowler Graham Hunt, and also my punt gunning partner of thirty years Julian Novorol, whose local combined knowledge of the ways and habits of wildfowl is second to none; both amazing countrymen and ornithologists.

Acknowledgements are due to some truly special humans and animals:

To all of the wonderful people I have met and encountered over the years, whether it be wildfowling, or game or clay pigeon shooting, and to the owners and skippers of the fishing trawlers that I have enjoyed watching and working with, these dedicated professional men: you never fail to impress me.

To all of my wonderful working gun dogs that I have owned, plus my father's dogs that he and I have shot over, beat and picked up on a shoot somewhere both since and before 1960. They were mainly black labradors with the exception of two: the first, a tall yellow dog that my sister brought back from Kent to Colchester on British Rail, and then from Colchester to Mersea on an Eastern National bus, for my father's 55th birthday; and the second, a gift to my father from Alan Gray at Bocking Hall – an absolute treasure.

Three other people have given me unflinching support for my way of working and social life: my wonderful wife Heather, and Peter, my son, who has shared with me a clay pigeon shoot on numerous occasions and has enjoyed, with our dogs, a flight somewhere. I must also thank my daughter, Emma, who has given unconditional support by setting up my iPad, printing copies of the text for me to scrutinise, and providing encouragement for this project.

I would also like to thank Trevor Hearn for his diligence and expertise in bringing this book to fruition.

I just bless the day when William Hoy first came to Mersea Island all those years ago. What made him leave his siblings to follow his nose and instincts from Fingringhoe to Shop Lane? Was it the promise of work or the hand of a pretty girl? Whatever the reason, I thank the Lord that he discovered this wonderful place.

Tis now the fowler man's his little barque,
equipped with gun and dog of sturdiest strain.
Prepared to weather the relentless blast, to try
his skill, and luck mid the feathered train.

Mr T Hughes

Picture Credits

Chapter 1: Silhouette picture of curlew courtesy of Creative Commons (https://creativecommons.org/licenses/by-nc-sa/2.0/#)

Chapter 2: Silhouette picture of wildfowler courtesy of Udayvir sohi07 Pinterest account (https://www.pinterest.co.uk/pin/notebooks--296674694202714700/)

Chapter 3: Picture of wildfowling by 1stdibs.com (https://www.1stdibs.com/art/prints-works-on-paper/more-prints-works-on-paper/frank-benson-winter-wildfowling/id-a_3404043/)

Chapter 4: Silhouette picture of wildfowling courtesy of adobe.com (https://www.google.com/url?sa=i&url=https%3A%2F%2Fstock.adobe.com%2Fsearch%3Fk%3Dduck%2Bhunting%2Bsilhouette&psig=AOvVaw3U83GAQ9qGAb8k-q-zxruo&ust=1702399249212000&source=images&cd=vfe&opi=89978449&ved=2ahUKEwihhbLF6YeDAxVNpycCHcRqCoIQr4kDegUIARDUAQ)

Chapter 5: Silhouette drawing of labrador and hunters wildfowling courtesy of Jagdhund — Vektorgrafik (https://www.google.com/url?sa=i&url=https%3A%2F%2Fdepositphotos.com%2Fde%2Fvector%2Fhunting-dog-13953760.html&psig=AOvVaw1MYkgqgL8wspr8Bga-oy5J&ust=1702399913713000&source=images&cd=vfe&opi=89978449&ved=2ahUKEwjO9p-C7IeDAxWtpicCHUHQB6MQr4kDegUIARD7AQ)

Chapter 6: Silhouette of trawling boat courtesy of shutterstock.com (https://www.shutterstock.com/image-vector/vector-sketch-commercial-fishing-boat-on-1595596333)

Chapter 7: Silhouette picture of wildfowler and dog courtesy of vexels.com Pinterest account (https://www.pinterest.co.uk/pin/1113937289053481509/)

Chapter 8: Silhouette picture of wildfowlers shooting ducks courtesy of shutterstock com (https://www.shutterstock.com/search/duck-silhouette)

Chapter 9: Silhouette picture of flight of ducks, copyright: Igor Zubkov | Dreamstime.com (https://www.google.com/url?sa=i&url=https%3A%2F%2Fwww.dreamstime.com%2Fillustration%2Fhunter-silhouette.html&psig=AOvVaw06QrxpxQK4SeoxhrKpDk2d&ust=1703763584574000&source=images&cd=vfe&opi=89978449&ved=2ahUKEwiyg5iLxK-DAxWdAfsDHT4yAlEQr4kDegUIARCaAQ)

Chapter 10: Silhouette picture of clay pigeon shooting courtesy of illustAC (https://www.google.com/url?sa=i&url=https%3A%2F%2Fen.ac-illust.com%2Fclip-art%2F24542486%2Fclay-pigeon-shooting-silhouette&psig=AOvVaw1qkSPY4LdipaKwsTDabA-j&ust=1704298614521000&source=images&cd=vfe&opi=89978449&ved=2ahUKEwi0uqydjb-DAxWHfqQEHWWiDtwQr4kDegQIARBy)

Chapter 11: Drawing of punt gunning courtesy of Vintage Guns (https://www.google.com/url?sa=i&url=https%3A%2F%2Fwww.vintageguns.co.uk%2Fmagazine%2Fpunt-gunning&psig=AOvVaw3lNslJjdY2_h_2JiYdkg9a&ust=1704478886537000&source=images&cd=vfe&opi=89978449&ved=2ahUKEwiNid_lrMSDAxV4rycCHZQYANcQr4kDegQIARB6)

Chapter 12: Drawing of ferret hunting prey courtesy of alamy. com (https://www.google.com/url?sa=t&rct=j&q=&esrc=s&source =web&cd=&ved=2ahUKEwiElqmU98aDAxVp6AIHHW9nCj0Qh- wKegQIDxAD&url=https%3A%2F%2Fwww.alamy.com%2Fstock-photo%2Fferret- hunting.html&usg=AOvVaw3ahxD27A3p7FKNR-jn2PvC&opi=89978449)

Chapter 13: Silhouette drawing of hunting courtesy of freepik.com (https://www. google.com/url?sa=i&url=https%3A%2F%2Fwww.freepik.com%2Ffree-photos- vectors%2Fhunting-clipart&psig=AOvVaw27PuCLf3ZZOn3VCyuQlWUT&u st=1704997173009000&source=images&cd=vfe&opi=89978449&ved=0CBU QjhxqFwoTCIi5kNq304MDFQAAAAAdAAAAABAI)

Chapter 14: Picture of punt gunning courtesy of www.shootinguk.co.uk (https://www.google.com/url?sa=i&url=https%3A%2F%2Fwww.shootinguk. co.uk%2Fguns%2Fhistory-of-punt-gunning-119189%2F&psig=AOvVaw1X2R4HzmffI NfyG4B2N3r_&ust=1705430340230000&source=images&cd=vfe&opi=89978449&ved =0CBIQtaYDahcKEwjI0sinheCDAxUAAAAAHQAAAAAQBg)

Chapter 15: Picture of fishing trawler courtesy of istock photo

https://www.istockphoto.com/vector/small-fishing-boat-in-sea-seagulls-and-vessel-ship- on-the-water-seascape-fishery-gm1428266047-471819516

Chapter 16: Picture of tawler courtesy of adobe.com (https:// www.google.com/url?sa=i&url=https%3A%2F%2Fstock.adobe. com%2Fsearch%3Fk%3Dfishing%2Bboat%2Bvector&psig =AOvVaw2dPTmsTcZmL9t45x_JeK7i&ust=1705679854366000&source=images&cd=vfe &opi=89978449&ved=2ahUKEwiCl-rfpueDAxXApycCHanJBs0Qr4kDegQIARBk)

Picture of Fry's Chocolate Cream from author's collection.

Chapter 17: Picture of punt gunner courtesy of Wikipedia.org (https://www. google.com/url?sa=i&url=https%3A%2F%2Fen.wikipedia.org%2Fwiki%2FPunt_ gun&psig=AOvVaw0pvYHzWkEvvdb6P1lDwAye&ust= 1705698308861000&source=images&cd= vfe&ved=0CBUQjhxqFwoTCMiH7 NPr54MDFQAAAAAdAAAAABAJ)

Endpiece: Picture of wildfowl gunner with dog courtesy of istock photo

https://www.istockphoto.com/vector/hunter-with-retriever-gm500737063-43070592?sear chscope=image%2Cfilm

Acknowledgements: Photograph taken at Maydays point courtesy of Trevor Hearn.